Digital TV - ISDB-T
~The Origin, R&D and Growth~

Aiming at mobile and portable TV
The basic concept and
how the taboos were broken

Appendix : The specifications of ISDB-T

Osamu Yamada
Fernando Bittencourt

Copyright © 2017 by Osamu Yamada and Fernando Bittencourt

Digital TV - ISDB-T
~The Origin, R&D and Growth~

Translater: Yoshiko Isahaya
Coordinator: Junko Rodriguez
Formatting: Sota Torigoe

Published by Babel Press U.S.A.
All rights reserved

ISBN: 978-0989232692

Babel Corporation
Pacific Business News Bldg. #208,
1833 Kalakaua Avenue, Honolulu, Hawaii 96815

Contents

Preface ... 10

Chapter 1
  INTRODUCTION ... 16

Chapter 2
  "LEARNING WITH THE BODY, NOT WITH THE HEAD" AS A NEW COMER TO NHK ... 20

Chapter 3
  MATURING STAGE OF DTTB TECHNOLOGY ... 26
  3.1 Still-Picture Broadcasting (1967-1977) ... 26
  3.2 Teletext (1977-1985) ... 31
  3.3 FM Multiplex Broadcasting (1985-1995) ... 46

Chapter 4
  JAPANESE DTTB : ISDB-T (1986-2003) ... 56
  4.1 Proposal for Mobile/Portable Reception ... 57
  4.2 DAB and OFDM ... 59

4.3 Trial Production of OFDM and Experiment in Mobile Reception ... 64

4.4 Basic SFN Experiment ... 67

4.5 Standardization of ISDB-T ... 70

4.6 Mobile/Portable Reception for TV : No One Noticed Its Potential and Importance ... 77

Chapter 5
CHARACTERISTICS AND TRANSMISSION METHOD OF ISDB-T ... 82

5.1 Characteristics ... 83

5.2 Transmission Method ... 89

Chapter 6
DIFFUSION ACTIVITIES ABROAD for ISDB-T (1990's-2010's) ... 100

6.1 Situation in Each Country ... 103

6.2 Diffusion Activities to Other Countries ... 105

6.3 Everything Started in Brazil ... 107

6.4 Diffusion Activities in Other Countries ... 112

Chapter 7
DTTB in BRAZIL ... 122

7.1 A Ten-Year Saga ... 122

7.2 Comparative Tests ... 131

Chapter 8

RESEARCH MANAGEMENT ... 152

8.1 Researcher ... 154

8.2 Research Manager ... 158

Chapter 9

ACKNOWLEDGEMENTS ... 166

REFERENCE ... 170

ABOUT THE AUTHORS ... 184

INDEX ... 192

APPENDIX ... 210

TRANSMISSION SYSTEM FOR DIGITAL TERRESTRIAL TELEVISION BROADCASTING ARIB STANDARD, STD-B31

PREFACE

The digitalization of broadcasting, which was the change from analog to digital technologies, similar to the shifts from radio to TV, black-and-white TV to color TV, and from color TV to HDTV, was one of the most challenging subjects technically and economically for broadcasting engineers to achieve in the 90's. The technical elements involved in digital broadcasting technologies include audio/video digital compression technologies, digital transmission technologies, high-speed and high-integration technologies for LSI, and so on. Through competition and cooperation among engineers in this field from all over the world, digital broadcasting technologies have advanced and blossomed into the current era.

While international system study groups such as DAVIC, MPEG, ATSC, DVB, and ITU-R/TG11-3 contributed to the establishment of digital broadcasting research in the world, new advances were regrettably delayed in Japan even though the study of HDTV had started earlier, because the experimental analog broadcasting system MUSE had already been implemented. However, since the 1970's, NHK STRL had been carrying out the basic research for digital terrestrial transmission.

Through the research and development of Teletext which is text data broadcasting multiplexed with TV blanking periods for stationary reception and FM multiplexed broadcasting for mobile reception, we developed a very flexible system called ISDB-T, and thereby contributed to the international technology community. One of the most peculiar characteristics of ISDB-T was that the research and development of the system had been focused not only on high-definition broadcasting, of which broadcast engineers had no notion at the time, but also on mobile and portable reception, the importance of which I noticed through outdoor experiments carried out in the 1970's.

Thanks to the efforts of many people concerned, ISDB-T, having been researched and developed by NHK STRL, was standardized in the domestic market in 1999, and standardized internationally by ITU-R in 2000. In Japan, HDTV services started to be offered in 2003, and One-Seg services for cellular phones started in 2006.

In Brazil, American and European broadcasting systems were being studied since the 1990's with Mr. Fernando Bittencourt of TVGlobo as a research leader. Comparative studies in ISDB-T were started in 1999. Then, in April 2000, Brazilian researchers proved for the first time that Japanese ISDB-T was the best among the three systems under development in Japan, the USA and Europe. The announcement of this discovery was persuasive because it was based on comparative experiments carried out in Brazil, which was a third party, not in Japan. The

PREFACE

announcement also had a great impact on broadcast engineers and researchers all over the world, sparking their interest in the characteristics of ISDB-T. Following the announcement of the results of the experiments, ISDB-T was further adopted in South-American countries. Mr. F. Bittencourt publicly recommended HDTV technologies developed by NHK to be the most suitable for viewing soccer, which is the national sport in Brazil, in the mid-1990's. After that, he further endorsed ISDB-T, publicly stating that multichannel broadcasting was meaningless and that ISDB-T, which permitted HDTV and mobile and portable reception was the most suitable choice for Brazil. Though there were many obstacles when it came to integrating the opinions of domestic broadcasting stations in Brazil, the Brazilian government finally decided in 2006 to adopt the ISDB-T system. Broadcasting services in ISDB-T started to be offered in 2007. Owing to activities promoting Mr. F. Bittencourt's findings in South America undertaken through cooperation between Japan and Brazil, all countries in South America, except Colombia, decided to adopt ISDB-T, and started offering broadcasting services using the system.

I have received several requests for an English version of a book on ISDB-T from people both in Japan and abroad. I also received an enthusiastic request from the MIC to publish the book, though it was not completed at the time. But now, with the cooperation of many colleagues, I have finally managed to complete the manuscript and to publish this book after having spent more than two years preparing it. This book is focused on the characteristics of the ISDB-T transmission system. Aspects of the system's performance are described through a history of the research and development that went into the technology, and the promotional activities to expand its use abroad.

The research and development, standardization, practical application, and promotional activities abroad for ISDB-T have been carried out with the cooperation of many people including NHK technical staff, MIC, ARIB, commercial broadcasting stations, manufacturers and universities, etc. in Japan. Therefore, I would like to express my gratitude to all those concerned, and especially to Mr. F. Bittencourt for his leadership in Brazil.

Osamu Yamada
Tokyo, Japan

I would also like to express my gratitude to Ana Eliza Faria and Vitor Chaves de Oliveira for helping me in the Group Abert/Set chapter.

Fernando Bittencourt
Rio de Janeiro, Brazil

We are also deeply grateful for the precious advice of Babel

PREFACE

Corporation, which has helped me publish this book, regardless of any trouble I gave to the staff due to delays in preparing the manuscript.

We are proud to have finished writing this book with our expertise as a researcher and a research manager, having devoted ourselves to the study of DTTB for more than 30 years. We hope our work will be able to give guidance to young engineers who want to become researchers in future and to other research managers.

This is the story of breaking the taboos to bring out new technologies.

Mr. Yamada was in charge of Chapter 1-6, and 8, 9 and Mr. F. Bittencourt was in charge of Chapter 7 (DTTB in Brazil).

The specifications of ISDB-T are attached at the end of this book as an appendix with permission from ARIB. Please refer to the appendix if you are interested in finding more detailed specifications.

Osamu Yamada
Fernando Bittencourt
January 2017

Chapter 1
INTRODUCTION

Looking back on the long period during which I was a salaried employee, I had a streak of rebelliousness that led me to choose a subject for my research in a field that diverged from the main stream at every essential point. Now that my period as an employee is finished, it seems that all the research I did in those days was related to the development of ISDB-T, which is the main theme of this book.

In 1967, I joined NHK, where I sought a job as a researcher. I worked at NHK Aomori (the northernmost prefecture of Japan's main land) broadcasting station as a broadcasting engineer until I was transferred to NHK STRL in 1971. At NHK STRL, I became thoroughly engaged in the research and development of digital broadcasting. Until 2002 when I left NHK because of my retirement age, I had dedicated myself to the development of digital broadcasting systems in Japan, though my abilities were limited.[1]

While the role of product manufacturers is to introduce many new products to the market every year, broadcasting companies are not so hasty to introduce new broadcasting systems because it takes a long time to research and develop them. Thanks to the efforts of senior staff and other interested parties in Japan, up to 10 broadcasting systems have been researched and developed, some of which have been in use since the start of radio broadcasting in 1925 up through the present day. I myself have been involved in the research/development and practical implementation of four such broadcasting systems: Teletext[2], FM Multiplexed Broadcasting[3], Satellite Digital Broadcasting[4],[5], and DTTB[5],[6]. It has been my great pleasure to play a leading role in the rapidly-advancing technical innovation that has been standard in digital broadcasting technologies from the emerging era of digital broadcasting technologies up through the era of fruition that we are witnessing today.

After leaving NHK in 2002, I joined Pioneer Corporation. Since then, I have been engaged in promotional activities for ISDB-T, which have been continued from the 1990's in South

Chapter 1 INTRODUCTION

America, as a member of DiBEG[7] in ARIB[8],[9]. Currently, all the South American countries except for Columbia are using the Japanese ISDB-T system (as of December, 2013). Moreover, the countries in Central America, Southeast Asia, and Africa have also become adopters of the system.

Looking back on the work I did in NHK STRL and the research activities I was involved in thereafter, I never could have imagined then that such a highly advanced digital terrestrial television broadcasting system would be realized within my 30-year career, though I always did my best at each task. I feel as though all the work I did over those years was somehow directly connected to my research on ISDB-T, in the end[10],[11]. In those days, the final goal of my work was to spread ISDB-T technologies abroad, because I believed that research was meaningless unless the results became useful to as many people as possible. I worked with particular interest on difficult problems that others might have passed over, since I was not very interested in deriving easy solutions.

I decided to write this book about how the ISDB-T transmission system was born, how the research and development of it was carried out, and how promotional activities for disseminating ISDB-T technologies abroad were carried out in order to be remembered by history. I also included my suggestions about how to manage research groups for young researchers and engineers who may play active roles in the technology's future advancement.

Chapter 2
"LEARNING WITH THE BODY, NOT WITH THE HEAD" AS A NEW COMER TO NHK
(1967-1971)[1]

In 1967 when I graduated from university, Japan was in the throes of a severe economic depression. While in normal circumstances, companies would send invitations to those graduate students who had been recommended by their professors, that year the university did not receive any invitations from the major electric-appliance manufacturers: NEC, Hitachi, Toshiba, etc. As such, I had a hard time finding a job. But luckily, a professor in charge of recruitment called me up, and said, "How about NHK?" I hadn't known prior to then that engineers could have career options as technology users, which is NHK's specialty, rather than as manufactures. It was then that I decided to join NHK.

As a university student, I was interested in the field of automatic control theory upon which many mathematical techniques have been based. I was also an utter amateur as far as communication, broadcasting and wireless communication were concerned. Therefore, during training seminars for newcomers to NHK, I found it difficult to understand the lectures. To make matters worse, those around me seemed to be very bright. At the time, this situation made me feel like an inferior employee.

The first office assigned to me after the training seminars was NHK Aomori broadcasting station, where senior employees taught me the basics of broadcasting technologies step by step over the course of 4 years. The experience of working in this provincial city as well as the network of personal relations that I established there became precious assets for the research activities I was to conduct later. For example, in an experiment for FM multiplex broadcasting (VICS) (see 3.3), I was able to use operative broadcasting equipment after broadcasts were concluded for the day, thanks to a senior staff member who I knew from NHK Aomori broadcasting station but was working in the Tokyo Tower at the time. He kindly allowed me to use the broadcasting equipment at my request.

In those days, the engineers at local broadcasting stations in Japan were mostly high-school graduates, and were all excellent workers. Back then, entry into industrial high schools was not easy because, unlike today, few local universities had engineering departments. I found out that the top one or two students from each industrial high school had joined NHK.

Though as a university graduate I was mostly respected by other staff members, I could not sufficiently do the jobs that were assigned to me at NHK Aomori broadcasting station, which made me feel inferior. In those days, I would often wonder why the high-school graduates were so good at their jobs, and I came to the understanding for the first time in my life that the work should be learned with the body, not with paper and pencil. This understanding became the foundation of my work as a researcher.

I was the first in NHK STRL to deal with such basic technologies as error correction code technologies and digital modulation technologies in the broadcasting field. I proposed the research and development of FM multiplex broadcasting[3], BS digital broadcasting[4], DTTB[5] with mobile/portable receiving functions, and Super-High Definition TV with 4,000 scanning lines (Super-Hivision)[12],[13], which NHK had not planned to research and develop at first. This put me at odds with people around me. If I had not continued to carry out my work in all aspects of the job site, I could not have come up with the idea of proposing research and development for these new technologies.

I was a complete amateur in the field of television back then. I had a very shameful experience at the job site when I could not repair a vacuum tube type master monitor that was out of order. After that experience, I bought a TV kit for a price almost equivalent to my first salary, and assembled the kit privately at home, which helped me to better understand television receivers. Still, I was too ashamed to tell my colleagues about this secret experiment. I wanted to acclimate to my job as quickly as possible and to be able to improve my performance until I could become a full-fledged researcher.

I brought home spare operation manuals for broadcasting equipment and studied the manuals earnestly. During my studies, I became particularly interested in a synchronized signal generator. I wondered why phase synchronization (*Gen-lock*) could not be achieved instantaneously but required a period of several seconds. I sought the answer through study, and as a result, I discovered that instantaneous phase synchronization was possible by adding a simple circuit. I prepared a test circuit, and confirmed the effect of it. From the result of that study, only NHK Aomori broadcasting station decided to use a Gen-lock circuit and continued to do so until the equipment in the master control room was updated due to the colorization of the TV broadcasting system from black and white. Thinking back, it is incredible from an accountability standpoint that a handmade circuit designed by site-

Chapter 2 "LEARNING WITH THE BODY, NOT WITH THE HEAD" AS A NEWCOMER TO NHK

based engineers, rather than a fully consigned one produced by a manufacturing company, was incorporated into working equipment. After all, management was not so strict and it seemed everything was possible. When I reported the result of the study and the experiment at a broadcasting technology convention at NHK all over Japan, my report earned an award of excellence, whereby the sense of inferiority that I had felt on several occasions was partly wiped away.

While it was my dream to be a researcher ever since I was a university student, I put STRL as my desired office in a personal statement form that had to be submitted every year because I wanted to venture into areas of research that others might consider unworkable.

After the broadcasting technology convention at NHK, I was invited to join the Studio Equipment Division by the upper management of NHK Broadcasting Center, who had heard of my report at the convention. I politely declined the offer because I wanted to be a researcher as I mentioned, and as a result, I was transferred to STRL in 1971. In those days, the Studio Equipment Division was positioned higher than STRL in terms of importance, playing an important role in the automation and colorization of broadcasting systems at NHK broadcasting stations all over Japan. I was continuously blamed by the management of the division for my transfer to STRL instead of the Studio Equipment Division. "You are foolish enough to decline our offer but to go to STRL ", they said whenever I met them. I was not interested in promotion at all in those days. My only intention was to contribute to the development of society with the results of my research, through which I intended to leave a mark on the world. After that, my boss occasionally got offers to transfer me to the Broadcasting Center, though I was to remain in STRL at my boss, Mr. Koichi Nio's discretion, until my retirement age. If my boss had accepted the offer to transfer me to the Broadcasting Center, the current digital broadcasting system that I put in place would not have existed, and a different digital broadcasting system would have been developed.

Looking back on the past, it seems to me that my admittance to NHK, my transfer to STRL, and my acquaintance with my boss, who was kind enough to allow me to devote myself strictly to research, were all major turning points in my life.

Chapter 3
MATURING STAGE OF DTTB TECHNOLOGY

My research and development of DTTB technologies are based on results of the long-term basic research carried out by many engineers in the world.

3.1 Still-Picture Broadcasting (1971-1977)[14]

In 1971, I was transferred to STRL as I had desired. NHK had decided, following the Tokyo Olympics in 1964, which would later be called the "Broadcasting Olympics", to focus its research on two main types of technology[15]: HDTV technology and "multi-information" technology, such as Teletext.

I had an opportunity to be a researcher. But I was not confident of myself at all to be a researcher, and I always felt uneasiness in those days. Anyway, I tried hard because it was my first aim to become a full-fledged researcher as soon as possible.

I was first assigned to a "Research Group for New Broadcasting Systems", which was to study "multi-information" technology. I was appointed as a member of the "Still- Picture Broadcasting" section of the group. In those the days, the current multi-channel satellite broadcasting era could not even be imagined. The challenge then was in finding how to use terrestrial broadcasting radio frequencies effectively. A normal TV program shows motion pictures by transmitting 30 frames per second, however educational programs can often be provided without using motion pictures. Accordingly, if an educational program shows still instead of motion pictures, then several dozen programs can be broadcasted through a single 6MHz channel. This is known as the "still-picture broadcasting" system. Under that system, approximately 50 programs could be provided by transmitting pictures at a rate of two audio frames per one video frame. However, since digital compression technology was not in use at that time, the system was incomplete showing analog pictures with digital sounds. And since there was also no error correction technology, noise mixing sound came out under even low bit error rate. A single frame memory for pictures was necessary on the receiver side.

Chapter 3 MATURING STAGE OF DTTB TECHNOLOGY

In those days, semiconductor memory was beyond imagination. A metal-plated disk was used as a memory medium. Thinking back to then, the speed at which recording technologies have progressed is remarkable.

As for the field of research assigned to me, I was in charge of transmission files for still-picture broadcasting and single frame memory on the receiver side. I learned about designing analog and digital circuits as well as magnetic recording technologies, etc. Furthermore, as 8-bit one-chip CPUs such as the Intel 8080 and the Motorola 6800 with only 64k bytes memory space had just been launched on the market[16], I was able to learn about these technologies on microcomputers including software, which became the foundation of the next theme of my research, Teletext. I was very happy to get the job I wanted as a researcher. I did what I could at home when it came to researching patents, doing other basic research and designing test equipment as much as possible. At work, on the other hand, I focused on conducting experiments in STRL's laboratory that allowed me to efficiently carry out my research, in which I was absorbed from Monday to Friday, and even on Saturday and Sunday, though I did play baseball for relaxation. Technical research is a sort of competition "the early bird catches the worm", therefore I devoted as much of my time to it as I found reasonable. While there is a limit to the number of working hours one can spend in the office, the amount of time required for research is limitless. Most researchers are constantly thinking of their work even when at home. Still, since I devoted almost all of my time every day to doing research, I had few hours left for my family, whom I regret now having burdened as I did due to my work.

In 1972, one year after my job transfer to STRL, I had the opportunity to give a research talk entitled "One-frame Memory for Still-Picture Broadcasting" for the first time at a national convention of ITE. Before the national convention, I prepared a paper for the research talk and showed it to my boss for his comments. I was greatly shocked then at a comment that my boss made about my paper. He said, "Mr. Yamada, your writing is awful". Because of this, I bought several books on writing, and tried hard to improve my writing skill by copying out a report written by a senior staff member, and other similar exercises. However, my efforts have yet to prove fruitful, even up to the present. I am now trying only to make my writing easy for readers to understand. Back then, while I mainly liked conducting research, I was very afraid of speaking in front of audiences at academic meetings. You may not believe it, but I was so nervous at times that I could not eat lunch if I had to give a speech at a meeting in the afternoon. Looking back on it, after having accumulated experiences, that lack of writing skill pointed out by my boss and my nervousness when it came to speaking might have been due to an insufficiency in my research and to lack of experience.

Unfortunately, still picture broadcasting was not realized

because of the progress of new technologies such as the digital, satellite transmission technologies, LSI memories, and the like. On the flip side, I was able to study important future technologies under the guidance of the late Mr. Hisakichi Yamane, who was my first boss. His leadership in research was ideal for me.

STRL had an athletic field behind the building. There I would enthusiastically play baseball, which has been my favorite sport since I was a child, during my lunch break every day. I carried out serious training there. For example, I would pull a tire by a rope that was tied around my waist, to strengthen the lower half of my body to be a good pitcher. My fellow researchers around me seemed to be dumbfounded at the strenuous training I put myself through. I practiced with so much enthusiasm that my boss at times seemed more impressed by my baseball skills than my studies, I'm afraid. As a result, although I was deeply absorbed in my research, when it came to being promoted I was the slowest among my colleagues who joined STRL the same year. There was a time when I was very worried over whether I should quit NHK. However, it was this slowness at getting promoted that inspired me to work harder. I wonder whether I would have had such eagerness if I had obtained a better evaluation and had been promoted earlier.

3.2 Teletext (1977-1985)

In 1972, the BBC announced a new information service called Ceefax which displayed characters and figures by multiplexing coded signals within vertical blanking intervals in which no TV image signals are transmitted. Inspired by the BBC's new service, NHK STRL started researching a Japanese Teletext system in the same year[17]. At the time, the standardization of Teletext systems among four countries, England, France, the USA and Japan was a major subject for the CCIR[18]. In the case of the English language, if a word has errors in the spelling caused by a bit error, a receiver can still recognize the word to some extent. On the other hand, in the case of Japanese Kanji characters, the display of a word with a bit error is totally different from the correct word since written Japanese Kanji comprises ideograms. Different from English, listeners cannot understand the meaning of a message in Japanese with bit errors on the TV screen (Fig.1).

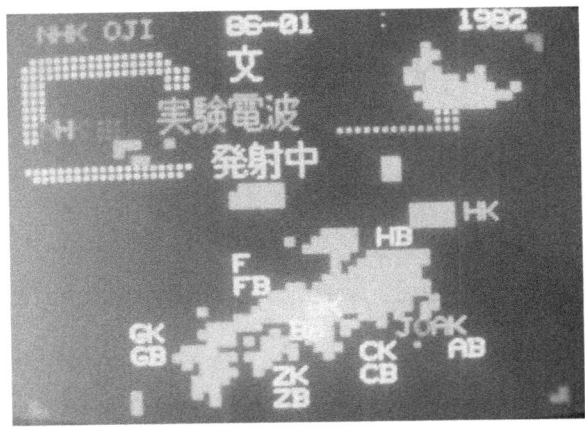

Fig.1 Teletext graphics with bit errors (The powerful error correcting code was needed.)

Chapter 3 MATURING STAGE OF DTTB TECHNOLOGY

Furthermore, error correcting technologies were not generally recognized all over the world in those days. Accordingly, based on the results of theoretical studies and transmission experiments, when it came to the initial Teletext in Japan, my predecessors at STRL thought that there would be too many bit errors to transmit Japanese character information in codes, and adopted the patterned Teletext system[19] to transmit signals by scanning the characters on an image screen in a like manner to a facsimile, instead of transmitting code information, as the initial Teletext in Japan. However, the speed of transmission under the patterned Teletext was about 1/20 the speed of transmitting the coded Teletext. Experimental Teletext under the pattern system was started in 1982. Researchers at that time considered that digital signals could not be transmitted through terrestrial transmission channels without there being any errors. They decided to start using the pattern system for Teletext after having thoroughly recognized the difficulty of digital transmission through terrestrial broadcasting by means of outdoor experiments. I believe the decision to use the pattern system was appropriate, considering the technological situation at the time.

After starting to study still-picture broadcasting in 1972, I initiated a colloquium with my fellow colleagues using "Error Correcting Codes" [20] written by William Peterson and E.J.Weldon,Jr as a textbook, which was not related to our primary subjects of study. In those days, there were no Japanese books on error correction theories, and I was uncertain whether the book would prove to be useful in the future. Nevertheless, I would spend several hours preparing for the colloquium, which was held once a week, only because the subject was mathematically interesting to me. I took on the role of manager of the colloquium. However, in spite of my efforts, more than half the members who attended the colloquium quit, because they thought it was useless to study error correction theories. Back then, Tokyo University and Osaka University were the only Japanese universities that carried out studies in error correction theories. At that time, error correction theory, which is one of the most important digital technologies in the current era, had been dealt with less seriously.

In 1977, I was told to take charge of the study of the coded transmission Teletext as a next-generation Teletext [21],[22]. We received information that one of the commercial broadcasting companies had started to study the coded transmission Teletext, and my boss was gripped by a sense of crisis, thinking that NHK too should launch into the study. But considering that it would still take NHK five more years before it started the experimental patterned transmission Teletext in 1982, it would seem that no one then believed much in the future practical use of the coded transmission Teletext. However, as I had been the manager of the colloquium, I voluntarily offered to take charge of the research and development of the error correction system for Teletext, a field in which STRL had no

Chapter 3 MATURING STAGE OF DTTB TECHNOLOGY

previous experience. Looking back, I must have been utterly reckless with eagerness to think I could take charge of the research and development myself simply because I had been the manager of the colloquium. I did not have any particular idea of the subject at the time.

I started the research and development process with the analysis of the situation regarding digital transmission in terrestrial broadcasting. In order to examine ghost interferences in Tokyo and Osaka, noises from factories, trains and power cables, and the influence of broadcasting repeaters over 7 stages in Wakayama and Hyogo Prefectures, random pattern signals were transmitted during TV signal blanking periods, and bit error patterns were collected on the receiver side (see Fig.2).

Fig.2(a) Bit error pattern collection in the fields: Actual field

Fig.2(b) Bit error pattern collection in the fields: Bit error collection system

The bit error patterns were recorded on several hundred FDs. The hardware and software for the error collection equipment was hand-made, and my research of still-picture broadcasting was very helpful in developing it.

From the results of the analysis of the error data, I found that most bit errors could not be completely prevented with BCH codes[20] or shortened cyclic codes[23] for burst errors by using the hardware available at the time. Therefore I felt it natural that the patterned transmission Teletext was serviceable for the start. I demonstrated in the analysis the necessity of forward/backward guarding, which ignores framing errors to some extent, by maintaining the phase continuity of clock signals. A framing code, which detects the tip of a packet signal, is vulnerable to errors. In Teletext being carried out in the US and Europe, forward/backward guarding was not stipulated.

I reported about bit errors and problems with terrestrial digital transmission channels by submitting the paper each year at the National Convention of ITE. Time passed very quickly without my finding any solution to these problems while I continued scrutinizing the results of the data analysis every day, trying to come up with solutions[24].

While conducting research and development, I devised a new method of error correction by converting a convolution code to a block code. I took out a patent for the new method, while still failing to achieve a favorable result. What got me started on such a difficult task? I asked myself with regret, while this long period of frustration endured.

One day in November, 1982, when as usual I was at home studying the results of an analysis of error patterns by block length, I noticed that the data at almost all the measuring points were error data of 8 bits or less, when the block length was 272 bits, the same as a packet. Then, I remembered Prof. James L Massey's "majority logic error-correcting codes"[25], though there were not very many of such kinds of the codes, from among the error-correcting codes that I had studied with the group. The majority logic error-correcting codes can correct errors with a simple circuit. I devised the (272,190) code by shortening the (273,191) code[26] from Prof. Weldon Jr's difference set cyclic codes, which are kinds of majority logic error-correcting codes that can correct any 8-bit errors in a packet of 272 bits. The (272,190) code consists of 190-bit information and 82-bit parity. I then developed the new decoding algorithm for the (272,190) code, which can correct not 8-bit but nearly 11-bit errors in a packet of 272 bits. By using this algorithm, almost all the errors collected in the outdoor experiments could be corrected. Moreover, those data were collected at locations with particularly poor receiving conditions.

Fig.3 shows packet signals multiplexed in the TV blanking periods and protected by the (272,190) code. The block error rate is found by the following expression:

$$Be= \sum_{t+1}^{n} \left(\frac{n}{t+1}\right) q^{t+1} (1-q)^{(n-(t+1))}$$

Be: block error rate

n: block length

t: correctable bit number

q: bit error rate

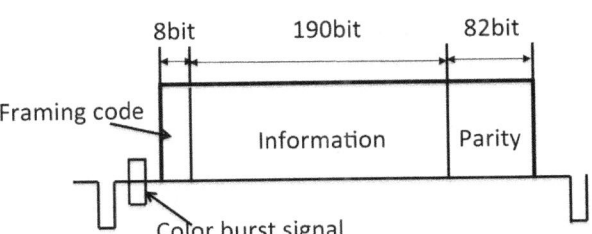

Bit rate : 5.73Mbps=8/5f_s f_s : Color subcarrier frequency

Fig.3 Teletext packet signals multiplexted with the TV blanking period

Though it took a bit of second guessing, it was clear that the longer the block length, the better the block error rates, under some ratios of the error correction bit number to the block length, as the block error rate is affected exponentially in relation to the bit number. One night after having been studying circuits until the darkness thinned and it became dawn, I noticed that it was past five o'clock in the morning by the time I finally found a possible solution to the problem with the error correction system that I had long been seeing. I will never forget the joy I felt when I discovered this. I thought, perhaps, the Goddess of Serendipity might have granted me her favor, and I could have confidence that I might become an independent researcher someday through the results of my own study following the achievement of Gen-lock at NHK Aomori broadcasting station. At the same time, I came to strongly believe that a solution would surely come, after having made every effort to find one.

I confirmed the effect of the decoding algorithm by conducting further experiments, in which received signals were decoded by software for 10-40 seconds. After confirming the strength of the decoded signals, the necessary hardware was made and its one-chip LSI was completed, so that signal processing in real time became possible. According to Professor Hideki Imai of Yokohama University, my study on the practical use of a high-quality error correcting code was almost equivalent to the Reed-Solomon code which has been adapted to CDs and was highly praised as an epoch-making invention. At least three young researchers in Japan and abroad have obtained a doctorate degree for their studies related to the (272,190) code. The efficiency of error correcting is evaluated based on Eb/No, wherein Eb is energy per bit of information and No is noise power per frequency. The performance of the (272,190) code is stronger than that of the convolution code which is 1/2 as efficient if the Eb/No is 5 dB or higher, as shown in Fig.4.

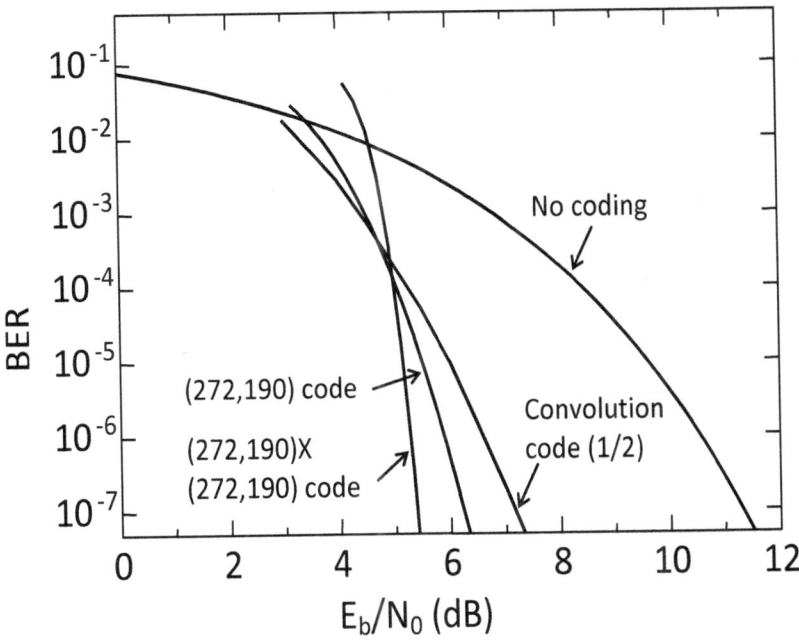

Fig.4 Error correction charasteristics of the (272,190) code

The error correcting capabiltiy is further strengthened if the code is double-coded such as (272,190) X (272,190), a characteristic of the double coding being that the curve is nearly perpendicular to the Eb/No (the horizontal axis). This double-coding method is used in FM multiplex broadcasting, which will be explained in the next section.

Teletext signals were received in their entirety under ghost interferences which would often become trouble in a terrestrial digital transmission channel. Fig.5 shows the analog TV reception of Teletext reception limit value of the ghost interference in the indoor experiment.

Fig.5 Analog TV signal with goast interferences at the limitation of the tetetext serviceusing the (272,190) code (D/U=9dB)

It took 5 years before the establishment of the error correction technology. Practical use of Teletext which is a kind of multiplex information broadcasting, started in 1985 as the first digital broadcasting service offered by NHK and other commercial broadcasting companies. That was also when the first error-free digital terrestrial television transmission channel in the world was completed. Thus, NHK STRL carried out detailed analysis into the problems that would come up when digital signals were transmitted over terrestrial broadcasting radio waves as described above. NHK STRL was able to present solutions based on its examinations, at a time when European and American researchers engaged in the teletext field didn't seem to be delving into the same basic research for digital transmission. Such detailed research, which led to the practical use of Teletext became the foundation for the research and development of DTTB.

I thought that if Teletext signals could be received in an automobile or by a cellular phone, data could become available for many people, and a whole range of services could be expanded. Based on this idea, we studied mobile reception in an automobile, but came to the conclusion that it was almost impossible. On the other hand, when it came to the reception of analog television broadcasting in automobiles, we found that the signals, though the quality was inferior, could be received to some extent. Therefore, an analog TV receiver was actually installed on an automobile in those days[27]. Accordingly, though digital compression technologies for pictures were yet to be developed at that time, the quality of digital terrestrial TV broadcasting might have been inferior to that of analog broadcasting without the development of mobile/portable re-

Chapter 3 MATURING STAGE OF DTTB TECHNOLOGY

ception. We feared that DTTB could not be realized in future. Thinking back, this concern was the starting point for me to launch into the research and development of DTTB for mobile/portable reception. Our team member, Mr. Muneyuki Tanaka[27] was in charge of implementing the comparative receiving tests between Teletext and analog TV (Fig.6).

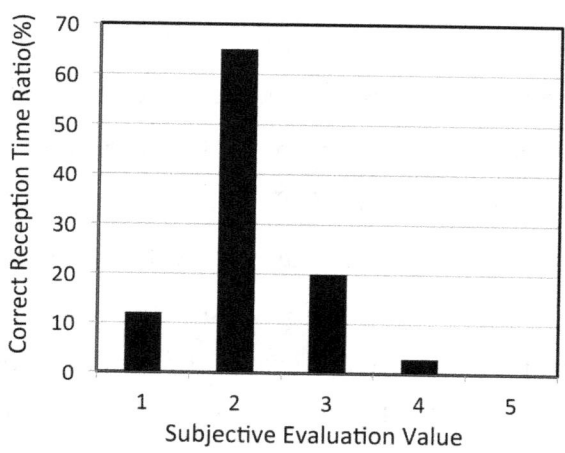

Fig.6 Results of comparative test between analog TV and Teletxt based on the five grade subjective test

In 1983, I submitted a thesis on the effects of the (272,190) code to IBC . However, the announcement of my thesis at the convention was rejected because it was too academic. The thesis I submitted was returned with a comment that it should go instead to the IEEE, etc. which in turn suggested that error correction technologies were not so generally known to the broadcasting community at the time. In fact, I didn't know the names of broadcasting researchers who had been studying the error correcting codes.

Instead of IBC, I submitted the thesis to the program committee of the 3rd IEEE GLOBECOM held in Atlanta in 1984. My paper was accepted and I presented the (272,190) code for the first time in the world. In the presentation room, I met Prof.H. Imai for the first time. Finally, my thesis on the practical use of the (272,190) code was published in a journal of the IEEE Communication Society in 1985[28], where submissions were said to be strictly examined. The thesis was evaluated highly by Prof. Mitsutoshi Hatori of Tokyo University and Prof. Imai, and I was lucky enough to have been awarded a doctorate degree. The (272,190) code was applied for FM multiplex broadcasting, the optical cards (ISO/IEC11693) [29] that were used in green cards in the USA, and TMCC signals, which are most important for defining various functions in Japanese DTTB and ISDB-T.

When I was invited to the first meeting of ISITA held in Hawaii in 1990, I presented the paper on an error correction method for the optical memory at the meeting. At the time, I visited the University of Hawaii and met Prof. Peterson and Prof. Weldon, both of whom were the authors of "Error Correcting Codes". We deepened our friendship at the opportunity. Since then, I have continued exchanging Christmas cards with Ms. Peterson, who was from Hiroshima of Japan. One day, I explained to her that I was studying the error correcting technology using her husband's "Error Correcting Codes" as the bible. Hearing my words, she was surprised and said to her husband, "Papa, you are so great!" I remember I was very impressed by her words at the time.

Prof. Peterson won the Japan Prize in 1999 for his establishing the coding theory for reliable digital communication, broadcasting and storage.

Furthermore, I became acquainted with Prof. Shu Lin [30] who was known as the author of the book, "An Introduction to Error Correcting Codes", and invited him to STRL to give a lecture for us. Then I dispatched Dr. Toru Kuroda to him at the University of Hawaii as a visiting researcher.

At the University of Hawaii, I also met Prof. Norman Manuel Abramson, who was very famous as a researcher of the ALOHA computer network. This network became the base of the Internet.

In those days, there were a lot of information theory researchers at the University of Hawaii, which was said to be Mecca of the information theory. The university accepted most students from Asian countries to the USA.

During the research and development process for Teletext technologies, I learned the following facts:

(1) A colloquium is indispensable for researchers, and they should choose a theme for study that is too difficult for anyone to understand alone.

(2) Though complex logistics can be understood theoretically, they cannot be realized as an actual circuit. However, rapid progress in LSI technologies made it possible to realize the circuits. Incidentally, the current degree of integration of LSI is more than 1 million times that in 1970's, still following Moore's law based on the rule that came from his experiences when he was working for Intel: "the number of transistors in a dense integrated circuit doubles approximately every 18-24 months".

(3) The digital terrestrial transmission characteristics of DTTB are not necessarily in accordance with theoretical evaluations that assume random noise. A real transmission channel is very hard to develop because there are various interferences. It cannot be predicted whether signals can really be received correctly or not before the signals are actually transmitted.

(4) Digital transmission over terrestrial TV broadcasting is robust against random noises but extremely weak against ghost interferences and signal distortion. Furthermore, group delay caused by a filter may occur in the broadcasting repeater, thus an equalizer is necessary every three stages.

(5) Impulse noises from home electrical appliances or from power cables hardly cause trouble on an analog TV screen, although noise appears on the screen. And in Teletext they cause random burst errors, which are very difficult to correct.

Accordingly, powerful error correcting codes are required to overcome this problem. The result for Teletext is the (272,190) code.

(6) Mobile reception is possible to some extent in analog TV broadcasting, but is completely impossible in Teletext. A special modulation system is necessary for DTTB.

3.3 FM Multiplex Broadcasting (1985-1995)

In the 1950's in America, many FM broadcasting stations had implemented analog FM multiplex broadcasting to broadcast background music programs called SCA. But in Japan, NHK considered FM broadcasting to be capable of high quality sound, however it had not yet implemented FM multiplex broadcasting because of problems with quality deterioration caused by ghost interferences, etc. The research of FM multiplex broadcasting was a kind of taboo in NHK.

At the request of Tokyo FM, we at NHK STRL developed 48kbps ADPCM sound multiplex broadcasting for stationary reception by FM multiplexing for correspondence education[31], which not NHK but a commercial FM broadcasting station, FM Tokyo, wanted to start at that time. We coped with their request as a public broadcasting station. Practical use of the FM multiplex sound broadcasting was started by FM Tokyo one year after that. However, as for myself, I was particularly interested in mobile reception of digital signals having realized first hand that Teletext signals could not be received at all in an automobile. In Sweden, Swedish Telecom, with Mr. Osten Makitalo as its leader, developed the *PI system*[32],[33] which was a kind of pager, wherein digital calling signals were multiplexed with FM broadcasting signals. That PI system has been used practically since 1978. EBU had worked with the CCIR (previous name of ITU-R) on the international standardization of RDS [33],[34] of FM multiplex broadcasting using the same transmission system as the PI. RDS is a simple system, the main function of which is to put out a command to automatically turn on an FM radio whenever traffic information services are being provided on a front FM broadcasting program to let a driver know the traffic condition. This RDS system is still used for automobiles in European countries.

In RDS, the (26,16) shortened cyclic code is used. The information bit rate of RDS is 0.7 kbps, and the (26,16) code[23] has the capability of correcting 5-bit burst errors. The code was developed by Prof. Tadao Kasami of Osaka University. The capability of correcting burst errors might seem sufficient as 5-bit burst errors in a block of 26 bits could be corrected, but a simulated Teletext with an actual error pattern made it clear that the (26,16) code was not so effective because bit errors generated in an actual transmission channel were not always within the range of 5-bit burst errors, in a block of 26 bits. When I visited Swedish Telecom, I discussed this approach to error correction with the researchers of it. They thought that when

Chapter 3 MATURING STAGE OF DTTB TECHNOLOGY

it came to block length, the shorter the better, and therefore, I failed in making them recognize the benefits of the (272,190) code. As for me, I had a certain hope that the transmission bit rate would be increased and that performance would be significantly improved by double-coding the (272,190) code used in Japanese Teletext, and applying a time interleaving method to deal with the signal shut-off.

Before 1985, NHK STRL had expressed approval of RDS, as proposed by EBU at a meeting of CCIR as I had no concrete plan for implementing FM multiplex broadcasting either analog sound multiplex broadcasting like SCA or digital multiplex broadcasting. But when I was informed that EBU had submitted a proposal on RDS as a recommendation to the meeting of the CCIR in 1985, I urgently asked a senior staff member, Mr. Yutaka Masuko, who had come to Geneva as a member of the Japanese delegation of CCIR to make arrangements to prevent RDS from being the sole recommendation. In the end, thanks to his efforts, he succeeded in adding a foot-note that "Another system has been researched and developed in other countries", suggesting that RDS was not the only system available. Looking back, being so young and never having attended a CCIR meeting before, I was reckless to have made such a difficult request to a senior staff member. I heard later that he strongly pressed the EBU staff to add the above footnote by saying, "I cannot go back to Japan if my request is rejected, and if it is rejected, I will have to jump into Lake Leman".

This eager suggestion from a Japanese representative seemed like a joke to the EBU side. And they told him not to commit Harakiri in the ITU room as that would surely cause terrible trouble. In the end, they decided to hear what he wanted. This is a story I heard after the meeting. Though it is an old story, I give thanks to Mr. Y. Masuko for his effort.

I participated in a transmission experiment in Germany in 1988 as requested by a Japanese manufacturer developing LSI for reception for RDS. I also recognized the outline of characteristics of mobile reception of RDS, for which as I had rightly expected and confirmed through experiment that the information could not be stably received. In fact, RDS adopted a system of repeatedly transmitting same signals as commands instead of transmitting messages that included sentences or large volumes of information such as traffic information. I thought, "I have got it! I was convinced that the (272,190) code developed in TELETEXT would make it possible.

As it turned out, strong demands had been made for better traffic information in order to cope with growing traffic jams in Japan, and the Metropolitan Police Department had begun to study traffic information services using Teleterminals. To meet these demands, and because of other reasons such as my publicly expressed opposition to RDS at the CCIR meeting, I promoted the research and development of FM multiplex broadcasting with young researchers (such as Dr. T. Kuroda and Mr. Masayuki Takada) based on the original

Chapter 3 MATURING STAGE OF DTTB TECHNOLOGY

Japanese (272,190) code, which could securely transmit a large volume of information to vehicles. In those days, since the main research theme of NHK was Hi-Vision, the research of FM multiplex broadcasting was not considered a main subject of research, and therefore, I had no supporters except my team members, Dr. T. Kuroda, Mr. M. Takada, Mr. Tomohiro Saito, and Mr. Tadashi Isobe. I felt miserable sometimes as if almost everyone opposed the research I was doing. In fact, a Director of the NHK engineering group dropped in at our experimental site and he said to my subordinate with anger, "What are you doing? Stop this experiment". But thinking that digital mobile reception technology would be very important in the future, I persuaded the management of STRL to continue with it, insisting that as the only public broadcasting organization in Japan pursuing research into a matter that was necessary for people, STRL should demonstrate its importance in the field, even if the theme was not directly related to the management of NHK. As a result of my persuasion, the head of the NHK Technology Group at the time, Mr. Shuich Morikawa, understood my intention, and allowed me to continue the research at STRL.

Finally, we succeeded in overcoming problems such as difficulties in mobile reception and the non-linear structure of an FM transmission channel, and established an FM multiplex broadcasting system using the (272,190) code, the time interleaving technology, and the demodulation system of level-controlled LMSK proposed by Dr. T. Kuroda[35]. LMSK is based on MSK, the band width of which is 1.5 times that of QPSK and noise is not so noticeable.

Japanese FM multiplex broadcasting had initially been strongly opposed by the EBU at a meeting of ITU-R in 1994, but with the cooperation of Sweden, which had friendly relations with Japan, and France, the host country of WG, and with support from the leaders of ABU, we managed to succeed in ITU-R standardization. We received approval for our proposal on FM multiplex broadcasting, which was a first for a Japanese Broadcasting system[36],[37]. Technical Director General of ABU, Mr. Om P. Kushu started supporting us in the standardization of ISDB-T from then on. We continued to cooperate with Mr. Perter Merburg and Tore Karlson of TERACOM exchanging DTTB technologies and digital FPU technologies developed by Dr. Shigeki Moriyama and other researchers. I learned that the technology cooperation and heart to heart exchange of information between organizations was extremely important.

The system was named DARC[39] by Mr. P. Melberg of TERACOM which has close ties with STRL. Some people opposed the name because the sound of "DARC" had a dark or negative image, but the name was finally decided on because the corollary word "dark" could also be used in a bright sense, such as a dark horse. Fig.7 shows DARCs of stereo sound signals and multiplexed signals before using FM modulation.

Chapter 3 MATURING STAGE OF DTTB TECHNOLOGY

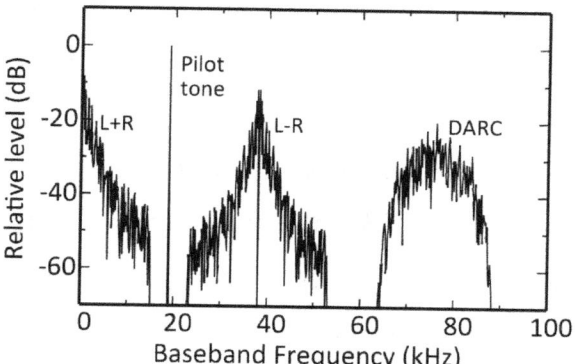

Fig.7 Frequency spectrum of FM audio signals and DARC
(RDS with the 57KHz subcarrier can be multiplexed.)

The frequency of the subcarrier of a DARC is set to be 76 KHz in order to be compatible with RDS. Currently, more than 4,800 units of DARCs have been commercially sold as the main media for VICS, which is a traffic information service started by MPT, MC and NPA, etc. on July 1, 1995. They have contributed in avoiding traffic jams by providing traffic information for drivers through car navigation systems (see Fig. 8).

This was the first practical use of the mobile reception of digi-

Fig.8 Car navigation system with the DARC receiving function
(Over 40.7milion VICS receivers has sold by Dec. 2013.)

tal broadcasting in the world. As a result, NHK received an additional income from VICS. Though a director of NHK at the time said to me, "Because of FM multiplex broadcasting developed by you, we were forced to start the service."

VICS have been practically used in Beijing, Shanghai and Guangzhou, and I hear that experiments on VICS are being carried out in other countries. A comparison between Japanese DARC and the European RDS is shown in Table 1. In fact, in Europe, the Swift project, Eureka 1197 which involved mainly broadcasting stations from France, Sweden, Norway, and Germany to develop a new data broadcasting network, was started based on both RDS and DARC in 1995.

Tabel 1 The transmission parameters of DARC and RDS

	DARC	RDS
Subcarrier frequency	76kHz	57kHz
Multiplexing level	4-10%	2-3%
Modulation	LMSK	BPSK
Information bit rate	8kbps	0.73kbps
Error correction code	(272,190)X(272,190)	(26,16)

What I learned in the research and development of FM multiplex broadcasting was that:

(1) A business model is important. There have been strong demands for traffic information services to avoid traffic jams[39].

Chapter 3 MATURING STAGE OF DTTB TECHNOLOGY

(2) A great deal of cross-talk interferences between multiplexed signals and stereo signals are caused by ghost interferences.

(3) The difference between mobile reception and stationary reception caused by reception conditions such as the height and gain of an antenna is about 19dB.

(4) FM multiplex broadcasting signals are further affected in various ways by fading interferences, as well as ghost interferences and impulse noise caused by omnidirectional antennas.

(5) While the agenda for the management of NHK included high-definition TV technologies rather than FM multiplex broadcasting technologies, the result of the research and development of FM multiplex broadcasting led to mobile reception technologies for Japanese DTTB.

Chapter 4
JAPANESE DTTB : ISDB-T (1986-2003)

Japanese DTTB, ISDB-T, is based on Teletext for stationary reception and FM multiplex broadcasting for mobile reception[40]. Fig.9 shows the overall history of the research and development of Japanese DTTB, which will be explained in detail in the following sections, including previously mentioned teletext and FM multiplex broadcasting technologies for transmitting digital terrestrial signals.

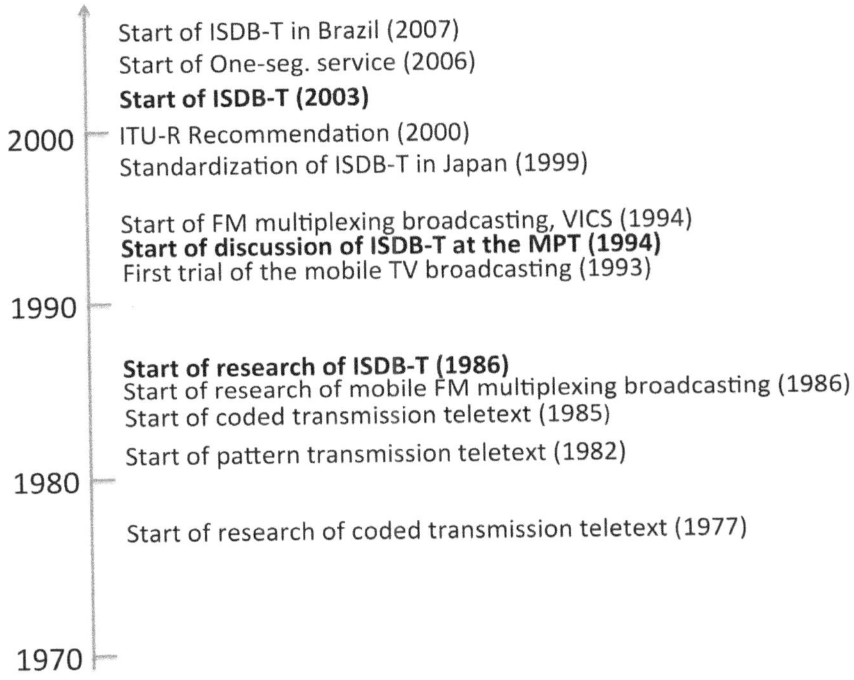

```
2000 ─┬─ Start of ISDB-T in Brazil (2007)
      │   Start of One-seg. service (2006)
      │   **Start of ISDB-T (2003)**
      │   ITU-R Recommendation (2000)
      │   Standardization of ISDB-T in Japan (1999)
      │
      │   Start of FM multiplexing broadcasting, VICS (1994)
      │   **Start of discussion of ISDB-T at the MPT (1994)**
      │   First trial of the mobile TV broadcasting (1993)
1990 ─┤
      │
      │   **Start of research of ISDB-T (1986)**
      │   Start of research of mobile FM multiplexing broadcasting (1986)
      │   Start of coded transmission teletext (1985)
      │   Start of pattern transmission teletext (1982)
1980 ─┤
      │   Start of research of coded transmission teletext (1977)
      │
      │
1970 ─┘
```

Fig.9 History of R&D of DTTB in Jaoan

4.1 Proposal for Mobile/Portable Reception

In digitalizing television, I thought that everything analog TV could do should also be possible for digital TV, as I had judged when I had been engaged in the research of coded transmission Teletext 10 years earlier. Specifically, I thought that mobile and portable reception should be possible for DTTB and that the sound from DTTB should be able to be heard on a digital radio, etc., as mentioned in Chapter 3. As satellite broadcasting technologies, CATV and optical communication advanced, people would be able to watch any type of program at home in future. But when it came to mobile reception, the problem was how to transmit important information to people while they were outdoors, which was one of essential roles of broadcasting. I soon came to firmly believe that DTTB via VHF and UHF was the most suitable for this purpose because of the characteristics of radio waves for transmitting information.

 I had studied the SS[41],[42] system for cellular phones, etc. as a modulation system suitable for mobile reception before 1986, but I knew that the SS system would not have a favorable bit rate, and therefore it would not be suitable as a broadcasting system for transmitting broadband TV signals. However, an American researcher made a proposal for the SS system to ATSC of the USA. He maintained that SS could avoid the "cliff effect", which in digital broadcasting is when signal reception abruptly ceases[43],[44]. There was also a group in Japan that strongly suggested the SS system should be studied for Japanese DTTB. We lost more than one year to persuade them that the SS system was not suitable for DTTB.

 According to the Shannon-Hartley theorem,
 The formula $C = B \cdot \log_2(1+S/N)$
  where C is transmission speed,
  B is band width,
  S is signal power, and
  N is noise power,

establishes that if the transmission speed is kept constant, then the larger the bandwidth (B) is, the lower the S/N will be. However, those who supported the SS had little knowledge that in TV broadcasting the service bandwidth is limited to 6MHz, which is different from cellular phone communication, where narrow-band audio signals are shared, and from deep space communication, where a wide band is used to transmit narrow band signals. They also did not take into account that TV pictures themselves were broadband signals, and that ghost interferences from distant buildings would disturb the orthogonal time conditions of the transmitted signals.

4.2 DAB and OFDM

In 1986, a general meeting of CCIR was held, where the EBU presented DAB technologies for mobile reception. I was strongly impressed by the presentation, and felt that we at STRL should also examine the technologies[45]. The DAB technologies were configured based on audio compression technologies developed by IRT of Germany, Switzerland, and Austria, and OFDM[46],[47] transmission technologies for mobile reception developed by CCETT of France.

They insisted that high-quality audio signals could be compressed by 1 bit per sample using a masking effect like that in the function of human hearing. These audio compression technologies for DAB are currently the standard. I have heard that OFDM was proposed by CCETT as a cellular-phone modulation system for the next generation, but was rejected for adoption. On the other hand, in Japan, Dr. Boutaro Hirosaki[48] of NEC had studied OFDM technology in 1980's. In the OFDM system, the transmission bit rate per carrier is reduced several thousand times by using that many carriers, which is different from a conventional system that uses a single carrier. Each carrier is allocated at an interval of 1/T (where T is a cycle of one symbol) to prevent interference between symbols. The number of carriers is very high, while the transmission bit rate per carrier is extremely low. As shown in Fig.10, both the generation of signals and wave detection can be calculated.

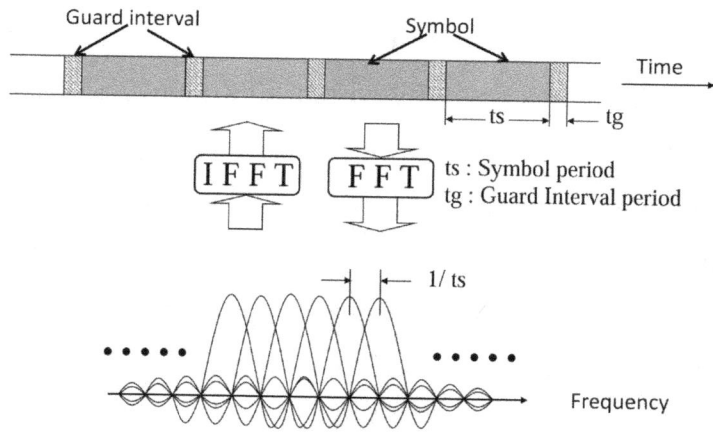

Fig.10 Principle of OFDM

Signal generation can be calculated by Inverse FFT as follows:

$$x(t) = \sum_{i=0}^{i=N-1} Re[c_i e^{j2\pi f_i t}] = \sum_{i=0}^{i=N-1}[a_i \cos 2\pi f_i t - b_i \sin 2\pi f_i t]$$

N: Number of carrier waves

Transmitted data $c_i = a_i + j b_i$

f_i: the i-th frequency of carriers.

Frequency interval $f_i - f_{i-1} = 1/Ts$

Ts: symbol length

Wave detection on the reception side can be calculated by FFT as follows:

$$f(n) = \sum_{i=0}^{i=N-1} x(i) e^{-\frac{j2\pi n i}{N}}, \quad n = 0, 1, \cdots (N-1), \quad N = 2^m$$

As I mentioned, the most difficult problem when it comes to DTTB channels is ghost interferences, which are time-axis interferences caused by buildings. OFDM signals are orthogonal on a frequency axis. If a symbol length of each signal is long on the time axis, the signals are hardly affected by ghost interferences, making OFDM signals an advantageous measure against them. Furthermore, guard intervals can be provided between frames to absorb ghost interferences. Research into OFDM signals had already been carried out in the communication field in the 60's. The practical use of OFDM became possible in the period from the late 80's to the 90's because of the development of discrete Fourier transform and the development of semiconductor technologies.

I have heard that research of DAB was carried out by the EBU as one of the important subjects of research as Eureka 147, a European research project. On the other hand, regrettably, STRL's research into OFDM was delayed.

When I went to Europe on business in 1988, I had an opportunity to visit the CCETT. I was introduced there by a friend from TDF and was able to confirm the benefits of OFDM by examining the difference between DAB with no noise and FM broadcasting with noises caused by ghost interferences, using an experimental vehicle at CCETT. Having seen for myself the difficulties involved in digital terrestrial transmission, I was greatly impressed by OFDM. Here, I would like to express my gratitude for the kindness of the researchers at CCETT who showed me the results of their experiments, regardless of how valuable they were.

At STRL, I started the research and development of OFDM with some young researchers, Dr. M. Saito and Dr. T. Kuroda, Dr. S. Moriyama, Mr. M. Takada, etc. in the late 80's. We started full-scale research in 1990. Though OFDM of CCETT was for DAB, we adopted OFDM as a countermeasure to overcome the difficulty of mobile reception DTTB which I experienced when researching Teletxt. Dr. M. Saito evaluated the performance of OFDM against ghost interferences by means of simulation. Fig.11[49] shows a comparison of the simulation carried out by him, OFDM and QPSK under conditions for reception with a DU signal ratio at 5 dB and with a plurality of ghosts, which were the strictest conditions for the ghost data obtained in the outdoor Teletext experiment.

In QPSK, the error ratio didn't decrease to 10^{-2} or lower no matter how high CN ratio increased, which indicated that QPSK could not cope with the ghost interferences. On the other hand, in the case of OFDM, the error rate was practicable if the CN ratio was at a certain level, which indicated that OFDM was effective against the ghost interferences, which were the most troublesome problems in our research of Teletext, for DTTB. The results of his simulation were the first data I saw that led me to decide that OFDM should be adopted for DTTB in Japan.

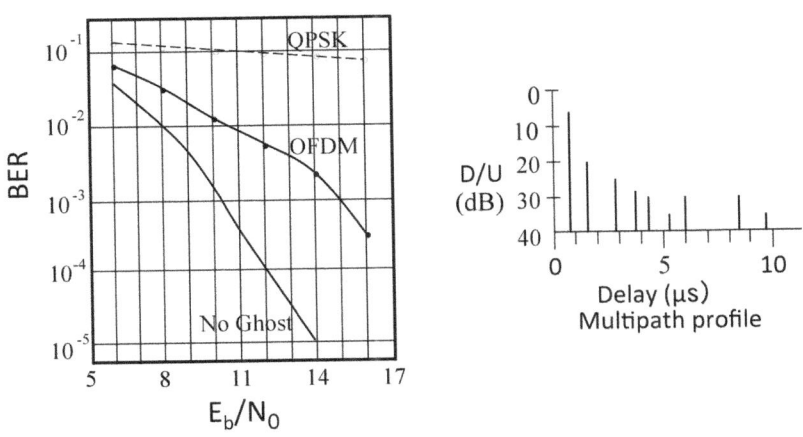

Fig.11 Comparative simulation between OFDM and QPSK (by Dr. M Saito)

4.3 Trial Production of OFDM and Experiment in Mobile Reception

In the latter half of the 1980's, the main subject of research for STRL was MUSE, a kind of BS analog HDTV. In addition, the development of the terrestrial analog MUSE transmission system was also carried out[50]. Therefore, although the OFDM, which was still totally unfamiliar to STRL researchers, was being studied by a few of our staff members, STRL had no room for a trial production of the experimental equipment. No one was expressing interest in OFDM.

STRL, meanwhile, had submitted the proposal for the narrow MUSE system to transmit analog signals terrestrially at 6MHz, to the ATSC in the USA. In both indoor and outdoor environments, to actually proceed with the research of DTTB was a kind of taboo at NHK. Nevertheless, I continually explained the importance of OFDM research, which I expected to come to the fore over the following 10 or more years, to the top management at STRL until finally I managed to obtain reserve funding for research into OFDM. Mr. Seikichi Sakakibara, then the Section Chief of the Broadcasting Engineering Section of MPT, indirectly supported us, because he shared the same opinion as me that STRL should focus not only on MUSE but also on research subjects that would likely become more relevant in future. Now I realize that it is difficult to carry out research on a subject that diverges from the course that has already been taken by the management or the research organization, especially when the importance of that subject is insisted upon by one person alone. Therefore, I think it is necessary to carefully explain a new subject to those both in and out of STRL to make them understand its importance and future relevance. In research organizations, if the researchers only follow the directions that have already been set by managers, the organization will be far behind with the research of new technologies and suffer from a fatal blow caused by the delay. The managers should study the organizational management of new technologies, recognize its importance and make the members of the organization understand it sufficiently.

I started working with our young researchers, Dr. M. Saito, Dr. T. Kuroda, Dr. S. Moriyama, Mr. M. Takada, etc. to plan to fix the specifications and design our original test equipment for confirming the actual performance of OFDM for DTTB. But it was too hard for a single manufacturing company to accept our order for a set of hardware and complete the test equipment alone. First, we had to educate the laboratory researchers at the manufacturing company before starting production. As we could not achieve our expected performance standards, a staff member, Dr. S. Moriyama who was in charge at STRL went to a manufacturing company's factory to stay there for more than one month and instruct the engineers with great care and patience, until finally the first generation of test equipment was completed[51],[52]. Dr. S. Moriyama's leadership of the manufacturer's operations enhanced their technology and they became the first manufacturer of OFDM equipment in Japan. They deeply appreciated Dr. S. Moriyama and NHK.

In 1993, a new experimental transmitter was established at STRL. The mobile reception of DTTB was exhibited at a public open house at STRL held in May to the public for the first time in the world by Mr. Shunji Nakahara (Fig.12). In the demonstration, we presented reception with no flickering on the screen, even in a traveling vehicle by combining a modulation system of OFDM, using the (272,190) code and time interleaving. However, visitors at STRL raised questions about why television should be watched in a traveling vehicle, and the exhibition did not attract any particular attention. Also there were people at STRL who opposed the exhibition itself. No one at that time recognized the importance of mobile reception.

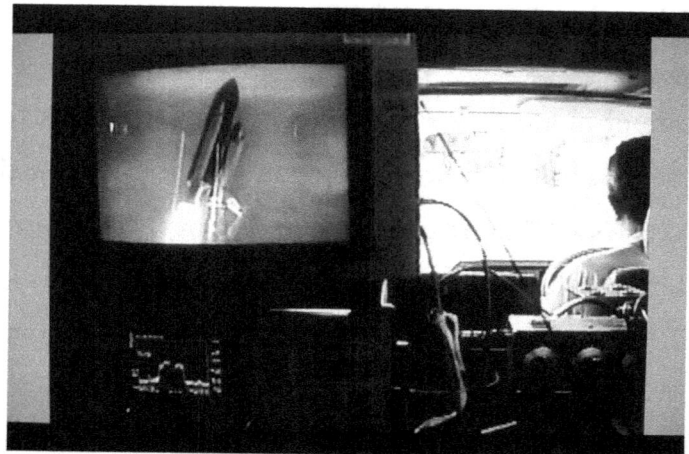

Fig.12 Demonstration of mobile TV reception for the first time in the world
(at NHK STRL Open Hous in May, 1993)

4.4 Basic SFN Experiment

In the OFDM system, which is different from analog broadcasting, a broadcasting repeater may be used at the same frequency if the contents of the programs to be broadcasted are the same. Since Japan is a mountainous country where many frequencies are used to broadcast programs to mountainous areas, SFN would likely contribute greatly in reducing the number of broadcasting frequencies, which are the property of the people of Japan, if an SFN were established. Naturally, the conditions for SFN vary according to such factors as transmission power, service areas, the lengths of ghost interferences, etc.

In 1995, Mr. S. Nakahara and other staff members carried out an experiment of an SFN between NHK Broadcasting Center and STRL (a distance of about 7.5km) using a test-produced transmitter/receiver. For the experiment, the same TV program was OFDM-modulated at a single frequency and radio waves were emitted to and from both sites to confirm the effect of SFN. Fig.13(a) shows what happened at the location of reception when radio waves were emitted from a transmitter on the STRL side only; Fig.13(b) shows what happened when radio waves were emitted from both transmission towers at the Broadcasting Center and at STRL.

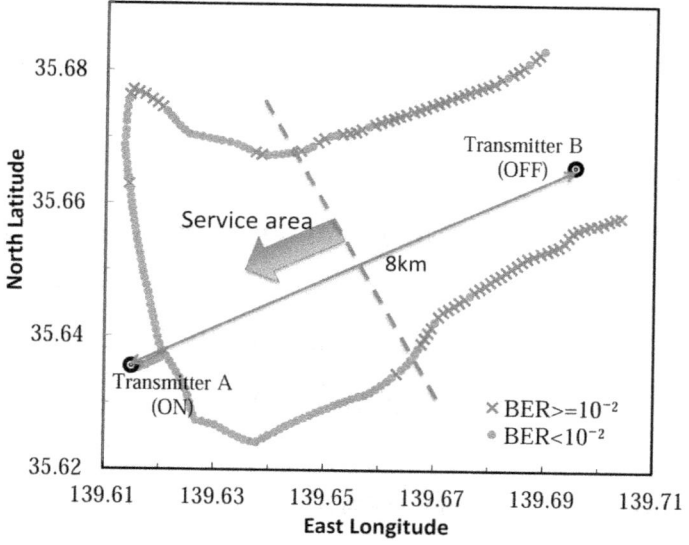

(a) A : power on, B : power off

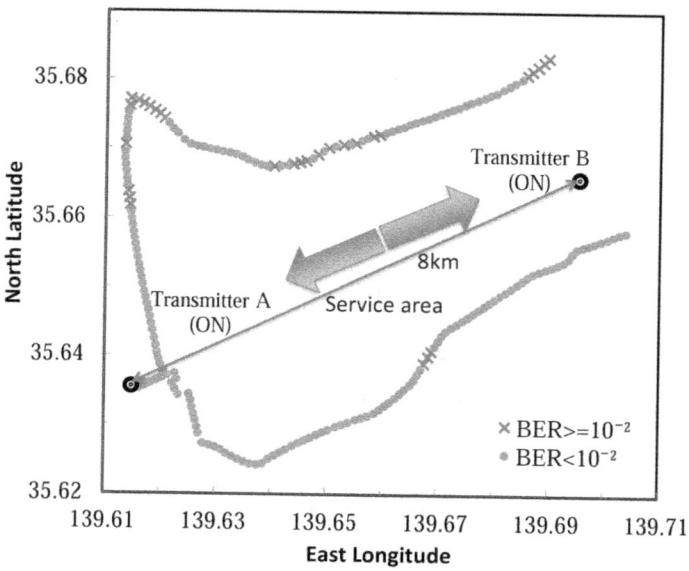

(b) A : power on, B : power on

Fig.13 SFN field trials between NHK broadcasting center (A) and NHK STRL (B) (by S. Nakahara)

The results of the experiment confirmed that although interferences occurred in analog broadcasting when radio waves were emitted at the same frequency, the service area in digital broadcasting could be extended[53] if the radio waves were OFDM-modulated. In other words, the results indicate that the OFDM system can greatly contribute to the reduction of broadcasting frequencies. By introducing SFN, the frequency bandwidth used for broadcasting could be reduced by 130 MHz after completion of analog switch off. The frequencies of 130MHz have been used for cellular phones and other purposes (Fig.14). More than 80% broadcasting stations in Japan have been adopting SFN.

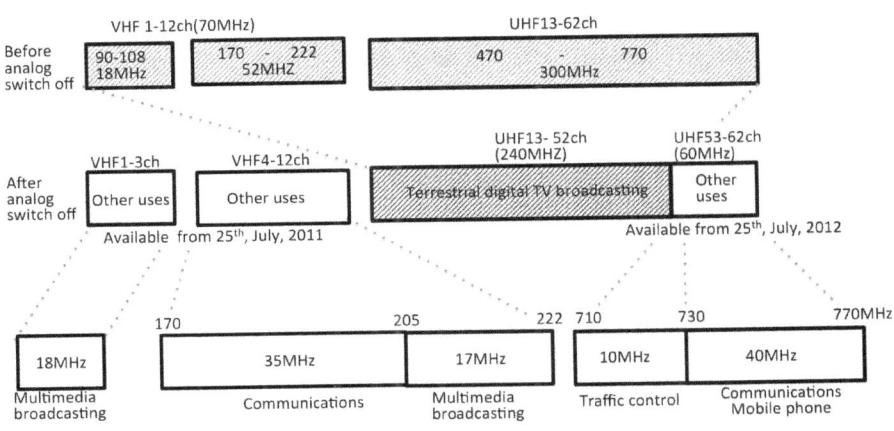

Fig.14 Frequency reallocation of TV channels after analog swich off
(130MHz can be used by TV digitalization)

4.5 Standardization of ISDB-T

4.5.1 Start of formal discussions to decide on DTTB system

In 1994, consultations with MPT were held to arrange a discussion forum on the future of digital broadcasting in Japan. As a consequence, the digital broadcasting systems committee chaired by Prof. Yasuhiko Yasuda of Waseda University was established in the Electric Communication Council of MPT. As shown in Fig.15, the committee organized 5 WG's on the common technologies such as audio/video compression technologies, DTTB, digital satellite broadcasting, digital cable TV, and digital audio broadcasting. As for specific technologies related to DTTB, a DTTB System Development Committee was organized within the ARIB in September 1996. The committee mainly comprised members of MPT, NHK, commercial broadcasting stations and manufacturing companies with the purpose of deciding the specifications, and conducting detailed examinations into DTTB technologies. From that point, I made efforts as a member of the WGs and chaired the DTTB System Development Committee of ARIB to establish DTTB technology in Japan.

Fig.15 The members of Japanese digital broadcasting working group (WG)

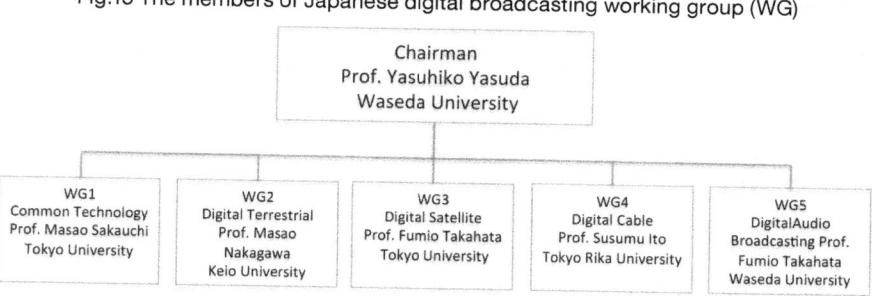

Fig.16 shows the history of this area of research and development from 1994, when discussions were initiated in MPT aiming at the implementation of DTTB. As a first step, the following system requirements for DTTB were established during the discussions:

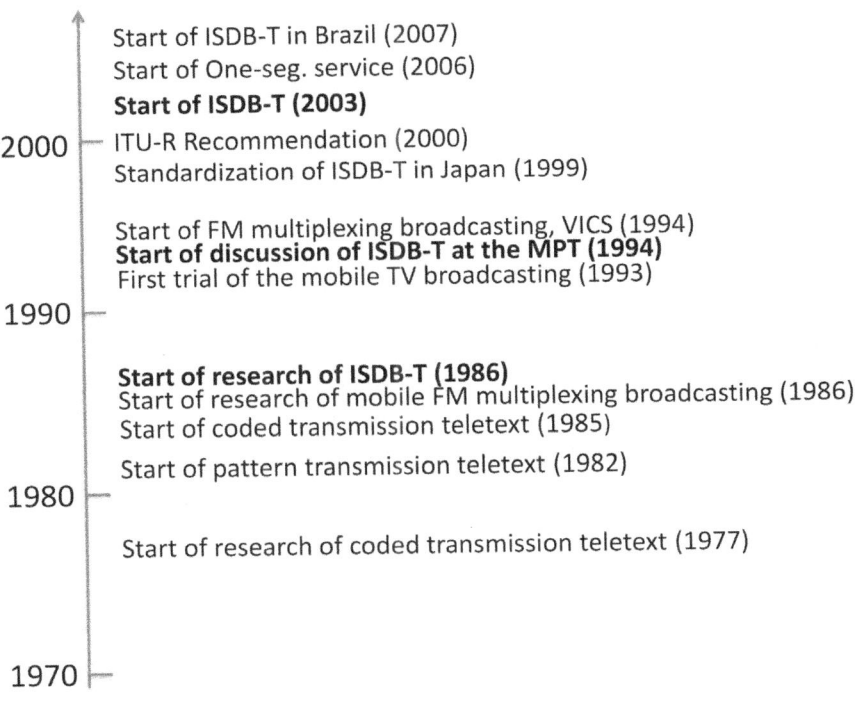

Fig.16 Formal DTTB development plan in Japan

(1) HDTV services should be available.

(2) Multi-channel standard TV services should be available.

(3) Mobile broadcasting services should be available.

(4) The system should contribute to the effective use of SFN frequencies.

(5) Commonality to BS digital broadcasting on base band signals should be secured.

(6) International standards should be adopted.

(7) Commonality across digital terrestrial audio broadcasting should be established.

4.5.2 The proposal of BST-OFDM

Though the system requirements were set as listed above, the field research carried out by Mr. S. Nakahara, etc. revealed that many frequencies had already been used for broadcasting repeaters in the mountainous regions of Japan, with few left for digital broadcasting. Therefore, we thought that under these circumstances, we had no other option than to use adjacent vacant channels in the same area in order to implement DTTB. We conducted an examination of a system (shown in Fig.17) utilizing the advantages of the multi-carrier system, because we expected there would be no problem in terms of the protection ratio if several central parts of adjacent channels could be used. By using multiple adjacent channels to obtain 6 MHz in total, a system of 6 MHz could be obtained after the termination of analog broadcasting. We reported it as a BST-

OFDM system at an ITU-R meeting. After that, we conducted various examinations, but during this process MPT announced that they would reallocate frequencies for DTTB. The idea of using multiple adjacent channels led to the development of the final specifications of BST-OFDM using 6 MHz split into 13 segments.

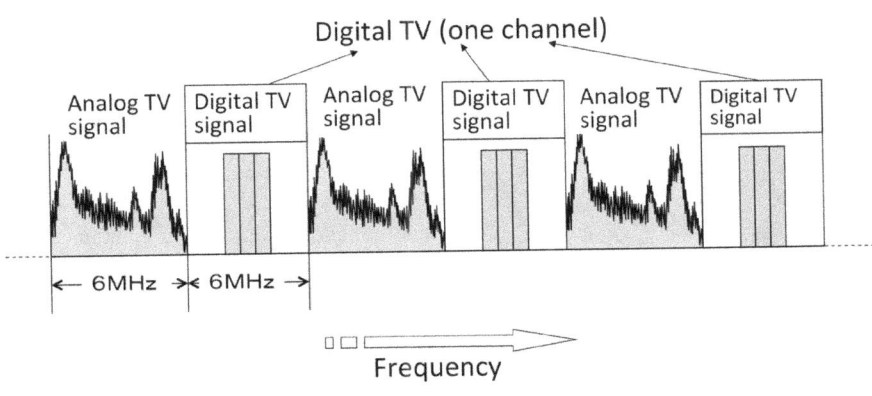

Fig.17 Original idea of BST-OFDM

Since such a complicated system as described above had to be studied further before DTTB could become practically usable, it seemed as if it would take more time before such technology could be implemented in Japan. Therefore, we tried to use OFDM technologies, which facilitate reception with omni-directional antennas, for FPU under the television marathon relay system, which can use conventional analog technologies, and requires many engineers, such as antenna repairmen, to climb on the rooves of relay vehicles in order to adjust the directions of the antennas. But Dr. S. Moriyama developed 800

MHz band relay equipment, the effect of which was confirmed for the first time in the Lake Biwako Marathon in 1995[54]. Thanks to this FPU, the cost of the marathon relay was significantly reduced. That represented the first practical use of digital FPU for mobile reception in the world. Based on the results achieved by STRL, similar FPUs using OFDM for wireless outside broadcasting are currently being used in most countries (Fig.18).

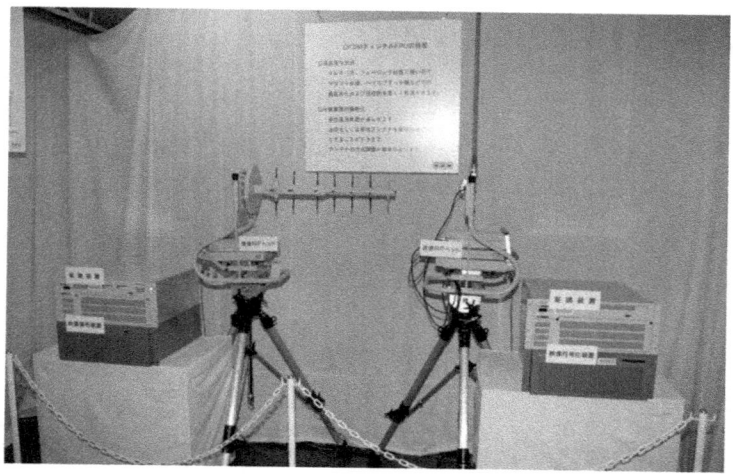

Fig.18 Field Pick Up unit (Developed by Dr. S. Moriyama)

4.5.3 Analog-analog conversion and realization of DTTB

After that, frequency bands for digital broadcasting were allocated at key stations located in provincial capitals. MPT then carried out a frequency allocation plan. Starting with the conversion of analog TV frequencies to other frequencies (so - called analog - analog conversion), MPT was able to make room in low UHF channels that were used for DTTB. By these means, 6MHz DTTB was finally achieved in Japan (Fig.19).

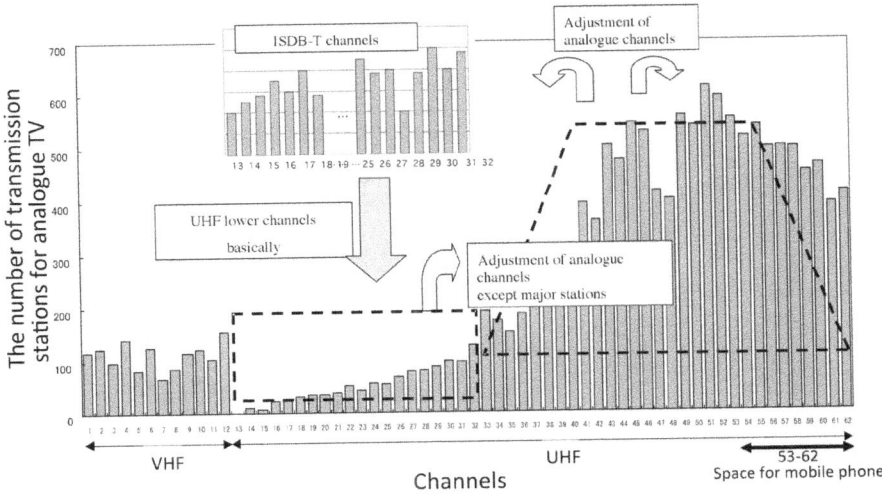

Fig.19 Analog-Anaqlog conversion for introduction of DTTB

In 1995, MPT established the DTVL which consisted of the researchers of STRL, manufactures, and commercial broadcasting stations. Dr. M. Saito, and Mr. Tetsuomi Ikeda transferred from STRL to the DTVL and contributed to the development of detailed system parameters. The final system parameters such as the number of the segments of 6MHz were decided based on the agreement between STRL and DTVL. Mr. Seiichi Sasaki, director of digital broadcasting division of STRL, managed both STRL and DTVL.

The examination of the system was carried out under the DTTB Development Committee of ARIB. The original plan for a provisional system was established at a committee meeting in September 1997, and a trial transmitter/receiver was produced by STRL to carry out various transmission experiments.

Based on the results of these transmission experiments and various simulations, a provisional system based on segmentation was decided in September 1998. Large-scale transmission experiments including measurement of the service area, were conducted[55] in order to confirm SFN functions using a broadcasting repeater at Tokyo Tower from November 1998 to March 1999. Apart from these experiments, 11 transmitters were set up from Hokkaido to Okinawa using funds from the national budget. Efforts were also made to publicize the experiments and to raise awareness around DTTB. The results of the experiments were organized, and based on these results, updates to the DTTB system were officially proposed in September 1999[56].

At the Okinawa Summit meeting in 2000, the superb merits of Japanese DTTB which can broadcast HDTV and mobile reception services were demonstrated to world leaders. The proposed system was approved and recommended at the assembly meeting of the ITU-R in May 2000. Dr. T. Kuroda and other members started the work of deciding on the parameters for actual system implementation, and set up a detailed operation guide[57] for broadcasting stations and manufacturers. Japanese DTTB was finally put into service in December 2003.

The provision of One-Seg services, which can also be received by cellular phones, started on April 1, 2006. Currently, almost all cellular phones have a One-Seg receiving function.

It has become one of the most attractive merits of Japanese DTTB, which is called ISDB-T when it comes to the promotional activities for the system all over the world (Fig.20).

Fig.20 Celler phones with one-seg receiving function
(Over 40milion one-seg receivers has been sold by the end of 2012)

4.6 Mobile/Portable Reception for TV

Before the start of discussion on digital broadcasting in Japan among MPT in 1994, a discussion on the international standardization of DTTB for the ITU-R was started in 1992 as proposed by the USA. I attended the first meeting of TG11/3 of the ITU-R as vice chairman, where I demanded to talk with Mr. Stan. Baron, Chairman, and Mr. Tery Long, vice chairman, regarding mobile reception, but I received no response from either of them. All they said was that portable liquid crystal receivers for analog television had been on the European market, but had hardly sold. Ultimately mobile/portable reception was not put on the agenda at the meeting of TG 11-3; in 1997, the European system DVB-T and the USA system ATSC were recommended as ITU-R systems. The Japanese system ISDB-T was attached to this recommendation as the future system because of it being underdeveloped. Namely, no one noticed its potential and importance. I felt at the time that a higher priority had been given by commercial leadership to the standardization than the development of broadcasting technologies in Europe and the USA. On the other hand, the Japanese system developed by STRL was technologically difficult, and detailed experiments for transmission/reception had to be conducted. As a result, the Japanese system wasn't recommended until as late as May, 2000[58],[59].

During a panel discussion at a symposium for the 70th anniversary of NHK STRL, which STRL held in the hall of the Japanese Federation of Economic Organizations in July 2000, a famous engineering critic asked me, "Mr. Yamada, do people really want to watch TV in moving automobiles or on cellular phones?", casting some doubt on the practical use of mobile/portable reception. Digital broadcasting in Japan was not looked upon too favorably back in 2000.

However, DTTB services were finally implemented in Japan in 2003 with the cooperation of MIC, ARIB, NHK, commercial television stations, manufacturers and academics, etc. One-Seg services for watching TV on cellular phones started in 2006. Currently, the One-Seg receiving function has been incorporated in almost all cellular phones. For example, at the final game of the WBC in 2009 when the Japanese team finally won, many passengers in trains watched the game on their handheld cellular phones, and applauded Ichiro's game-winning hit in the 10th inning. In the great earthquake on March 11, 2011, when all transportation systems in Tokyo were stopped, communication through cellular phones was blocked, and it became difficult for commuters in Tokyo to get back home. But One-Seg services played an important role as the only source of reliable information. This may show that it is not the image quality but the immediateness and accuracy of information that is usually most important. The ISDB-T system has a unique function as an EWS, which no other systems have. This function is understood to be greatly useful for saving lives in case of a disaster, and is used as the standard specification for receivers in Chile[60], etc.

Lately, many people can be seen using ear-phones and watching TV on cellular phones on trains. With the increased use of smart phones, an environment has been established where people can access various TV programs or other types of programs via the Internet even if they are not at home. Currently, the development of content to further advance the mobile/portable reception functions of ISDB-T is still required.

Mobile reception was not considered at all, either in terms of ATSC or DVB-T. However, recently new systems have been proposed to cover mobile reception such as MPH, an improved ATSC system,, and DVB-H and DVB-T2, which is different from the DVB-T system. It seemed to me that to change broadcasting systems, was very difficult because of many receivers spreading among people. These days, I sometimes hear people involved in broadcasting in Europe and the USA say, "We envy Japan because services can be expanded to many applications including mobile services." I now feel that the direction our research has taken toward the development of mobile/portable reception was right.

Chapter 5
CHARACTERISTICS AND TRANSMISSION METHOD OF ISDB-T

The image in Fig.21 shows services provided by ISDB-T[61]. The system can provide several unique services, which the European and American systems do not provide, in this era of integration between broadcasting and communication.

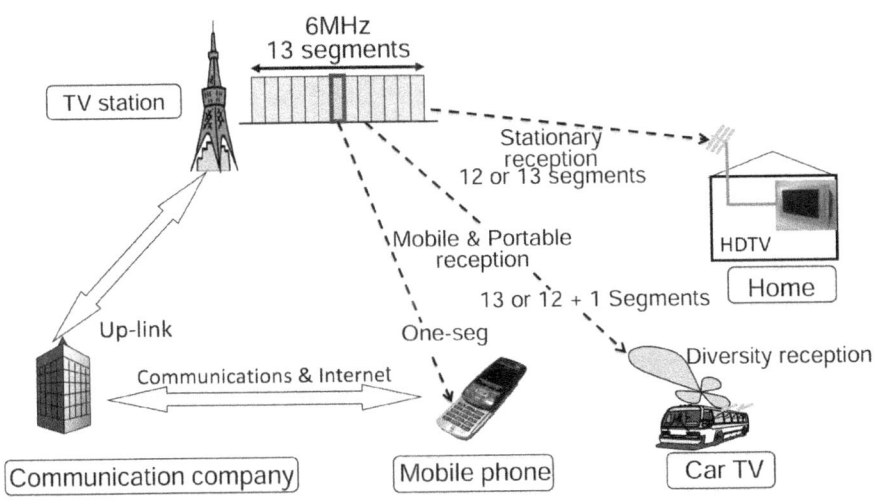

Fig.21 Service images of ISDB-T services (from DiBEG)

5.1 Characteristics

5.1.1 Provision of various services

In analog broadcasting, a single standard television program is provided by using the entire band of 6MHz. On the other hand, ISDB-T enables the provision of HDTV broadcasting services with mobile/portable reception services or three standard television programs with mobile/portable reception services if the video compression is based on MPEG-2. Furthermore, if the video compression is based on MPEG-4, the amount of possible services doubles. As a cellular phone has a TV receiving function, or so-called One-Seg function, emergency information etc. can be received anytime and anywhere. In an extreme situation, people could watch TV in a place with no electricity as long as their cellular phones could be charged and radio waves can reach the location. Furthermore, integrated Internet services could be possible by using the uplink from cellular phones to the Internet.

As for emergency information, ISDB-T is the most suitable system for providing information on a state of emergency especially for people in an outdoor area where they cannot easily access information, because ISDB-T has a mobile/portable receiving function. Since the occurrence of the Tsunami that was caused by the Sumatra Andaman earthquake in December 2004, the use of digital broadcasting as a means of transmitting information in an emergency has been discussed as a theme for research by ITU-R. Finally, ITU-R recommended the "'use of digital broadcasting as broadcasting infrastructure for warning the public and rescuing them from disaster'"[62]. The only device with an emergency warning function is an ISDB-T receiver.

5.1.2 Flexible system by segmentation

The ISDB-T system is based on the concept of segmentation studied at the initial stage of research and development of digital broadcasting. NHK STRL and DTVL discussed and decided the detail segmentation structure. As shown in Fig.21, a 6MHz band is divided into 14 segments (a single segment is approximately 429 kHz), 13 segments (about 5.7 MHz) of which are used for signal transmission with respect to adjacent signals. In this system, the maximum number of three modulation methods is set by flexibly combining the 13 segments to allow hierarchical transmission which permits change in the modulations and the coding ratios of the error correcting codes for different services.

5.1.3 Possible single frequency network (SFN)

In conventional analog broadcasting, the same frequency could not be shared in the same service area because interferences might occur between adjacent broadcasting stations or relay broadcasting stations. For example, the closest place that had the same frequency as Channel 1 of the NHK Tokyo broadcasting station was the NHK Kofu broadcasting station, approximately 100 km away from Tokyo. However, as ISDB-T adopts the OFDM modulation system which is strong against multi-path interferences, as shown in Fig.14, the same frequency as the main station can be used at relay broadcasting stations, and thus, the ISDB-T system can contribute to the effective use of frequencies. More than 80% of relay broadcasting stations have adopted SFN thus contributing to the reduction of the 130MHz frequency band by digitalizing broadcasting.

5.1.4 Efficient mobile/portable reception

Efficient mobile/portable reception is possible in ISDB-T by combining a suitable modulation system with strong error correction, and adopting time interleaving. Fig.22 show the effects of time interleaving, meaning that time interleaving is the most important function for mobile/portable reception, as confirmed through experiments conducted by Mr. M. Takada, etc.

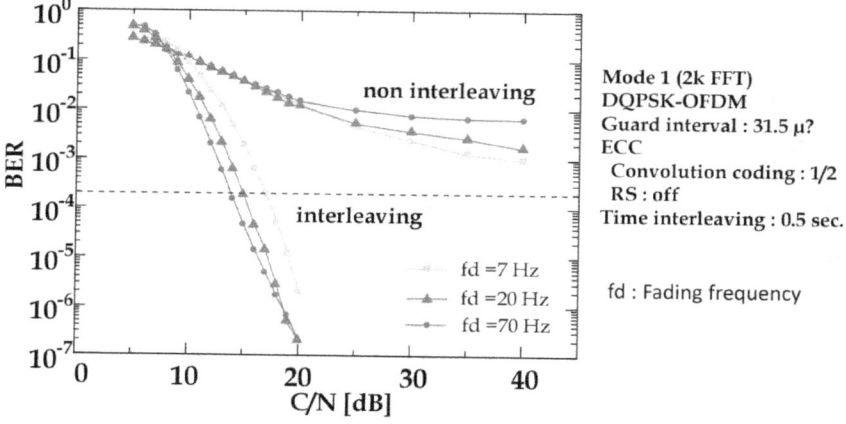

Fig.22 Effect of interleaving (by Mr. M. Takada)

5.1.5 Service area and protection ratio [63]

Field strength is expressed in dB with $1\mu v/m = 0dB$. The service area for analog broadcasting is set to be $70dB\mu v/m$ at a ground clearance of 4m while that for digital broadcasting is set to be $60dB\mu v/m$ at a ground clearance of 10m. In the case of digital broadcasting, reception is possible with about 10dB lower signal level against noise than analog broadcasting.

When V=receiver input voltage (μv),

   E=Field strength (μv/m),

   G=Antenna gain,

   H=Antenna effective length (m =λ/π)

   and L=Cable loss,

   V(dB)=E+G+H-L-6.

One of the most important parameters to determine broadcasting frequency is the protection ratio. This is the ratio used to determine the difference in signal level to permit broadcasting without interferences when the same frequency and the adjacent frequency in an area are used. Table 2 shows the protection ratio in the case of ISDB-T. The data are set based on experiments carried out by NHK in the 90's. ISDB-T signals are based on 64QAM and an error correcting rate of 7/8 which is the weakest against interferences, in order to make the channel plan perfect.

Chapter 5 CHARACTERISTICS AND TRANSMISSION METHOD OF ISDB-T

Tabel 2 Protection ratio of ISDB-T and NTSC

Desired	Undesired	Undesired Channel	Protection Ratio(dB)
Analog	Analog	Co-channel	45
		Lower- Channel	10
		Upper-Channel	0
	Digital	Co-channel	45
		Lower-Channel	10
		Upper-Channel	0
Digital	Analog	Co-channel	20
		Lower-Channel	-21
		Upper-Channel	-24
	Digital	Co-channel	28
		Lower-Channel	-26
		Upper-Channel	-29

Analog : NTSC, Digital : 64QAM(7/8)

When the desired wave is for analog broadcasting, the interfering wave is -45dB, whether in analog or in digital broadcasting. On the other hand, when the desired wave is for digital broadcasting, the interfering wave of digital broadcasting is -28dB, so that there is no problem even if the interfering wave is greater by 17dB in digital broadcasting than in analog. Particularly, in an adjacent channel, no problem occurs if the interfering wave is greater by 20dB or more. The option of using vacant channels mentioned in Section 4.5 is based on the advantage of digital signals which are strong against interfering waves. Table 2 suggests that digital broadcasting is strong against interference and easy for making a channel plan.

5.1.6 Compatibility with other media

For audio/video compression technologies and multiplex broadcasting, MPEG-2 is adopted because it is desirable to use a common system among various digital broadcasting media.

5.2 *Transmission Method*

Table 3 shows the segment parameters of ISDB-T.

Tabel 3 The segment parameters of ISDB-T

ISDB-T mode	Mode 1	Mode 2	Mode 3
Occupied bandwidth	5.6MHz [Segment bandwidth : 430kHz]		
Number of segment	13		
Carrier spacing	3.968kHz	1.984kHz	0.992kHz
Total carriers	1405	2809	5617
Carrier modulation	DQPSK, QPSK, 16QAM, 64QAM (OFDM)		
Effective symbol duration (Tu)	252μs	504μs	1008μs
Guard interval length(Tg)	1/4, 1/8, 1/16, 1/32 of Tu		
Number of symbols / frame	204		
FEC (Inner code)	Convolutional code (Coding rate : 1/2, 2/3, 3/4, 5/6, 7/8)		
FEC (Outer code)	(204,188) Reed-Solomon code		
Interleaving	Frequency and time interleaving (0 - 0.5s)		
Information bit rate	3.7 – 23.2 Mbit/s		

5.2.1 BST-OFDM

Since mobile and portable reception is considered to be essential in ISDB-T, as mentioned above, BST-OFDM, which is a multi-carrier segmentation system, has been adopted as its transmission system. It has been confirmed through various simulations and indoor/outdoor transmission experiments that data can be securely received by using this system, even under the worst conditions for DTTB. Adoption of this system was also necessary because Japan, a mountainous country, needs a wide range of frequencies to expand serviceable areas, and because the number of frequencies can be reduced by SFN.

Through BST-OFDM, various broadcasting services such as HDTV and multi-channel television broadcasting services, stationary reception services, and services combined with mobile/portable reception can be offered under flexible bandwidth specifications.

The structure of segments and other parameters are specified by TMCC signals, which will be explained later.

5.2.2 Mode

In order for receivers to cope with a sudden change in environment, such as occurs in mobile reception, the symbol period (Ts) should be shortened. On the other hand, in the case of stationary reception where conditions rarely change, a long Ts is permissible. Basically, three modes are provided for ISDB-T: Mode 1 (1405(13X108+1), 2000-carrier system), Mode 2 (2809(13X216+1), 4000-carrier system), and Mode 3 (5817(13X432+1), 8000-carrier system). Since control signals are included, the actual number of data carriers per segment is 96 in Mode 1, 192 in Mode 2 and 384 in Mode 3 respectively. Carriers of control signals such as TMCC, are added in the final stage of OFDM modulation.

5.2.3 Guard interval

The most difficult problem to be solved in the DTTB channel is ghost interferences in the transmission channels, as mentioned previously. Even a regular OFDM system is more effective against ghost interferences than a single carrier system, because the bit rate for each carrier in the OFDM system is lower than that in the single carrier system. In order to further improve effectiveness, guard intervals are provided in ISDB-T to absorb ghosts. As shown in Fig.23, ghost interferences are absorbed by re-transmitting the head of a symbol. ISDB-T also has a symbol synchronization function to transmit the same signal twice to the head and the end of the symbol.

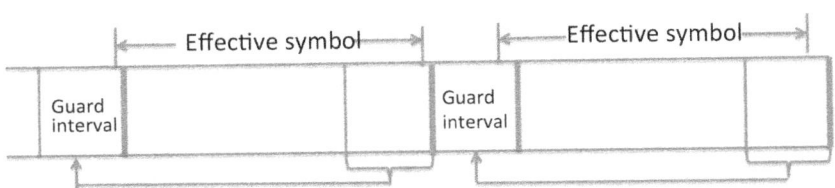

Fig.23 Guard interval of ISDB-T for gost interferences

Defining the actual symbol length Ts to be effective, each guard interval is set at 1/4, 1/8, 1/16 or 1/32 of the effective symbol length. For example, if the guard interval is 1/4, the signal is transmitted to the effective symbol length at an interval of 5/4 the effective symbol length.

Chapter 5 CHARACTERISTICS AND TRANSMISSION METHOD OF ISDB-T

The guard intervals, though effective against ghosts generated in an actual transmission channel, are disadvantageous in terms of the static performance that is produced with respect to the Eb/No (Eb=energy/bit, No=noise power/frequency) due to the energy from the guard interval not being used. This is the main reason why ATSC without guard intervals is advantageous.

5.2.4 Segment and hierarchical transmission

In ISDB-T, 13 data segments can be transmitted by freely dividing the segments into at most three hierarchies with different transmission characteristics. The hierarchies can be classified by a carrier modulation method, a coding ratio for inner codes (convolutional codes), and parameters of interleave length can be specified by TMCC signals.

In this system, a segment at the center is reserved to allow frequency interleaving within that segment only, making partial reception by a receiver possible. Furthermore, the transmission is compatible with digital radios.

The maximum capacity of information transmission is 23.234 Mbps (in the case of 64 QAM, the coding rate being 7/8, and the guard interval ratio being 1/32). With respect to interferences in adjacent analog signals and the protection ratio against interference, the digital signals are entirely shifted by 1/7 MHz to higher frequencies within the 6 MHz band.

5.2.5 Signal generation

The main flow of signals is shown in Fig.24[64]. For further details on the transmission method, refer to the appendix attached separately.

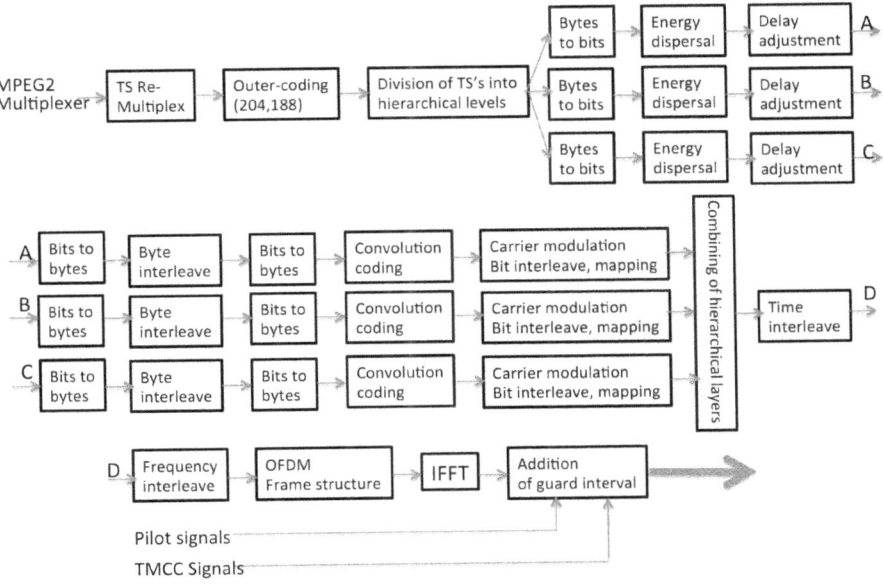

Fig.24 ISDB-T signal flow

(1) TS re-multiplex

ISDB-T may offer the hierarchical transmission of the maximum number of three hierarchies, the modulation system by carrier, a coding ratio of inner codes, the time-axial interleave length, three modes, and four guard interval ratios, as will be explained later. The actual bit rates are varied. In order to adapt the bit rates, a null packet is inserted so that a TS can be processed at a fixed interval. A clock frequency is set at four times the sample frequency of IFFT (4 x 8.12698 - MHz=32.5079

MHz).

In this way, several TSs are always included in every frame composed of 204 symbols of the OFDM signal. Excessive null packets are removed in each hierarchy signal process.

(2) Outer code

188-byte information in each packet is encoded by using the (255,239) RS code which can correct 8-byte random errors. In the encoding process, 51-byte information at the head is considered to be zero, and is not actually transmitted. The 239-byte information is shortened to 188 bytes of TSs, to which 16-byte parity is added to be shortened through the (204,188) RS code.

(3) Division of hierarchy

204-byte TS's are allocated respectively to their specified hierarchies to be processed in each one respectively. A synchronous signal at the head of each TS and null packet is removed.

(4) Hierarchy compound

After being processed in each hierarchy, such as inner coding, setting amplitude and phase of I-axis and Q-axis, carriers are allocated to respective data segments in each hierarchy. In the case of Mode 3, the number of carriers is 432, 348 of which are used for data transmission.

(5) Modulation and error correction [65]

The modulation method can be specified for each of the maximum three hierarchies, among DQPSK, QPSK, 16QAM and 64QAM. The coding ratio of inner codes can be specified at 1/2, 2/3, 3/4, 5/6, and 7/8, and so on. Compared with the 64QAM method, which has the largest transmission capacity, the 16QAM, DQPSK and QPSK methods have stronger receiving strengths, but their respective volumes of transmitted information are smaller than those in 64QAM. The volume in the case of 16QAM is 2/3 that of 64QAM, and the volumes in DQPSK and QPSK respectively are both 1/3. A 188-byte TS base band signal is encoded by using the error correction (204,188) RS code, which can correct 8-byte random errors, to be a 204-byte code, and all the signal processing thereafter is based on that code. The error-correcting code is made compatible with international standards, the BS digital broadcasting system in Japan, etc. and other media. Fig.25 shows relationships between C/N and the speed of information transmission when the modulation system and the efficiency of convolutional code are changed.

Chapter 5 CHARACTERISTICS AND TRANSMISSION METHOD OF ISDB-T

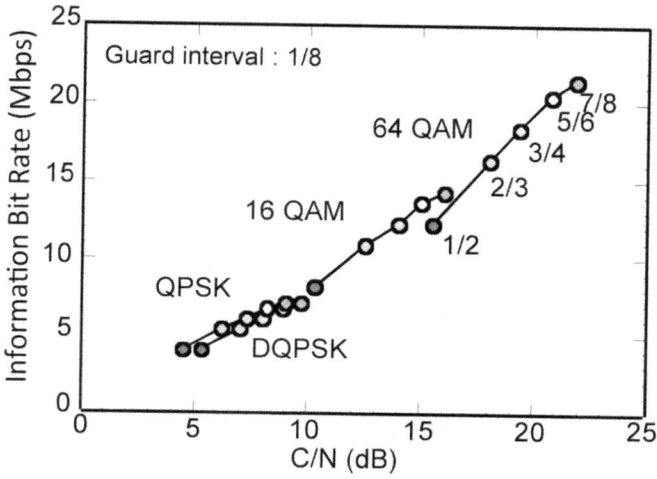

Fig.25 Relationship between C/N and modulation schemes

(6) Time-axis interleaving

Among ATSC, DVB-T, and ISDB-T, only ISDB-T is adaptable to time-axis interleaving in order to cope with sudden changes in reception such as fading and signal interruption during mobile/portable reception. Accordingly, symbol data after modulation are temporally dispersed, and by restructuring the symbol data on the reception side, burst errors are changed to random errors to be easily corrected. A maximum number of four interleaving lengths, including zero interleaving, can be specified for the respective hierarchies. ISDB-T can cope with signal interruption of about 0.4 sec at the longest.

(7) Frequency interleaving

The frequency interleaving process occurs in two stages; a stage of inter-segment interleaving to be carried out widely across a plurality of data segments and frequencies, and a stage of intra-segment interleaving to be carried out within each data segment. Only intra-segment interleaving is carried out in the single-segment in the center.

(8) Frame structure

An OFDM frame before OFDM modulation is composed by adding various pilot signals needed on the receiver side to the symbol data that is subjected to time-axis and frequency-axis interleaving.

(9) TMCC signal

The TMCC signal includes the most important transmission parameters, such as discrimination between differential and synchronization, discrimination of systems between television or radio, indexes for switching transmission parameters, a flag for emergency warning systems with or without partial reception, and transmission parameters for each hierarchy such as the carrier modulation method, convolutional coding ratio, time-axis interleaving length and the number of segments.

The TMCC signal is the most important signal in the system. Since it has to be decoded immediately before signal processing, DBPSK-modulated information is transmitted by using the (184,102) code, which is obtained by shortening the (272,190) code, developed for Teletext, by 88 bits. The TMCC signal can correct errors of nearly 11 out of 184 bits. As all TMCC signals are the same in terms of transmission to their respective data segments, they are further strengthened by correcting errors after subjecting the signals in 13 segments to the majority decision processing.

Thus, ISDB-T has many transmission parameters that are variable, while the mode, guard interval and the symbol length are fixed.

5.2.6 Restriction on system operation

ISDB-T was officially decided in 1999 to be the Japanese DTTB system. From 2000 through 2003 when DTTB services started, NHK, the commercial broadcasting corporations and the manufacturers concerned had reduced the parameters for operating the system and for reducing loads on the receiver side. The reduction of parameters was decided because it was found that broadcasting was possible either in Mode 2 or in Mode 3 based on the results of various experiments on stationary/mobile reception. As for the modulation method, DQPSK for mobile reception was canceled because QPSK was found to be sufficient.

5.2.7 ISDB-T for 7 and *8MHz*[66]

TV frequency bands all over the world are 6, 7, and 8MHz. A band of 6 MHz is used in Japan and in South-American countries, etc. and therefore, the transmission system for 6MHz is the one explained in this book. For bandwidths of 7MHz and 8MHz, though the bit rates are different from the 6MHz system, transmission systems with the same structure and same number of segments as those for 6MHz can be used. Furthermore, the ISDB-T systems for 6, 7, and 8MHz were standardized by ARIB and recommended by ITU-R. As a result, countries where the frequency band of 8MHz is used have adopted this system with the same structure as for 6MHz.

As in the system for 6MHz, one TV frequency bandwidth is divided into 14 segments, among which 13 segments are used. Specifically, the frequency bandwidth of one segment for 7MHz and 8MHz is 7MHz/14 and 8MHz/14 respectively. Since the symbol frequency in the case of Mode 1 is 252μs for 6MHz, the frequency is set to be 216μs (6/7x252μs) for 7MHz and 189μs(6/8x252μs) for 8MHz.

A receiver LSI, a signal generator, and a measuring device, etc. in which components for 6, 7, and 8MHz are integrated, are provided by manufacturers. Experiments in the transmission on ISDB-T for 8MHz were carried out in Botswana, Africa. For the detailed results of these experiments, refer to Reference [64].

Chapter 6
DIFFUSION ACTIVITIES ABROAD for ISDB-T (1990's ~2010's)

Ideally, the results of research, once their practical use has been demonstrated, should be implemented as widely as possible. Since the final goal of our research is the diffusion of its results, it is our responsibility as researchers to spread them in foreign countries. To this end, we implemented a public relations campaign abroad for systems which I had been in charge of before the development of the DTTB system. Before that, we had implemented a public relations campaign for Japanese Teletext system and FM multiplexed broadcasting, but failed[67].

In the late 1980's, we made efforts to explain the merits of Japanese Teletext to China, where ideograph characters including as much information as Japanese characters are used, though China did not start using Teletext including WST until the 2000s. As for DARC, or FM multiplex broadcasting, we had been promoting DARC to both European countries and the USA, but neither of them decided to adopt it.

As for the HDTV system, our predecessors at NHK made great efforts in diffusing and standardizing it before it was recommended by ITU-R in March, 2000[68]. Though Japanese digital phones are excellent in terms of performance, Japan failed to spread the technology to the world. Japanese ICT was said to be Galapagosized[69] because the technology, though highly sophisticated by itself, had not been spread to other countries. I thought at the time that we would surely be questioned about our diffusion activities for the Japanese DTTB technology a few decades later if no country adopted ISDB-T, and I firmly believed that we should leave proof of our having implemented the public relations campaign throughout the world, whatever the results might have been. At that time, I thought that other countries adopting ISDB-T would be a dream of a dream, and I never expected it to happen.

However, in further advancing our diffusion activities, I looked back on past failure and troubles on the activities, and decided to take action in the year 2000 based on the following

Chapter 6 DIFFUSION ACTIVITIES ABROAD for ISDB-T (1990's ~2010's)

two points.

(1) Considering that the Japanese documents had not been effectively circulated to the world and that broadcasting engineers in the world didn't know much about the results of researches at STRL, I decided to let the results of our research at STRL be known by circulating the document called BT in English three times a year.

(2) I made STRL choose 2-3 excellent young researchers in the countries of ABU, allowing them to stay at STRL as resident researchers, to learn state-of-the-art broadcasting technologies such as ISDB-T so that sympathizers with STRL would be increased among other countries.. I thought, from a long view, that increasing friends was effective in the activities of ITU-R for standardizing broadcasting systems. Further, I thought there could be merits in achieving wider sourcing and coverage of breaking events among broadcasting stations. In 2002, STRL accepted three young engineers including Ms. Ana Eliza Faria e Silva from Brazilian TVGlobo to learn about ISDB-T technologies. I believe that it led to the adoption of ISDB-T by Brazil in 2006.

These two actions have continued steadily for more than 15 years, resulting in the spread of the research results of STRL all over the world.

6.1 Situation in Each Country

We have pushed our public relations campaign for the research and development of digital terrestrial broadcasting for mobile reception in Japan at every opportunity such as at meetings of the ABU, NAB, Broadcast Asia, IBC, SMPTE as well as ITU-R. In the 1990's, Mr. Robert Graves of ATSC, Mr. Mac Avoc of DVB, and myself as a representative of ISDB-T participated in a series of international meetings held throughout the world where we presented each system.

Our relationship became so intimate that we made jokes among ourselves at conferences about replacing one another in our respective positions.

In the early 1990's, though the industrialization of digital broadcasting was an urgent issue for broadcasting companies all over the world, most of them were still like penguins in the second line, who jump into the sea after observing those in the front line and confirming there is no shark, do the same, and successfully catch game. Such industrialization required extensive cost and facilities investment. The situation was the same in Japan, where most broadcasting companies were hesitant to implement DTTB which would require a high level of facilities investment.

On the other hand, I was afraid that the broadcasting system might not catch on in Japan because analogue broadcasting was inferior in usability and could not be interchanged with other media which were being digitalized. In NHK, some of directors said that NHK should not start implementing ISDB-T because the financial affairs of NHK would fail due to the construction costs of the digital broadcasting transmitters all over Japan. But I believed that the digitalization of broadcasting would become a necessity in future, and to take an extreme view, that the digitalization of broadcasting should be a national project of high importance to the future of our country.

DTTB services started in Great Britain in September in 1998 and in the USA in November of the same year, as if those countries were competing for first place. Discussion over the matter held at the technical session of IBC '99 the following year was focused on which countries DTTB systems should be adopted in next, and frankly, the general tone of the meeting was one of bewilderment[70],[71]. All the parties there, including Japan, European countries and the USA, claimed that their own system was the best, and no objective broadcasting company was able to decide which was the best system until a comparative experiment among the three was carried out in Brazil in April, 2000. The comparison of the three systems is shown in Table 4.

Tabel 4 The comparison of the three transmission systems

Item	ISDB-T	DVB-T	ATSC
Modulation	BST-OFDM	OFDM	8VSB-AM
Hierarchical transmission	Yes	No	No
Time interleave	Yes	No	No
Mobile & portable	One-seg	No	No
Artificial noise	Excellent	-	-
EWS(Emergency Warning System)	Yes	No	No

6.2 Diffusion Activities to Other Countries[72],[73]

In Japan, the DiBEG was organized within ARIB in 1996 to compete with DigiTAG which was an organization to diffuse the European DVB-T. The DiBEG consisted of broadcasting companies and manufacturers. It was organized by Mr. Noboru Yoshida of MPT and was chaired by Mr. Atsushi Sugimoto who belonged to NEC at the time. Diffusion activities for ISDB-T were implemented by DiBEG. We had tried to promote the diffusion of ISDB-T since the early 1990's through my friends in Korea, China, Taiwan, Singapore, Hong Kong, etc., but our promotional efforts did not result in the system's adoption.

In 1997, we participated in a comparative experiment among the three systems at the request of the Singaporean Government. It was found, through the experiment, that ISDB-T was the best in terms of performance of mobile reception, etc., but

Chapter 6 DIFFUSION ACTIVITIES ABROAD for ISDB-T (1990's ~2010's)

ISDB-T was not adopted because services had not been sufficiently implemented[74],[75].

Reflecting on the failure in the comparative test carried out in Singapore the year before, I thought we should advertise more the performance of ISDB-T to the world and asked Mr. O. Kyushu, Technical Director of ABU, to hold a workshop on ISDB-T at BroadcastAsia'98 in Singapore. Mr. Masato Shinagawa, Director of Broadcasting Administrative Director of MPT, Mr. N. Yoshida, Director of Broadcasting Technology Division of MPT, Mr. A. Sugimoto, Mr. Masao Shimizu of TBS, Mr. Yasuo Takahashi of Toshiba, Mr. Toyoaki Hasegawa and myself from NHK, etc, participated in the workshop and the panel discussion. In those years, we began to recognize the necessity of diffusion activities for ISDB-T, but I didn't see any prospects for it in the future.

In 1999, we, Dr. S. Moriyama and Mr. S. Nakahara and other researchers, participated in an experiment to test the transmission capacities of the three systems through a friend of ABC in Hong Kong, Mr. Lin Sang Ng. The result of the experiment indicated that our system was the best in mobile reception through tunnels in expressways, but our efforts did not result in the adoption of the system because, according to their explanation, a decision would not be made until results of an examination in mainland China were provided.

6.3 Everything Started in Brazil

SET'98 became a historical meeting for Japanese TV engineers. I was invited to introduce ISDB-T at the broadcasting technology exhibition SET'98 in August 1998[76], even though in those days, all the people around me were against my business trip to faraway Brazil. They thought that it would be impossible for Brazil to adopt ISDB-T and my business trip would be fruitless. Therefore I thought I had to make my trip very short and returned to Japan as soon as possible after my presentation at SET'98. Actually, I traveled 5 days in total but spent just 1 night in Brazil.

At SET'98 (Fig.26) the representatives of ATSC, DVB-T and ISDB-T presented each technology. The presenters were Mr. R. Graves, Mr. M. Avoc, and myself. Among the Brazilian audience were Mr. Olimpio Jose Franco, President of SET, Mr. F. Bittencourt, Ms. *Liliana Nakonechnyj* of TVGlobo, etc. I had the opportunity to give a speech at the exhibition and a talk at a meeting of the Brazilian digital broadcasting committee after the exhibition to explain the importance of mobile/portable reception. However, my explanation didn't seem to be sufficiently understood at the time. At the end of the meeting, I anxiously asked Ms. L. Nakonechnyj, "Is there a possibility for Brazil to adopt ISDB-T? " Her answer was no. She said, "Japan is too far from Brazil, which is on the other side of the earth". I felt very miserable thinking that I had come such a long way to Brazil against all opposition, but in vain. The situ-

Chapter 6 DIFFUSION ACTIVITIES ABROAD for ISDB-T (1990's ~2010's)

ation in the year when SET'98 was held in Brazil was such that Brazil didn't seem ready to adopt ISDB-T at all.

Fig.26 At SET'98 (Ms. Liliana, Yamada, and Mr. Bittecourt)

At the ITU-R/TG11/3 meeting in autumn of 1998, Mr. Carlos de Brito Nogueira of Brazil TVGlobo gave me a message from Mr. F. Bittencourt. He asked us in his message to lend Japan's ISDB-T equipment for evaluation in Brazil because Brazil would, in making a decision for the adoption of digital broadcasting, take the purely technical matter into consideration while other countries, following the examples of Singapore and Hong Kong, would make the decision depending on the political entanglement in those countries; a purely technical discussion would be difficult for them.

After I returned to Japan, I discussed the Brazilian proposal at a DiBEG meeting. In those days, DiBEG didn't have the money to send the requested equipment to Brazil. I asked MPT, NHK, and other organizations to bear the shipping costs but their answers were, "Why must Japan use money for Brazil ?" . After all, the Brazilian side decided to bear the cost for shipping the equipment. Such was the situation at that time. Brazil started conducting the mobile comparative tests among ATSC, DVB-T and ISDB-T in Rio de Janeiro where receiving conditions were very severe because of the mountainous terrain. Based on that experiment, the country publicly announced the superiority of ISDB-T at NAB in April 2000 for the first time in the world[77],[78] (Table 5). Though the meeting held early in the morning had not been officially announced in advance, many people involved in broadcasting including ITU-R members, attended. The meeting was packed with an enthusiastic attendance. This indicates the great interest that the broadcasting industry took in the new Brazilian trend.

Tabel 5 Comparative mobile transmission tests carried out in Rio De Janeiro in 1999

Standard	Parameter				Transmission Rate (Mbps)	Errors (Times)
	Modulation	Convolution	Guard Length	Carrier		
ISDB-T	16QAM	2/3	1/16	2k	11.45	0
	64QAM	2/3	1/16	2k	17.18	6
	16QAM	2/3	1/16	4k	11.45	0
DVB-T	QPSK	1/2	1/16	2k	4.39	1
	QPSK	2/3	1/16	2k	5.85	Many
	QPSK	1/2	1/32	8k	4.52	Many
ATSC	8VSB				19.39	Out of measurement

Using the Brazilian announcement that ISDB-T indicated the best performances among three systems as an opportunity, I persuaded Mr. T. Hasegawa who was the head of NHK's engineering group, to visit Brazil and to meet with members of the

Brazilian government. He willingly accepted my suggestion and visited Brazil in spite of his schedule to visit the Sydney Olympic games being held at the time as a responsible person in charge. Dr. T. Kuroda accompanied him.

In addition, I asked Mr. Yoshiyuki Takeda of MPT to visit Brazil with me, and he also willingly accepted my request. Mr. A. Sugimoto, representing the Chairman of DiBEG went together with us.

In 2005, a group under Mr. Akira Ohkubo of MPT visited Brazil and made efforts to persuade the governmental organizations related to DTTB in Brazil. Mr. Noriyuki Shigeta of ARIB, Mr. A. Sugimoto, myself, and other key persons from DiBEG accompanied the group.

At that time, Mr. F. Bittencourt was irresolute about video compression technologies, and could not decide which was the best for ISDB-T in Brazil, MPEG2 or MPEG4. The MPEG2 technology had been completed and already used for the Japanese ISDB-T while the MPEG4 technology was still under development at that time. I advised him that Japan could not change MPEG2 but Brazil should adopt MPEG4. As a result, Brazil decided to adopt MPEG4 and since then, they have been broadcasting two HDTV programs over one channel. I believe his decision was correct. Up until that time, I had visited Brazil more than ten times and persuaded the country to adopt ISDB-T.

In 2002, the Brazilian side asked me to recommend a kind of combined system with ISDB-T and DVB-T. Though they fully recognized the superiority of ISDB-T to DVB-T, the DVB group strongly insisted that DVB-T be adopted in Brazil. In response to the request from the Brazilian side, I met with the people who supported the DVB-T. I took the opportunity to attend an annual meeting with ARIB and DVB at IBC2002, and showed them the new system called DVB-XT. The DVB-XT system consists of the basic transmission system of ISDB-T and the data broadcasting for the Portuguese language, which was called DVB-MHP of DVB-T. But finally, the DVB group rejected the system I proposed.

Brazil decided to adopt ISDB-T in 2006[79],[80], and then started providing ISDB-T services in 2007[81]. Mr. Muliro Pederneiras's cooperation as a consultant of ARIB was behind the success, too. The details of this will be explained in Chapter 7.

With the adoption of ISDB-T in Brazil as a catalyst, all South-American countries except Colombia adopted ISDB-T[82]. Since the latter half of 2007, I have visited various foreign countries to explain ISDB-T technologies and to lead comparative experiments on ISDB-T. I have been devoted to diffusion activities for ISDB-T in South-American and other countries. Mr. R. Graves, who was the president of ATSC, asked me if I lived in a South American Country. He might have believed I did. In the following section, I will describe the especially impressive diffusion activities that took place in Chile, Peru, Argentina, Uruguay, and the Philippines.

6.4 Diffusion Activities in Chile, Peru, Argentina, Uruguay and the Philippines

After Brazil's decision to adopt ISDB-T, our diffusion activities spread to other South American countries. A team consisting of MIC, NHK, as well as commercial broadcasters, and manufacturers, went around each South American country to explain the merits of ISDB-T and participated in the comparative tests of three systems. Under the leadership of MIC, Vice Minister, Mr. Akira Terasaki, Mr. Hideo Fuseda, Mr. Yasushi Furukawa, etc. we achieved fruitful results through good teamwork. Table 6 shows names of the promotion team members.

Tabel 6 The members of the DiBEG promotion group

MIC	Akira Terasaki, Hideo Fuseda, Yasushi Furukawa
ARIB	Kiyoshi Sekiguchi,
DiBEG	Yasuo Takahashi, Eiji Ropponngi
NHK	Takashi Yabashi, Masayuki Takada
Panasonic	Hirohiko Sakashita
NEC	Tomohito Ikegami
Toshiba	Yasuo Takahashi, Seiji Sakuma, Rafael Perez Cruz
Pioneer	Osamu Yamada
TV Asahi	Yoshiki Maruyama

(1) Chile[81],[82]

In 2007, when DiBEG's members recommended the adoption of ISDB-T to Chile for the first time, it seemed that the upper level of the Chilean government had decided to adopt DVB-

T for DTTB in the country. Although Mr. Cristian Rodrigo Nunez-Pacheco, Assistant Secretary of the Ministry of Communications of Chile, who used to be an engineer, quickly understood the superiority of ISDB-T, people at higher levels in the government hardly recognized the technological superiority of ISDB-T, and it seemed nearly impossible for us to persuade them.

Accordingly, we held meetings to explain ISDB-T at the university of UTEM, the university of Chile, the Industries Association, broadcasting stations and the Japanese Embassy, etc. in order to reach as many people as possible, such as members of Congress, government personnel, and people in the broadcasting industry. Mr. Roberto Plass Gerstmann and Mr. Luis Silva Tapia of Chile Vision understood the performance of ISDB-T, and always sat in the first row at the meetings. Supporters of ISDB-T gradually increased, including Prof. Hugo Durney W. of UTEM, Mr. Daniel HerriguezIlic of the Post-Production Film/HD, Mr. Rodrigo Torres Pena of AXIO BASE, and Mr. Jaime Mondria V. of SIDARTE, etc. who also sufficiently understood the technology of ISDB-T. We repeatedly explained that ISDB-T had excellent reception characteristics that mobile/portable reception was possible through ISDB-T, and that long-term thinking was important, considering that changes to a broadcasting system once implemented could not easily be changed. On the other hand, a member of the Chile Industrial Group visited the Japanese embassy and made a

Chapter 6 DIFFUSION ACTIVITIES ABROAD for ISDB-T (1990's ~2010's)

comment that as Chile was using analog NTSC TV developed by the USA, ATSC should be adopted in Chile and it would be the only possible way. He added, "Let's toast here to the final decision of ATSC."

In implementing a public relations campaign for ISDB-T, Mr. Hiroaki Kodama of the Japanese Embassy was very kind to assist us as leader, even though he was not an expert in this field. He seemed to think ISDB-T would be more quickly diffused if Chile decided to adopt ISDB-T following Brazil. I would like to express gratitude to Mr. Kodama here again.

The Chilean government entrusted an outside organization with the implementation of a comparative experiment among the three systems, and published the interim report, which clearly indicated the superiority of ISDB-T among the three systems in the area of stationary reception. In ordinary homes in Chile, broadcasting is usually received through interior antennas. Fig.27[84] shows the results of reception through an interior antenna as analyzed by Mr. M. Takada of NHK STRL.

On March 6, 2008, a public hearing on the three systems was held in Santiago by the Subsecretaria de Telecomunications of the Chilean government, where we gave detailed replies to 59 questions on 19 subjects which had been submitted to the Japanese representatives. I was leaving Japan when I was appointed by the Chilean side as the presenter on behalf of the Japanese side for the public hearing. So I had to prepare the materials for the presentation in the hotel lobby with Mr. M.

Takada all through the night.

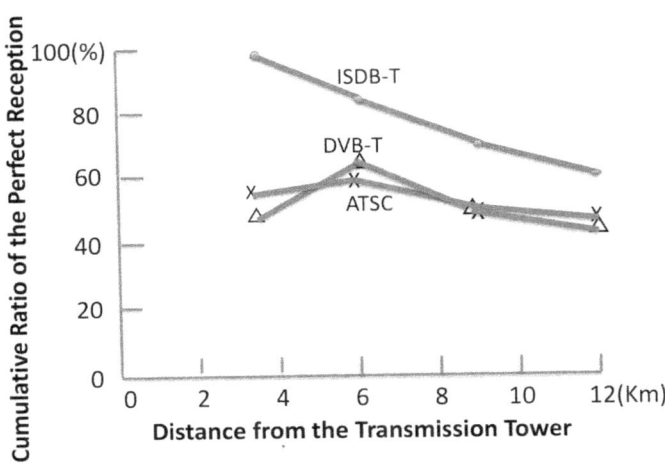

Fig.27 Result of receiving tests by indoor anntenas
(analized by Mr. Takada)

Mr. F. Bittencourt of TVGlobo and Mr. O. Franco of SET also came from Brazil to attend the meeting and explained the reasons why Brazil decided to adopt ISDB-T. Attendants at the public hearing were mainly members of the Chilean national committee consisting of engineers as well as university professors. They were particularly interested in experiments in mobile reception using a vehicle exhibited in the assembly hall. After the public hearing, we received some questions from them via e-mail, and continued exchanging mails with them for a while.

We corresponded in interviews and meetings with newspaper publishing companies and other publishers again and again, explaining why Japan placed greater importance on mobile/portable reception, and why we were eagerly promoting diffusion activities. As a result, our activities were widely reported through these media.

I explained that we were implementing diffusion activities not for financial gain, but because we wanted the Chilean people to use the Japanese ISDB-T system, which is really excellent in terms of performance. I also explained that, a broadcasting system, once decided, could hardly be changed, and that ISDB-T was, so to speak, a lubricant between countries. The best thing was to develop an interchange in the fields of industry, science, culture, education etc. because Japan and Chile are neighboring countries with the Pacific Ocean between them.

Finally, in September 2009, Chile decided to adopt ISDB-T.

(2) Peru

From early in January 2008, we, Mr. Kiyoshi Sekiguchi, Director of ARIB, and myself began to travel to other South American countries, and at the end of that month, we attended a field experiment for reception in Peru. As I mentioned, reception is usually accomplished via interior antennas in South American countries, so we proposed to measure resistance against impulse noise, which is generated from mixers and dryers, as the subject of our experiment. We often experienced failures in the digital system caused by impulse noise, which is hardly a problem in analogue broadcasting, in Teletext mentioned in

Chapter 3-2. Therefore, in these experiments, we introduced time-axis interleaving in FM multiplexed broadcasting as a measure against the impulse noise.

We clearly demonstrated in front of the MTC committee, which was chaired by Mr. Manuel Cipriano Pirgo (Director General of MTC), the greater strength of ISDB-T through time-axis interleaving against the noise from a home appliance such as a mixer (Fig.28)[83], as compared with ATSC and DVB-T, which are weak against such noise. The comparative tests were carried out under the direction of MR. James Martin Arellano of MTC[85]. We also carried out an experiment in which a vehicle traveled along 6 routes of normal roads. In the experiment, signals could be received on all the routes by ISDB-T, while signals could not be received completely on all the routes by either of the other two systems (Fig.29). Mr. Cesar Gallegos of NEC always supported us during the comparative tests.

Fig.28 Imunity tests against electrical appliances carried out in Peru

Chapter 6 DIFFUSION ACTIVITIES ABROAD for ISDB-T (1990's ~2010's)

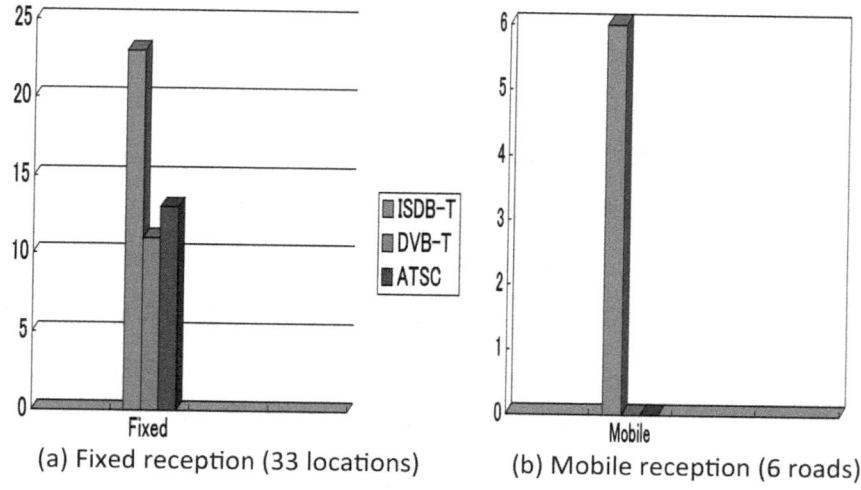

(a) Fixed reception (33 locations)　　(b) Mobile reception (6 roads)

Fig.29 Mobile receiving tests in Peru

The late Mr. Carlos Romero who was the Director of MTC, regretted that Peru politically decided to adopt the analog NTSC, and advised me to explain the technical performance of ISDB-T. He was a real engineer and he believed that the Peruvian DTTB should be decided from a technical point of view.

In April 2009, Peru, following Brazil, decided to adopt ISDB-T. Mr. M. Cipiriano and the committee members did make a right decision.

(3) Argentina

In 2006, Mr. H. Fuseda, Mr. M. Takada, Mr. Eiji Roppongi and other members of DiBEG demonstrated ISDB-T in Buenos Aires for the first time.

We attended a meeting of CAPER held in Buenos Aires in December 2007 and a digital broadcasting seminar sponsored by the Industries Association, where we explained the superiority of ISDB-T and deepened our exchanges with people in charge in the country. Prof. Luis Valle of the University of Palermo who understood the performance of ISDB-T, was a leader in the evaluation of digital broadcasting, and he kindly held seminars two years consecutively.

In August 2009, Argentina decided to adopt ISDB-T.

(4) Uruguay

Uruguay decided to adopt DVB-T in August 2007 before we started our promotion activities for ISDB-T in South-American countries other than Brazil. After that, Uruguay recognized the significance of other countries' decisions, and reconsidered their DTTB. Japan, Brazil and Argentina explained to Uruguay the superiority of ISDB-T, and they finally decided to adopt ISDB-T in December 2010.

(5) Philippines

We attended a comparative experiment among the three systems in cooperation with the Philippine government in 2009. The experiment was implemented mainly for stationary reception along roads at the request of the Philippines, because there was a lot of traffic particularly motorbikes. Each system was evaluated by counting the frequency of errors during a

Chapter 6 DIFFUSION ACTIVITIES ABROAD for ISDB-T (1990's ~2010's)

predetermined measuring time. As illustrated in Fig.30, ISDB-T with the time interleaving function was superior to DVB-T without time interleaving with an error correcting efficiency rate of 3/4 and a 50% reception rate by 18dB[86].

Mr. James Rodney Santiago stayed in STRL from 2007 to 2008 to study ITDB-T technology. So he greatly supported us in the comparison tests held in the Philippines as he sufficiently recognized the performance of ISDB-T.

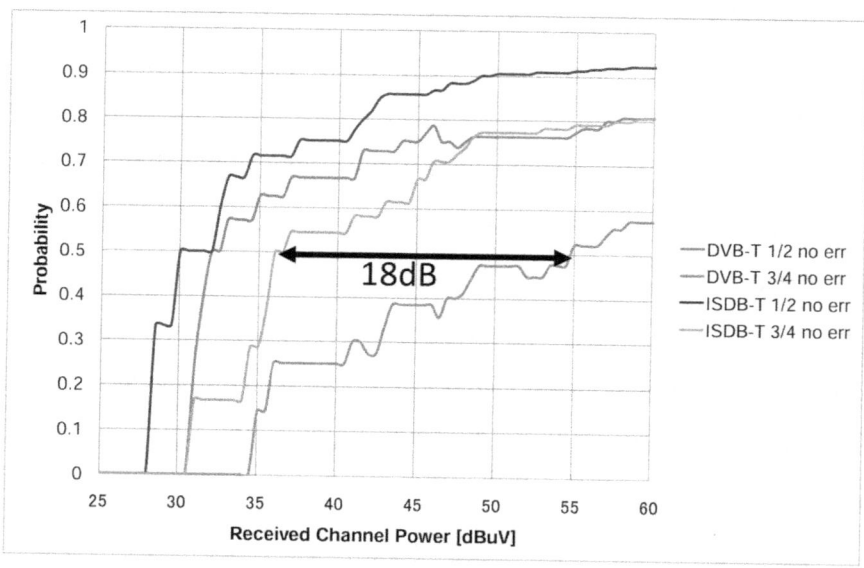

Fig.30 Field receiving tests in the Philippines

In June 2010, the Philippines decided to adopt ISDB-T.

(6) Looking back on the Diffusion activities

Throughout our diffusion activities in the South-American countries, our interactions with engineers from governments, universities, and broadcasting stations, and their support in their respective countries were very helpful. In addition to the above-mentioned key persons, I received support from many other people including Mr. H. Kodama of the Japanese embassy in Chile, Prof. H. Durney who publicly announced his preference for ISDB-T based on his studies before the official decision was made by the Chilean government, Mr. L. Tapia of Chilevision who kindly attended every lecture, Mr. R. Gerstmann of CH-13CH, Mr. Hajime Ogawa, the former Japanese Ambassador to Chile, who came a long way to Chile from Tokyo and introduced ISDB-T to the Chilean government and the country's industries, Mr. J. Dodria, Chairman of the Chile Artist Association and Mr. D. Ilic who were not directly related to the broadcasting industry but were captivated by the excellent characteristics of ISDB-T, Mr. C. Gallegos of Peru NEC in Peru, and the late Mr. C. Morero, the former representative of ITU-R Peru, and so on. If it had not been for the cooperation of these people, today's success in diffusing ISDB-T in South American countries would have been impossible.

The diffusion activities for three years from 2007 through 2009 depended especially on Mr. E. Roppongi, consultant of DiBEG, who lives in Argentina. He has strong links with leaders in South America, and an excellent ability to cooperate with the kind of tough negotiation partners typical in Latin-America. Without the cooperation of Mr. E. Roppongi, there would not have been success in South America. Here, I would like to express my gratitude also to him.

Chapter 7
DTTB in BRAZIL[87]

In Brazil, the discussion about the digitalization of broadcasting started in 1994, and they have faced on a lot of difficult problems since then. Brazil carried out the comparative tests between ATSC, DVB-T and ISDB-T, and showed them for the first time to the world in 2000. As for the implementation of the pure technologies, Brazil decided to adopt ISDB-T in 2006 and started it in 2007.

7.1 A Ten-Year Saga
7.1.1 Multi-SDTV vs HDTV

It was on June 29, 2006, that Brazilian President Luiz Inácio Lula da Silva officially decreed SBTVD as the Digital TV standard to be adopted in Brazil. After more than ten years of studies, laboratories and field tests comparing the ATSC, DVB-T and ISDB-T systems, and after years of negotiations concerning the three systems, the Brazilian government finally made the decision to go ahead with the ISDB-T technology as the standard for Brazilian Digital TV. The decree also made HDTV mandatory at the time when digital TV was being implemented by broadcasters, and set 2016 as the final year of using analog TV in Brazil.

The wrong business model, which had been adopted by the Europeans and which was called "multiplexes", had a very strong influence among many different people in Brazil, including some broadcasters and lobbyists. Europe had chosen the option of multi-SDTV programs on the same TV channel and argued that this was the best choice for developing countries, where people would not be able to buy any expensive HDTV receivers ; in addition, it would give them more choice of programs. This was a big mistake, as later proven in Europe.

We were able to convince the Brazilian government that HDTV was the future of television. If not adopted by broadcasters, only those able to subscribe to cable TV would have access to high- definition TV. With the help of NHK, we implemented a very successful HDTV demo in São Paulo, during the 1998 World Cup. Key personalities attended this demo and

Chapter 7 DTTB in BRAZIL(87)

were impacted by the new technology, thus reinforcing the importance of HDTV for the future of Brazilian TV.

7.1.2 Activities of ABERT

In 1994, ABERT and SET formed a study group, whose objective was to suggest the best choice for making the standard in Brazilian digital TV. I was appointed as the chair of this group, and between the time of its formation and 2006 we had the most important job of our professional lives, not only technically but also politically: trying to convince the whole broadcasting community and the government of our conclusions, after more than ten years of intense study, seminars and discussions[88].

The most important task was to set up a comprehensive evaluation of the three existing systems, both in the lab and in the field, in order to verify their performance. The results of this study were published in 2000 and reported in different forums, including at one historic SET panel at the NAB'2000 show in Las Vegas.[89],[90]

We were the first study group in the world to perform such a comparison and the broadcast community was anxious to see the results, which would have a big impact throughout America. The summary of this study is described in Chapter 7.2.

The conclusion of the study was that ISDB-T was, by far, the most appropriate technology for terrestrial digital transmission. The main reasons for this were :

(1) It had the most robust transmission modulation scheme and error correction required for rough over-the-air transmission and reception, especially for "rabbit ear" antennas, which are very common in Brazil.

(2) It offered the option of mobile reception, which was a unique feature among the three systems. ATSC and DVB-T did not offer this feature, which we considered strategic for the future of broadcasting companies in Brazil. It would not make sense to allocate one 6-MHz TV channel, but not to be able receive it on mobile devices in the future, when most TV receivers at home would be connected to cable, fiber-optics or satellite.

(3) The Japanese offered exemption from royalties in exchange for the adoption of their technologies, and offered by far the most collaborative and reliable long-term support, not only from the Japanese Ministry of Communications, but from ARIB, NHK and private Japanese broadcasters.

7.1.3 Brazilian broadcasting and the final decision

TV broadcasting plays a very important role in Brazilian culture and life. It is responsible for keeping the population well informed and has one the world's largest audiences, who like to watch entertainment programs, mainly telenovelas. In addition, important sporting events, such as World Cup soccer and the Olympics are aired by broadcasters free-of-charge for millions of people around the country. Today, 70% of Brazilians still watch TV purely by over-the-air reception. For this reason, many outside communities and politicians viewed the transition from analog to digital as an opportunity to intervene and reduce the power of the broadcasters. Of course, we could not accept this, not only because it was our role to defend our companies' interests, but mainly because we were absolutely convinced that we were defending the best choice for our country and for Brazilian society.

The ATSC and DVB reps, and companies associated with them - either via royalties or for market competition - had launched a war against our group and did not spare any effort to degrade and manipulate our work. In addition, we unfortunately had no support from Japanese TV manufacturing companies operating in Brazil; they all reported to their American or European subsidiaries, favoring their origins. In summary, we were very much alone in that war! Some important scientific experts and research centers were convinced by the committees representing these systems (ATSC and DVB) to vote against our report and declare their support for our opponents without any deep analysis, or purely for political reasons. During this time, to insist on ISDB-T was a taboo in Brazil.

Our group of SET/ABERT engineers, together with the Mackenzie lab professors and students, based our reports only on technology and business strategy, without any political bias, and we were very much determined to fight to the end for what we considered to be the best thing for our country.

The final decision on which technology to be adopted was always in the hands of the Brazilian Communications Minister, a position that had changed hands four or five times over the course of these 10+ years. One of them decided that Brazil should develop its own technology; he was completely unaware of the challenges, the cost, and the delay that such a decision would represent for the country.

We made this decision and suggested that we should adopt ISDB-T and replace some of the technologies that would be easy to replace, and were not essential to the performance of the system. After so many years, MPEG-2 could be replaced by MPEG-4 and the middleware could be replaced by Ginga, a top proposal by some Brazilian Universities, without any major changes to the ISDB core technology. In addition, we had to struggle against the stigma of the Pal-M which was a big mistake made 30 years ago, when the Brazilian government decided on the NTSC modified version as the color TV standard in Brazil. Fortunately, our proposal of adopting ISDB-T with some updated technology was accepted by the Minister of Communications and the Office of the President's Chief of Staff.

However, the struggle was not yet over. Even after the decree was signed, we would have to fight against an action in the supreme court against the executive decision, and there would be a presidential election a couple of months later, which could have changed everything if a new president was elected, replacing President Lula and his ministers. Meanwhile, a forum was created to regulate and draft the SBTVD standard, harmonizing the new technologies (MPEG-4 and Ginga the new middleware) with the existing Japanese ISDB-T. The SBTVD Forum was created with the participation of broadcasters, the TV reception industry, TV manufacturers, software companies and the universities responsible for the newly introduced technologies. Finally, on December 2, 2007, in São Paulo, President Lula (then re-elected), along with the most important broadcasters in Brazil, unveiled the digital TV with what should be considered the best digital TV system in the world[?], since it integrated the ISDB-T with a MPEG-4 compression scheme and the new Ginga middleware.

As a proof that it was the right decision, over the following years all South American countries began following the Brazilian standard and a TV market of half a billion TV receivers in total has by now been reached[91].

It is extremely sensible for me to name the people who contributed to this battle. They were not very many, believe it or not, but they really were warriors. It was thanks to these warriors that we finally achieved our goal, which had initially seemed almost impossible.

7.1.4 Cooperation with NHK

I would also like to express our gratitude to Osamu Yamada-san, then STRL NHK General Director, who was the first person who trusted us and provided us with all of the ISDB-T equipment and NHK's support for the tests and the HDTV demo. Yamada-san visited us more than ten times, supporting us tirelessly, both technically and politically, and was present over all those years.

It was on the day President Lula signed the decree that I sent an emotional message to Yamada-san entitled "The Digital Marriage", which I transcribe below:

"Dear Yamada san,

Our first encounter was in 1998.

At that time, it was unrequited love from Japan. It was a long and difficult relationship before this wedding day.

Initially we were shy and suspicious of each other. After some time we started getting close and appreciating each other.

As time went by, we (the Brazilians) did not decide to marry you (the Japanese).

You became skeptical about our real intentions.

But it was only because we wanted to make sure that our marriage would last forever! Finally we got married on this June 29th 2006!

Yamada san, you are the godfather of this marriage.

Fernando Bittencourt

Chapter 7 DTTB in BRAZIL(87)

The Priest"

7.1.5 Toward future cooperation

Through the technology exchange we engaged in with each other, Brazilian broadcasters were taught the patience of the Japanese people. Both of us had been eagerly discussing and insisting on digital broadcasting technology for years up to the final decision in June 2006. As a result, we received great gratitude and confidence, and now we are coming to a stage of starting a new relationship. Through the continuous relationship between Brazilian and Japanese broadcasters, we want this relationship between us to be further strengthened.

The immigrants from Japan have brought new technologies and a labor force in the field of agriculture to Brazil going back as far as 100 years ago. Thanks to them, agriculture has become an important field in the Brazilian export industry and it contributes 34% of the nation's GDP. With the keen insight of "perseverance" and "Vision for the Future" brought by those immigrants from Japan, Brazil has become one of the leading agricultural producing countries in the world.

History repeats itself. This time, in the field of broadcasting technology, Japan has helped Brazil again with the same "perseverance" and "Vision of the Future" of the Japanese people.

We hope our mutual cooperation between Brazil and Japan will be further strengthened through the development of digital broadcasting.

7.2 Comparative Tests

7.2.1 History

In 1998, ANATEL initiated the Digital TV system selection process in Brazil and work on the identification and description of the laboratory tests began.

In 1999, ANATEL and 17 companies concerned began to discuss and define the nature and timing of the experiments, the technical feasibility conditions of the channels that would be used and the installation of the digital systems that would be tested, the elements and technical parameters that would be considered as well as the structure of the reports that would be submitted. The test equipment of three systems (ATSC, DVB-T and ISDB-T) was provided by NEC, NDS and Zenith. The work was coordinated by the ABERT/SET Digital TV Technical Group, created in 1994 by ABERT and SET to include the private sector in the study and evaluation of the various Digital TV systems that were being developed and made available globally, and to enable Brazil to choose the best solution. The laboratory tests were practically closed in November.

In 2000, at the end of January, having already conducted numerous laboratory tests, with the coverage field tests in the final stage, but still lacking other tests to complete the work, the group judged that the data accumulated up to that time allowed a quite reliable technical evaluation regarding the performance of each system from the point of view of the development stage that pointed to the potential evolution of the system. It was therefore decided to bring forward the presentation of the final report in regard to the modulation used by the tested systems, since an analysis of the results led to the conclusion that the 8VSB modulation was not suitable for Brazilian needs. On February 9, 2000, the first part of the final report containing the results obtained so far, their assessment, and the subsequent proposal that the system be selected by ANATEL for adoption in Brazil as the COFDM modulation was submitted to ANATEL. ANATEL, in turn, submitted the report for public consideration.

7.2.2 Brazilian system requirements for DTTB

In the first half of 2000, it was already clear that the DVB-T and ISDB-T systems were capable of meeting the requirements to improve, or at least replicate reception of the current analog channels, enabling transmission of HDTV signals ("payload" greater than 18 Mbps), in addition to adding new applications for Brazilian broadcasters. It was also clear that the ISDB-T system was far superior to the DVB-T system with regard to its immunity against impulsive noise, as well as its performance through portable and mobile reception. These were important characteristics for ensuring the competitiveness of the sound and image broadcasting service in the future, in addition to offering greater application flexibility.

It was not the Japanese who told us about this. The study, which covered various aspects involved in the implementation of DTTB in Brazil including social and economic aspects, conducted by the ABERT/SET GROUP, concluded that the ISDB-T Standard had a great advantage over the DVB-T Standard. The study highlighted:

(1) The greater ease of public access to the sound and image broadcasting service, enabling reception by fixed, mobile and portable receivers, thus contributing to the universalization of access to the service.

(2) Total adaptation to the country's medium-term needs, to enable the competitiveness of the service, given the expected evolution of broadcasting in a scenario where high-definition broadcast television signals for fixed reception, are already being offered by other media. This finding would lead broadcasters to seek the development of new markets that had not yet been reached, adding applications for mobile reception, without compromising high-definition broadcasting for fixed reception.

(3) Total adaptation to the country's long-term needs, to enable continued sound and image broadcasting services, given the expected technological evolution once the penetration of other media had already reached a high level and reception mobil-

ity played a totally different role for the service.

(4) The feasibility of converging the wireless worlds of information technology, the Internet and broadcasting, allowing Brazil to fully benefit from better use of the frequency spectrum.

The nearly 30 professionals involved in field and laboratory testing reached the conclusion that there is only one model capable of meeting the entire list of items relevant to the digital television system being adopted in Brazil. They proposed a system that would :

- Allow maximum application flexibility
- Promote universal access to the service
- Maximize the possibility of competition among the broadcasters
- Enable HDTV transmission and mobile and portable reception
- Enable better reception with an internal antenna
- Enable frequency reuse

The technical superiority and flexibility of the ISDB-T system was evident in every evaluation, particularly with regard to its behavior in conditions resembling real life situations. We were confident in our use of the Japanese model when, pursuant to

Brazilian law, we were required to create a national system. Faced with a chaotic scenario of diverse political opinions and interests, the former Minister of Communications, Miro Teixeira declared, in 2003, the need to develop a national model for Brazilian DTTB, marking the end of discussions regarding the possible use of American, European and Japanese standards. At that moment, a bucket of cold water was dumped over everyone's heads after nearly ten years of studies and struggles.

What we first saw as a trainwreck proved to be the perfect opportunity for creating the technology that would be best suited to the Brazilian scenario. With the truth in our hands, as proven by testing, although facing a great deal of resistance, the ABERT/SET Group managed to convince the agents that they could revolutionize television in Brazil. A Brazilian standard was created, based on the Japanese standard. This was an achievement that will go down in history.

7.2.3 The measurement of the laboratory and field tests[92]

During the testing period, thorough assessments were made, with topics grouped into families and characterized by their functionality.

(1) Interference Behavior
- Digital into analog PAL-M interference.
- Analog PAL-M into digital interference.
- Digital into digital interference.

- Continuous wave (CW) interference.
- Robustness of the COFDM and 8VSB systems against impulse noise.
- Simultaneous interference of digital channel and noise over the analog PAL-M channel.
- Simultaneous interference of analog PAL-M channel and noise in digital channel.
- Simultaneous interference of digital channel and noise in digital channel.

(2) Digital system robustness against interference
- Multipath interference without interfering noise.
- Multipath interference with interfering noise.
- Multipath interference – Simulation for channels with multiple echoes.

(3) Characteristics of reception performance
- Carrier-to-noise ratio threshold (C/N for a given error rate).
- Minimum input signal level (for a given error rate).
- "Error rate" vs. "Signal level".
- "Error rate" vs. "Carrier-to-noise ratio".
- "Carrier-to-noise ratio threshold" vs. "Signal level".

(4) Characteristics of transmission performance
- Transmitter calibration and spectral analysis of the transmitted signals.
- Transmitter compression performance.
- Out-of-band emission in adjacent channels.

(5) Characteristics of Digital TV systems for mobile reception (Doppler Effect)

All possible care was taken to ensure the reliability of the results and to make them reflect, as accurately as possible, the performance of several parameters analyzed, allowing proper comparison between the three existing standards at the time. The ABERT/SET Group had the huge responsibility of submitting technical analysis reports on the performance of the tested models to ANATEL, the Brazilian Federal Government's Telecommunications Agency.

7.2.4 Laboratory tests
7.2.4.1 Minimum signal power at receivers

Table 7 shows the minimum signal power of each receiver required to obtain good quality reception where there is no interference. This test is indicative of the technology used to implement the receiver, rather than the system performance. The system performance will not be commented on. The performances show improvement when compared to older versions of receivers.

Tabel 7 The consolidated data for the three systems

System and Configuration	dBm
ATSC – Zenith	-81.4
ATSC - Chip A	-82.3
ATSC - Chip U	NT
ATSC - Chip S	-81.4
ATSC - Chip T	-80.5
DVB-T - NDS - 3/4 1/16 2k	-80.9
DVB-T - Chip N - 2/3 1/32 8k	-78.8
DVB-T - Chip M - 2/3 1/32 8k	-81.5
DVB-T - Chip K - 2/3 1/32 8k	-71.2
DVB-T - Chip L - 2/3 1/32 8k	-81.7
ISDB-T-DiBEG- 3/4 1/16 4k 0.1	-78.6
ISDB-T –Chip J- 3/4 1/16 4k 0.1	-81.4

NT:Not Tested

7.2.4.2 Multipath Interference

In the Fig.31, a comparison between the three systems, ATSC, DVB-T and ISDB-T is shown. Observing the curves, a clear advantage of the systems that employ the OFDM modulation (DVB-T and ISDB-T) over the system that employs the 8VSB modulation (ATSC) can be seen, as these can tolerate a longer echo (especially when a larger number of carriers are employed) with greater intensity (0dB).

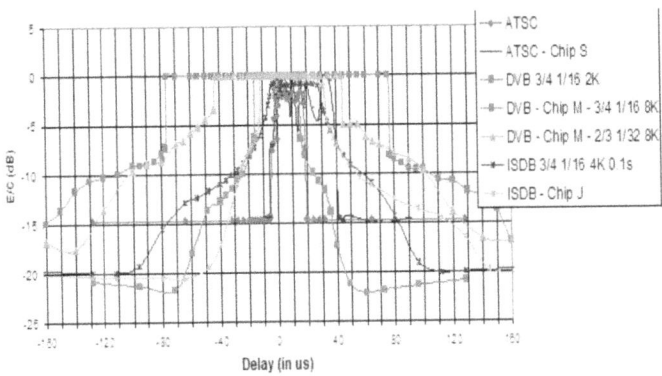

Fig.31 Relationship between delay and signal/ echo ratio for the error rate threshold-ATSC, DVB-T and ISDB-T

Another aspect of ATSC that can be seen is the abrupt transition between the region for which strong echoes are tolerated and the region in which the reflected signals need to be much attenuated. This behavior is characteristic of the 8VSB modulation and is determined by the equalizer length. Note that this also increases the tolerated delay for the new implementations, due to improvements in the equalizer.

A great evolution between the two ISDB-T receivers tested was seen: the first prototype tested could not tolerate echoes of 0 dB due to simplifications in signal processing algorithms, while the second receiver tolerated echoes of 0 dB without problems.

7.2.4.3 Impulse noise

This test was made to evaluate the degradation in a digital channel when interfered with by impulse noise, which in practice is generated by electric motors with brushes, power transmission lines, energy substations, engine ignitions, and other sources. This interference is measured by evaluating the- parameter called the equivalent carrier-to-noise ratio (C/Neq), which is the ratio in dB between the power of the desired signal power and the equivalent noise without switching. The lower the value, the more interference the digital system can support while maintaining its operation.

For this test, an ignition noise simulator was used, which consists of a coaxial switch, switched by a timer, and a combiner, which adds the desired white noise to the digital signal, which is applied to the input of the coaxial switch. The timer maintains the coaxial switch connected for a programmable period (called a window) from 1 to 999 μs, and the switching frequency varies from 12.5 Hz to 100 Hz every 30 seconds; i.e., at the beginning of the cycle, the window is connected 12.5 times per second for 30 seconds, and this frequency is increased up to 100 times per second, returning to 12.5 Hz at the end of the cycle.

As shown in Fig.32, the system that has a wide advantage over the others is clearly the ISDB-T system. The superiority of the ISDB-T's performance is due to the long interleaver used. This technique consists of scrambling data, in a way that in the occurrence of a burst error, continuous portions of data are not affected. All three systems employ this technique, but with different time intervals.

Graph 2.5.3.1: Relationship between the noise window width and the interfering signal for impulsive noise

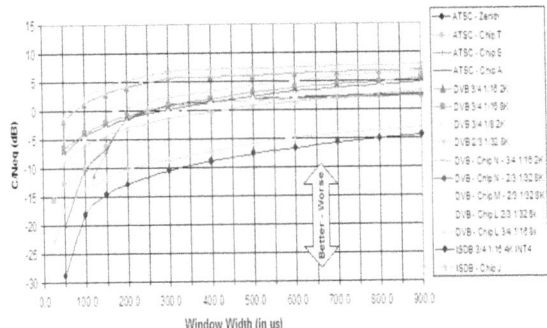

Fig.32 Relationship between the noise window width and the interfering signal for impulse noise

This is a very important factor in practice because, in field tests in about a quarter of the field locations, the presence of impulsive noise was observed.

In this test, two criteria were used to evaluate the robustness of the digital system against impulsive noise, which are described below:

Criterion 1: Maintaining a constant digital signal level, the window values were set and the noise level was increased until the system threshold was reached. The threshold was determined by the error rate after the Reed-Solomon parameter of less than 3×10^{-6} in exactly two minutes. The count started at the same time as the ignition noise simulator cycle, or an error in the video every twenty seconds for DVB-T chips K, L, M, and N.

Criterion 2: Maintaining a constant digital signal level, with the equivalent noise (i.e., the white noise level with the switch closed 100% of the time) 5 dB above the desired signal being varied until the system threshold determined in the same manner as test 1 was reached.

7.2.5 Field Tests

The vehicle reception system was composed of a professional Shaffner antenna, RF preamplifier system, white noise generator, the three receiver systems, HDTV decoder, and spectrum analyzer. The vehicle and its interior during the fields tests are shown in Fig.33.

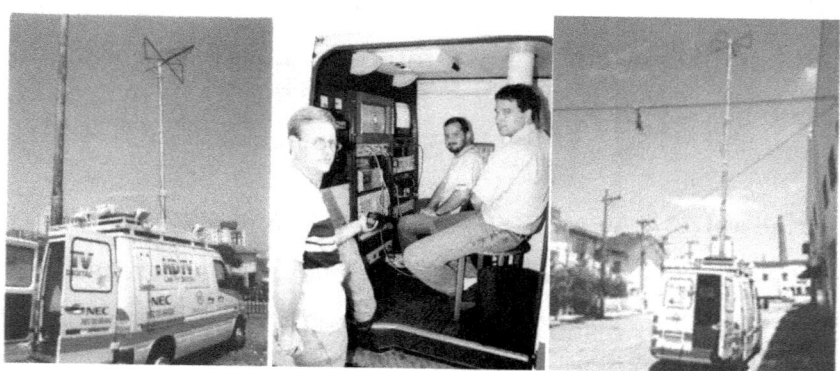

Fig.33 The vehicle and its inside during the field tests

7.2.5.1 Fixed reception

(1) Interferences in real reception conditions

The combination of laboratory and field tests allowed the characterization of the systems from a detailed analysis of each interference, and at the same time evaluated which effects were more significant in actual reception conditions. The field evaluations showed that the most important effects were multipath and impulse noise, as outlined in Table 8, which shows the percentage of locations in which each type of interference was considered significant.

Tabel 8 Percentage of locations with interference in real reception conditions

Interference	Percentage
Multipath	100%
Impulsive Noise	23%
Doppler	2%
Fluctuation	2%
Low Level (30 to 51 dBµV/m)	15%

(2) The results of the fixed reception tests

The fixed reception tests were carried out at 127 locations with field-strength higher than 50dBµV/m. The Fig.34 below shows the percentage of cumulative locations with the number of errors < 5. ATSC didn't show good performance even under a strong field strength.

Chapter 7 DTTB in BRAZIL(87)

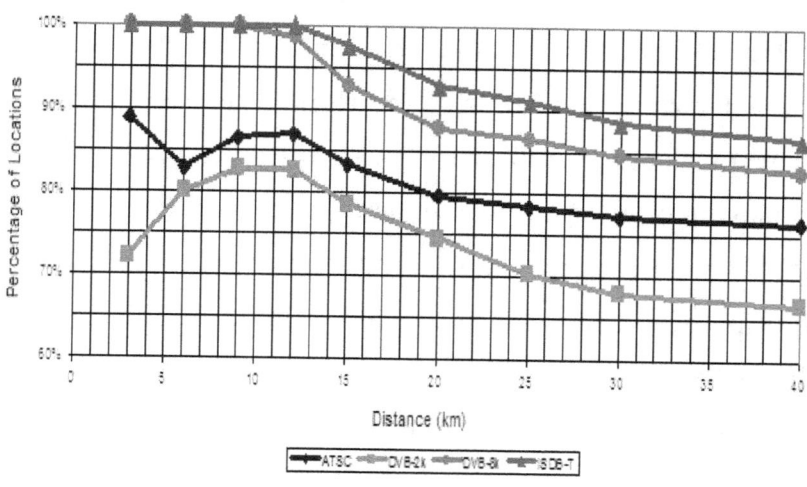

Fig.34 Percentage of cumulative location numbers with error<5

7.2.5.2 Mobile reception

As shown in Table 5, the mobile comparative tests between ISDB-T, DVB-T, and ATSC were carried out in Rio de Janeiro, which is a mountainous area and the most difficult area in Brazil for receiving digital signals in moving cars.

The ATSC signals couldn't be received at all. In the case of DVB-T, in spite of the lower bit rate compared to ISDB-T, its performance was poorer than ISDB-T.

ISDB-T showed the best performance because of the interleaving function. If Brazil wanted to add mobile reception services to fixed reception services, ISDB-T would be the best option.

7.2.6 Conclusions

The 17 companies authorized to carry out the tests on digital television systems expect that the work now complemented can contribute to the existing work completed by ANATEL in this endeavor in a competent and transparent manner.

The ABERT/SET Group shown in Fig.35 performed various analyses considering a lot of aspects. It offered the report to ANATEL, at the end of May, 2000 as an additional contribution to this important process for Brazil, namely the selection of a digital system to be used in sound and image broadcasting that considered:

(1) The objective of optimizing reception by air, improving or at least maintaining the free service currently provided to the population by analog broadcasting systems;

(2) The DVB-T and ISDB-T systems offer better performance in high multipath situations taking place in densely populated areas, areas that would be the first to be served by digital television;

(3) The DVB-T and ISDB-T systems allow the implementation of a high definition transmission model with adequate robustness;

Chapter 7 DTTB in BRAZIL(87)

ABERT/SET GROUP

TASK FORCE

(1) ABERT/SET Group
- **ABERT/SET Group Coordinator**
  Fernando Bittencourt Filho – TV Globo
- **Testing Subgroup Coordinator**
  Valderez de Almeida Donzelli – TV Cultura
- **Executive Consultant**
  Tereza Mondino – TM – Consultoria em Telecomunicações Ltda.
- **Laboratory Consultant**
  Eduardo de Oliveira e Silva Bicudo – EBCOM
- **Planning & Control Advisory Services**
  Carlos de Brito Nogueira – TV Globo
- **Coordinator:** Luís Tadeu Raunheitte
  Ana Cecília Munhoz Martins
  Carlos Eduardo Dantas
  Francisco Sukys
  Ricardo Franzen
  Cristiano Akamine
  Daniel da Costa Diniz
  Fábio Baiadori
- **Studio Subgroup Coordinator**
  Roberto Franco – Rede Record
- **Strategic Evaluation Subgroup Coordinator**
  Olímpio José Franco – SET
- **Channeling Subgroup Coordinator**
  Liliana Nakonechnyj – TV Globo
- **Consumption Subgroup Coordinator**
  Alfonso Aurin Palacin Junior – TV SBT

(2) Task Force
- **Broadcasters' Professionals:**
  Alfonso Aurin Palacin Junior - TV SBT
  Ana Eliza Faria e Silva - TV Globo
  Daniel Lourenço Domingos - TV Globo
  Edson Geraldo Benedito - TV Cultura
  Fernando Wictor Pietrukoviz Quinttela - TV Globo
  Francisco Sergio Husni Ribeiro - TV Cultura
  Maria Goretti Romeiro - TV SBT
  Paulo Henrique Corona Viveiros de Castro - TV Globo
  Roberto Tamotsu Aono - EPTV
  Sidnei Nogueira Pinto - TV Globo
  Sizenando José Ferreira Filho - TV SBT
  Sandro Rodrigues da Silva - ABERT/SET
- **Professionals of the Instituto Presbiteriano Mackenzie**
  [Mackenzie Presbyterian Institute]

Fig.35 The member names of ARBERT/SET group

(4) Only the DVB-T and ISDB-T systems achieved reception in 100% of locations within the area of greatest population concentration, closer to the point of transmission;

(5) The DVB-T and ISDB-T systems performed better than the ATSC system in coverage areas with shadows with the use of gap filler stations and, in general, in the employment of single frequency networks (SFN);

(6) The new ATSC receivers recently developed and made available for testing, despite the use of sophisticated equalization techniques, did not lead to real improvements in practical situations;

(7) With regard to planning, although the ATSC system has better efficiency than the others, the difference is not significant;

(8) The disadvantages previously seen in the DVB-T and ISDB-T systems for adjacent channel protection ratios were overcome by the implementations made available later;

(9) The advantage in the signal-to-noise ratio threshold presented by the ATSC system does not translate into practical outcomes to improve coverage for the typical configuration of the main Brazilian cities;

(10) Unfavorable results from the relationship between peak power and average power provided by the DVB-T and ISDB-T systems have low relevance because they only affect the broadcaster and not the population;

(11) The ISDB-T system has the best overall performance in domestic reception conditions using internal antennas (indoor reception), the DVB-T system provides adequate performance, and the ATSC system is inadequate in these conditions;

(12) The ISDB-T system has superior performance relative to the others due to its immunity to impulse noise and

(13) The ISDB-T system is the one with greater flexibility for the possible applications of sound and image broadcasting services, including mobile or portable reception.

Conclusions :

(1) The ATSC system does not meet the minimum technical requirements for the preservation of sound and image broadcasting in Brazil, mainly due to its low robustness in multipath and its low flexibility, compared to the DVB-T and ISDB-T systems.

(2) The DVB-T and ISDB-T systems are able to meet both the requirements to improve or at least replicate receiving the current analog channels, allowing the transmission of HDTV signals (with a payload of more than 18 Mbps), and to add new applications for Brazilian broadcasters.

(3) The ISDB-T system is significantly better than DVB-T with respect to its immunity to impulsive noise and its performance in portable or mobile reception; this is important to ensure the competitiveness of the sound and image broadcasting service in the future, in addition to offering greater application flexibility.

(4) Despite the technical superiority and flexibility of the ISDB-T system, other aspects need to be considered, such as the impact that the adoption of each system will have on the domestic industry, the conditions and implementation facilities of each system, the timing of its commercial availability, the price of receivers for the consumer, and the expected fall

in these prices, in order to enable faster access to all sections of the population.

In addition, starting in the year 2000, Prof. Gunnar Bedicks' group of Mackenzie Presbyterian University began carrying out lab and field tests to evaluate the performance of current DTV systems, with the aim of providing backing for the Brazilian Government's decision on the standard to be adopted. These results were presented in IEEE Transaction on Broadcasting, Vol.52, No.1, March 2006[92].

Chapter 8
RESEARCH MANAGEMENT[93]

For more than 40 years, I gained much experience as a researcher, and as a research manager. Thanks to my brilliant colleagues, I managed to achieve some results. During my years of experience, I observed the research and development practices of other companies as well as those of my senior and junior researchers. It is easier for a young researcher to follow the boss's instructions when conducting research. Since the time available for a researcher to be immersed in research work is often less than what one would like. A researcher should endeavor to make the best use of the time available as the workload can change dramatically once he/she rises in rank and is given the responsibility of managing subordinates.

Table 9 shows my ideas on the relationship between the position and the main task of the researcher. Each person has to achieve a completely different and more difficult task in the position he/she is in, to avoid the Peter Principle, according to which a person continues to be promoted until finally found to be incompetent.

Tabel 9 The relationship between the position and main task of the researcher

Main Task	Position			
	Researcher	Chief Researcher	Director of Division	Director General of Laboratory
Pursuit of technology	X			
Internal and external activities	X			
Acquisition of patent	X			
Training subordinates		X		
Creation of research theme		X		
Judge of the appropriateness of subordinates		X		
Familiarity with non-professional themes			X	
Cooperation with outside			X	
Scrap-and-build of research theme			X	
Medium- to long-term plan of laboratory				X
Appeal to other companies, governments and other countries				X
Building and implementing a management philosophy				X

Since research and development operations mainly deal with state-of-the art technologies and no one can tell for sure at the beginning whether the research is going to be successful or not, researchers should be offered wider flexibility, and

Chapter 8 RESEARCH MANAGEMENT

be appreciated for how greatly their approaches differ from standard business operations.

Broadcasting showed many advantages in comparison with communication, in terms of its broadband signals and widespread coverage areas. However, as the Internet has higher bit rates than broadcasting and its service area is wider, the advantages of broadcasting have now been fading away. Since the practical uses of digital broadcasting were first demonstrated, the environment for broadcast technologies has greatly changed with the commonization of baseband signals in communication, etc. Moreover, technology changes in the fields of camera, display, and recording devices are happening rapidly, and it is getting more and more difficult for broadcasting researchers to establish relevant study themes and to manage their subordinates.

For these reasons, I would like to express my opinion, which has been developed through my own experience as a researcher, on the course that research managers should take[94],[95].

8.1 Researcher

A good researcher is required to have unique qualities. Of course, basic academic skills are necessary, but not all those who earn high scores at school will become excellent researchers. Research comprises business practices that no one has ever worked with before, while academic study involves learning what has already been established as standard knowledge, in that test scores at school reflect students' ability to work with information they have already learned. Accordingly, the main quality required of a researcher is not brightness or sharpness of the brain but strength and tenacity of heart when facing challenging and difficult problems.

As a matter of course, a researcher who lacks in basic academic skills will not be able to progress to new stages in the research. As for me, my basic academic skills consisted of error correcting, digital modulation and digital terrestrial broadcasting channel technologies, etc., which no one knew very much about when I started doing my research. As a method of improving one's basic academic skills, I recommend holding a colloquium, or a study meeting among fellow researchers. My own basic academic skills were improved by attending study meetings where we covered information form the textbook "Error Correcting Codes" as mentioned in this book

Furthermore, it is also necessary for a researcher to always have his/her own opinion, though it may differ from others'. Naturally, the more a researcher's opinion differs from others' and the stronger his/her will to make that opinion be accepted, the more often conflict may occur between the researcher and his/her boss or manager. I have found through my experiences and studies that there are actually some taboos employees can't break as long as they are in an organization. If we can't break the taboo of the organization, we will certainly fall into dilemma of the innovation[96]. For example, the direction that some issues are headed in often cannot be changed, and an alteration of their course cannot be expected to come about in the future. When I belonged to STRL, FM multiplexed broadcasting, BS digital broadcasting, DTTB, and Super Hi-Vision were the taboo areas there.

However, researchers should not be afraid of taboos. Instead of aiming at high positions in an organization, they should earn their positions as a result of their research activities. A good researcher should be able to persuade his/her boss, and should not be afraid of disputing the matter if necessary. The researcher should pursue his/her research with a rebellious spirit and a desire to be the world's No.1. The boss or manager does not always have sufficient knowledge or understanding about advanced state-of-the-art technologies, while the young engineers doing the actual work are usually most familiar with such things. In other words, a yes-man or flatterer who is always obedient to his/her boss will not be good at doing research, and those who cannot assert themselves when stating their opinions or are afraid to enter into disputes with their bosses are disqualified from becoming top researchers.

Conducting research is like being in a race: one wants to come in first place. It also requires a strong intention to wrestle with a difficult task with a fighting spirit and a sense of rivalry, which at first glance may look hard to achieve. Yet another quality required of a good researcher is an honest mind, open to patiently listening to others' ideas for the benefit of his/her own growth and the ability to form one's own ideas with a full understanding of others' positions.

Unlike the olden days, themes of research have become complicated, and research cannot be carried out by one person alone. Therefore, skill in cooperation is also required. A researcher must cooperate with others in a group when conducting research.

As I explained previously, I was the kind of person who was always objecting to my bosses' directions. They might have seen me as a recalcitrant person, and a difficult subordinate for them to deal with. That is why I really appreciated the tolerance and generosity of NHK management when it came to accepting me. Though I tried various things from my childhood, I dropped them all except research, and concentrated my efforts on research as my life's work. I was not interested in what other researchers were doing or were able to do. I liked trying my hand at difficult research themes that nobody else dealt with. In a sense I felt that studying was a hobby for me. In this respect, I recall the following saying from the "Doji-kyo", a folk teaching for children, written in the Kamakura era, in the 1100's: If a person can find a thing he likes and make every effort to get it, he will be able to reach the top of his chosen field even if he is not so bright.

Here, I would like to suggest that young researchers should have a strong sense of purpose and a strong fighting spirit for

Chapter 8 RESEARCH MANAGEMENT

dealing with difficult and challenging research themes that may differ from those of others, in order to strengthen their academic skills.

8.2 Research Manager

A research manager should not forget the sense of tension he/she felt when appointed as a manager who would lead subordinates for the first time. In my case, I was appointed as a manager when I was 40 years old. At the time, I thought my work would be unsatisfactory if I could not succeed in raising my subordinates to newer levels of excellence. I always taught them as hard as I could, how to write papers, how to proceed with research, how to present papers, etc.

Naturally the future careers of young researchers depend not only on their potential but also on their superior's abilities.

The important requirements for a good research manager include the ability to specify the course of research to be taken in future, not by the research manager alone, but by the whole group of researchers. A good research manager should also be able to set new themes for research, to develop human resources, and to create a free and comfortable working environment, among others. I was given teachings and a free environment from my boss, the late Mr. H. Yamane, when I was a young researcher (refer to Chapter 3). A manager who doesn't propose new research themes, but rather conducts research in the standard way cannot be considered an adequate research manager. Unfortunately, however, there are some managers who only give orders to set a new theme for research without specifying the course that the research is to take. There are also those who cannot set the theme by themselves. Research managers are required as part of their responsibilities to honestly listen to what their young subordinates say, and to study independently in order to set the course of research in future. For this reason, it is important to create a working environment in which subordinates may freely express their opinions. Furthermore, it is also necessary for research managers to have a flexible way of thinking that allows them to change their ideas if they judge that another person's idea is right, while theirs is wrong. Once the theme of research has been decided, more than half of the work is practically done. At that point, the researchers will be able to become absorbed in their research without worry. The most important role of managers is to establish new research themes for their subordinates and the organization.

In my case, I was engaged in eight research themes in NHK STRL over 31 years, and all the research themes including DTTB but apart from the one I was first given when I was transferred to NHK STRL were initially proposed by me. However, the themes I proposed were not considered feasible because of the situation at that time, and therefore, I had a hard time persuading my boss and other people to accept those new research themes. Furthermore, at that time I was actively involved in spreading ISDB-T abroad, which was not directly related to research. At the beginning of this activity, I had to promote ISDB-T without support from any domestic organizations. I had to persuade the key people in these organizations to secure their cooperation, using all my ingenuity applied in various ways.

Researchers cannot fulfill their roles simply by responding to the current requests of management. They will save themselves from a potential crisis with their managers in future by challenging undesirable technologies with an independent spirit. If less attention is paid to research and development because the serious pursuit of it is against the policy of management, then the company will be sure to face a crisis in future. It is the responsibility of a business's management to determine how the results of research and development should be taken into consideration. FM multiplexed broadcasting and BS digital broadcasting, both of which had been my themes of research, were initially strongly opposed by management, and no one else tried to promote them.

When I was appointed as Director General of NHK STRL in 1999, I started worrying about how I would manage the research center after the advent of digital broadcasting.

One of my main worries was that I would have to explain the necessity of the new NHK STRL building built in March 2002. Also during this period, I had a hard time persuading the management of NHK about my proposal. I had proposed a TV system using 4,000 scanning lines after discussing the matter with the leader of NHK's engineering group, Mr. T. Hasegawa in 2000. But this proposal was strongly opposed by HDTV researchers initially. They said, "Dr. Yamada is not a specialist on HDTV, yet he is insisting on a strange thing. We should not obey his proposal". In the situation where HDTV was not put to practical use, it was a taboo in NHK to study TV systems with higher qualities than HDTV.

I tried hard as the head of STRL to persuade the Chairman of NHK at the time, Mr. Katuji Ebisawa, and finally succeeded in convincing him to establish the 4000 scanning line TV system, as the theme of research for the future NHK. He declared officially that NHK STRL would begin to study the 4000 scanning line TV system at a special lecture given at NHK STRL's 70th anniversary commemoration symposium on the 4th of July, 2000[13]. After that, the 4000 scanning line TV system was named "Super Hi-Vision" in 2003[12],[97].

I made up my mind to extend the scope of our research into broadcasting technologies to video archives, medical applications, industrial applications, etc. as well as new broadcasting, which I thought could contribute to making people happy. Prof. Toshio Chiba, Nippon University, and Dr. Kenichi Tanioka, ex-Director General established the MIC* consisting of 18 companies[98]. The MIC* has assisted with the development of Super-Hivision medical applications[99], including, for example, endoscopes, displays of surgical operations, etc. By using Super-Hi-Vision cameras, we can watch things in detail, which otherwise cannot be seen with usual cameras. That is why I firmly believe that the combination of medical and broadcasting technologies can contribute to people's happiness. Technology doesn't stop developing. It is always making rapid progress, and STRL aims to be at the head of that progress.

Concerning new research themes, they basically depend on how the top people in a laboratory look at them. If the top management doesn't have his/her own independent ideas and does thing under the instruction of other institutions, the government, commercial broadcasters, etc., the results might be irreparable. As the heads of research laboratories best know the latest technologies, a leader should not easily accept others' opinions, but should instead strive to persuade others of the validity of his/her own ideas. When I started doing research into FM multiplex broadcasting and DTTB, there were a lot of differences in opinion between the government and me, and we even yelled at each other even over the telephone. Finally, we came to understand each other and we were able to get fruitful results.

I believe a research laboratory should be a work place for people interested in seriously pursuing research and development together. It is desirable that the head of a laboratory should have experienced some of the pains and troubles that a researcher must undergo, and have wide-spanning bureaucratic links outside of the research organization with business management. It is further desirable that the head of the organization be someone who accepts when a person asserts an objection as this person evinces an important quality, instead of excluding the person. If the person's opinion is found out to be wrong, the head should carefully explain the reason why it was rejected so that the person can fully understand the error. If people who assert objections are excluded from the organization, it will soon be full of yes-men and flatterers, and will surely start declining. In other words, without people who assert their own opinions and are not afraid of disputing with their bosses, the kind of research and development that produces ground-breaking results will not be achieved. In order to prevent such brave people from being excluded from organizations, transparency is indispensable. I would like to recommend the type of system for junior staff and colleagues to evaluate their senior staff that is generally used in Europe and the USA, to secure the transparency of organizations.

There is a proverb, "The nail that sticks out gets hammered in". I think this is one of the causes of the recent slump at some Japanese companies. On the contrary, when I think about the current situation in Japan, I would say the nail that sticks out should not be hammered in, but rather be stretched out. Mr. Soichiro Honda, the founder of Honda Motor Co., Ltd once said, "Only those who disobey the President are necessary". And Mr. Masaru Ibuka, the co-founder of Sony Corporation once said, "The strong stone wall of Castle Sony is made of edgy people", according to their respective books.

I hope that young researchers will have flexible ideas and a fighting spirit, and that organizations will be flexibly managed by their heads, who will carry out their jobs with transparency.

Chapter 9
ACKNOWLEDGEMENTS

The research and development of DTTB in Japan has been carried out through the efforts of the excellent researchers at NHK STRL, who have realized the goal of HDTV and mobile/portable reception based on an understanding of the characteristics of Teletext transmission channels. Furthermore, thanks to a collaboration between NHK, MIC, ARIB, commercial broadcasting stations and manufacturers, among others, the standardization, practical use and overseas publicity of the Japanese ISDB-T system have been advanced, and diffused across the world despite many difficulties.

Mr. F. Bittencourt of TV Globo in Brazil, the coauthor of this book, announced the advantages of ISDB-T over other systems that have been introduced to the public for the first time in the world. His announcement was the starting point for all the above-mentioned activities, particularly the overseas publicity. Now, I would like to take this opportunity to express my appreciation to all the persons who have been concerned with ISDB-T.

As I mentioned, the most important step for a researcher to take is to propose a theme of research aimed at success over several decades in future, and to make his or her boss recognize the importance of the proposal. On the contrary, it is a boss's role to set new themes of research for his/her subordinates. Once the theme is set, at least half of the research can be said to have been completed. I have been away from the world of research for years, but I still experience nightmares in which I am suffering because I cannot propose a new theme of research, which may be natural considering the importance of the proposal of new themes. Both FM multiplexed broadcasting and ISDB-T, the themes I proposed while I was an active researcher, seemed to be against the stream and very difficult to achieve at the time. However, my boss and the management in place then were kind enough to stand by and give me the opportunity to continuously devote myself to the research. I am still deeply grateful for the kindness of my boss and management.

Chapter 9 ACKNOWLEDGEMENTS

Furthermore, as I mentioned, I was a poor researcher, without any particular knowledge and abilities when I joined NHK in 1967. I was young and I only wanted to do research. But with the guidance of many senor researchers in NHK STRL, I managed to become a fully fledged researcher. Now, I feel in my heart that people cannot grow alone, but must be part of an organization in order to develop their talents. I am always thankful to NHK for assisting me to grow as a researcher.

Finally, there are three things I have to mention that are of great importance to me.

The first one is my gratitude to: the late Mr. H. Yamane, my boss who gave me a chance to study error correcting codes which became a key technology in the digital age; Mr. Yasutaka Numaguchi, General Manager of NHK STRL; Mr. E. Sawabe, Chief Research Engineer of NHK STRL, and Mr. K. Nio, General Manager of NHK STRL, etc. who made efforts to start actual Teletext and FM multiplex broadcasting services; Prof. Emeritus M. Hatori and Prof. Emeritus H. Imai of Tokyo University who evaluated the (272,190) code I developed; and also the late Mr. Yoshiro Nakamura, Mr. T. Hasegawa, Mr. T. Izumi, and *Dr.* Takehiko Yoshino who were the heads of NHK engineers' group and appointed me as the leader of the digital broadcasting research group.

The second one is my gratitude to many of the bright researchers I have worked with, such as Dr. T. Kuroda, Dr. M. Saito, who participated in the research of DTTB the promising future of which could never have been predicted back in 1986; Dr. S. Moriyama, Mr. M. Takada, Mr. S. Nakahara; and the more than 30 research team members at STRL, who followed us and contributed their abilities to completing ISDB-T.

The third one is my gratitude to the MIC, ARIB, commercial broadcasting stations, manufacturers, and the universities, all of which contributed to the research & development standardization, and diffusion activities of ISDB-T.

Finally, I would like to dedicate this book with love and gratitude to my parents who raised me, and my wife and children who supported me in my career as a researcher, both publicly and behind the scenes.

REFERENCE

Chapter 1

(1) Osamu Yamada : Ichi Housou Gijutusha no Jijoden, (in Japanese),
---Describing R&D activities in NHK STRL for about 30 years by Mr. Osamu Yamada.
Institute of Image Information and Engineers (ITE), Vol.65, No.8, August 2011

(2) Eiichi Sawabe, Akio Yanagimachi, Yoshio Sugimori and Masanobu Morisita : Moji Taju Houso, Denshi Jouho Tushinngakkaishi (in Japanese),
---Describing the history of R&D of Teletex at NHK STRL through 1970's and 1980's.
The Institute of Electronics Information and Communication Engineers (IEICE), Vol.70, No.13, October 1987

(3) Toru Kuroda : Idojusinnyo FM Tajuhouso Kikaku, Eizo Media Gakkaishi (inJapanese),
---Describing the outline of specifications of FM multiplex broadcasting for mobile reception developed in Japan.
Institute of Image Information and Engineers (ITE), Vol.47, No.10, October 1993

(4) Hisakazu Katoh, Akinori Hashimoto, Hajime Matsumura, Osamu Yamada : A Flexible Transmission Technique for the Satellite ISDB, IEEE Transaction on Broadcasting Vol.42, No.3, September, 1996

(5) The supervision of Osamu Yamada, : Digital Housou Hand Book(in Japanese)
---Describing detailed specifications of digital terrestrial TV broadcasting in Japan.
Ohmsha, June, 2003

(6) Osamu Yamada : Chijo Digital Housou no Kenkyu Kaihatu wo furikaette,

(in Japanese),
---Describing the history of R&D of digital terrestrial TV broadcasting developed by Mr. Yamada at NHK STRL, and key points in the research. Institute of Image Information and Engineers (ITE), Vol.60, No.9, March, 2006

(7) ARIB : Transmission System for Digital Terrestrial Television Broadcasting, ARIB Standard B-31 Version 2.2-E1, March 2014

(8) Digital Broadcasting Experts Group : Digital Terrestrial Television Broadcasting, Brochure, April 2010

(9) Osamu Yamada : Chijou Digital Housou no Kenkyu Kaihatu to Kaigai Tenkai (in Iapanese)
---Describing R&D of digital terrestrial TV broadcasting in Japan.
Information Processing Society of Japan (IPS), Vol.52, No.7, July 2011

(10) Ministry of Information and Communications, Japan (MIC) : White Pater 2014 (in Japanese), 2015

(11) Osamu Yamda : Chijo Digital Housou Densou Gijutu ni Kaketa 30 Nen (in Japanese)
---Describing R&D of digital terrestrial TV broadcasting for 30 years at NHK STRL by Mr. Yamada.
Radio Engineering & Electronics Association, Future of Radio Network (FORN), No.287, July 2012

Chapter 2

(12) Tadao Chikuma : Yumeno Super-HDTV ni Idomu (in Japanese)
---Describing the background of the proposal of ultra-high-definition TV.
NHK Publishing Company March 2005

(13) NHK Housou Gijutu Kenkyuujo : Kaisho 70 Shunen Kinen Symposium (in Japanese)
---Describing the 70th anniversary symposium of NHK STRL held at the Japan Business Federation hall in July, 2000.
NHK STRL, July 2000

REFERENCE

Chapter 3.1

(14) Hisakichi Yamane, Takehiko Yoshino and Akio Yamagimachi : Seisigahousou Jikken System (in Japanese)
---Describing the still picture broadcasting, which had been researched since 1960's at NHK STRL, but did not result in its practical use.
Institute of Television Engineers (ITE), Vol.30, No.5, May 1976

(15) Yoshikatu Sawamura : Shourai niokeru Housou Gijutu (in Japanese),
---Describing the future of broadcasting technologies as Director General if NHK STRL at the time.
Institute of TV Engineers (ITE), Vol.26, No.2, February 1972

(16) Osamu Yamada : Minicon Micon no Shorisokudo Hyouka (in Japanese),
---Describing the performance of minicomputers and microcomputers which were popular in the 1970's.
NHK Monthly Technical Report, Vol.21, No.1, January 1978

Chapter 3.2

(17) Keisuke Murasaki, Maehara, Tadashi Isobe, Masao Fujiwara, Koichi Tanigaki and Isamu Misonoo : Mojihouso Pattern Denso Hosiki no Kaihatu (in Japanese),
---Report on the study of patterned teletext instead of code transmission which had been studied at NHK STRL.
NHK R&D Report, Vol.36, No.1, 1984

(18) ITU-R Recommendation BT.653-3 : Teletext Systems. 1986 - 1990 - 1994 - 1998

(19) Eiichi Sawabe : Mojihousouhousiki no Gaiyou (in Japanese),
---Describing technologies for Teletext developed in Japan to be practically used.
Institute of TV Engineers (ITE), Vol.40, No.1, January 1986

(20) W. W. Peterson and E. J. Weldon, Jr : The MIT Press, 1972

(21) Tadashi Isobe : Moji Code Housou no Kanousei (in Japanese),
---The first thesis on the possibility of code transmission of ideogram information such as Japanese Kanji characters.

Technical Report of Institute of Television Engineers (ITE), IT-32-1, January 1978

(22) Tadashi Isobe, Ario Yanagimachi, Osamu Yamada : Moji Kohdo Housou no Kentou to Jikken (in Japanese)
---Report on results of the indoor experiments of code transmission of ideogram information such as Japanese Kanji, instead of patterned information.
Institute of Communication Engineers (ICE), Technical Report, IE78-56, 1984

(23) T. Kasami : Optimum Shortened Cyclic Codes for Burst Error Correction, IEEE Trans.on Information Theory, VolIT-9 No.2, 1963

(24) Osamu Yamada : Fugou-ka Densou-housiki Mojihousou you Ayamariteisei Fugou (in Japanese),
---Report on the results of R&D for an error correction method using a patterned Teletext system.
Transaction, Institute of Communication Engineers (elevisionICE) J67-B, April 1984

(25) J. L. Massey : Threshold Decoding, Cambridge, Massachusetts, MIT Press, 1963

(26) E.J.Weldon, Jr : Difference-Set Cyclic Codes, BSTJ, Vol.45, No.7 (1966)

(27) Muneyuki Tanaka : Jidousha Soukouji no Television Jusin Gazou Chousa (in Japanese),
---Thesis on the 5-grade evaluation of average image quality when analog TV is received while moving on a vehicle.
Annual Meeting of Institute of Television Engineers (ITE), August 1986

(28) Osamu Yamada : Development of an Error Correcting Method for Data Packet Multiplexed with TV signals, IEEE Trans. On Cpmmunications, Vol.35, No.1, 1987

(29) Osamu Yamada, Koichi Yamazaki, and Didier Besset : An Error - Correcting Scheme for an Optical Card System, 1990 International

Symposium on Information Theory and Applications (ISITA'90), November 1990

(30) Shu Lin : An Introduction to Error-Correcting Codes, Printice Hall, 1970

Chapter 3.3

(31) Osamu Yamada : FM Multiplex Broadcasting, NHK Laboratory Note, No.372, October 1989

(32) Osten Makitalo : Utilization of the FM broadcasting network for transmission of supplementary, Swedish Telecommunications Administration, Radio Laboratory Report RI 001/77, 1978

(33) Swedish Telecommunication Administration(Televerket) : Swedish Public Radio Paging System, Ref76-1650-ZE 1976

(34) ITU-R Recommendation BS.450-1 : Transmissin Standards for FM Sound Broadcasting at VHF, 1982

(35) EBU : Specifications of the radio data system RDS for VHF/FM sound broadcasting, Tec. 3244-E 1984

(36) Toru Kuroda, Masanori Saitou and Osamu Yamada : Transmission Scheme of High-capacity FM Multiplex Broadcasting System, IEEE Transaction on Broadcasting, Vol.42, No.3, September 1996

(37) ITU-R Recommendation BS.1194-2 : Systems for Multiplexing Frequency Modulation (FM) Sound Broadcasting with a Sub-carrier Data Cannel Having a Relatively Large Transmission Capacity for Stationary and Mobile Reception, 1995-1998

(38) Osamu Yamada : DARC Housiki FM Taju Housou Gijutu (in Japanese), ---Book on technologies of FM broadcasting, DARC, developed by NHK. Torikeppusu, March 1997

(39) Osamu Yamada, Tadashi Isobe, Toru Kuroda, Shigeki Moriyama, and Masayuki Takada : Traffic Information Services Using FM Multiplex

Broadcasting, IVHS Journal, Vol.1(1), 1993

Chapter 4
(40) Masayuki Takada : Chijo Digital Housou Kaihatu no Michinori to Genzai, sosite Mirai (in Japanese)
---Describing the history of R&D of digital terrestrial TV broadcasting, and its technology.
RF World, CQ Shuppan, March 2008

Chapter 4.1
(41) Robert. C. Dixon : Spectrum Spread Systems, John Wiley & Sons, 1976

(42) Mitsuo Yokoyama : Spectrum Kakusan Tusin System (in Japanese),
---The first guide in Japanese on the Spectrum Spread technology written by Mr. Yokoyama, researcher at the Radio Wave Research Laboratory of the Posts and Telecommunications Ministry.
Kagaku Gijutu Shuppan, 1988

(43) William F. Schreiber : Spread- Spectrum Television Broadcasting, SMPTE Journal, August 1992

(44) Takehiko Yoshino, Masanori Saitou and Yasuyuki Ito : Study on Advanced Digital Modulation Method, OFDM and AW-CDMA, NAB Broadcasting Engineering Conference Proceedings, March 1994

Chapter 4.2
(45) ITU-R Recommendation BS.1114-7 : Systems for Terrestrial Digital Sound Broadcasting to Vehiclelar, Portable and Fixed Receivers in the Frequency range 30-3,000MHz. December 2011

(46) M.Alard and R.Lassalle : Principles of Modulation and Channel Coding for Digital Broadcasting for Mobile Receivers, EBU Review-Technical, No.224, Aug.1987

(47) Bernard Le Floch, Roselyne Halbert-Lassalle and Damien Castelain : Digital Broadcasting to Mobile Receivers, ITEE Trans. Commun. Vol.Com-29, No.7

REFERENCE

(48) Botaro Hirosaki : An Orthogonally Multiplexed QAM System Using the Discrete Fourier Transform, IEEE Trans. Commun., Vol.COM-29, No.7, July 1981

(49) Masanori Saitou, Sigeki Moriyama and Osamu Yamada :Ghost Kankyou kadeno OFDM Densouhousiki no Ayamariritu Tokusei (in Japanese),
---Proving that OFDM is very effective against the ghost interferences peculiar to the terrestrial broadcasting by finding the error correcting characteristics of OFDM through simulation using the ghost interference data of terrestrial broadcasting collected during R&D of Teletext.
The Institute of Electronics Information Communication Engineers (IEICE), 1991 Autumn Meeting, B-231, September 1991

Chapter 4.3

(50) Joel Brinkley : Defining Vision : The Battle for the future of Television, Harcourt Brace & Company, 1998

(51) Moriyama Shigeki and Masanori Saitou : OFDM Henchouhousiki no Shitunai Denso Jikken Kekka (in Japanese),
---Describing results of measurement in an indoor transmission experiment for OFDM modulator/demodulator for TV using the first prototype produced in Japan.
The 1993 meeting of Institute of TV Engineers (ITE), 14-7, July 1993

(52) Masanori Saitou, Shigeki Moriyama and Shunji Nakahara : Experimental and Simulation Results on an OFDM Modem for TV Broadcasters, SMPTE Journal, Vol.105, No.1 January 1996

Chapter 4.4

(53) Shunji Nakahara, Shigeki Moriyama, Toru Kuroda, Makoto, Sasaki, Shigeru Yamazaki and Osamu Yamada : Effective Use of Frequencies in Terrestrial ISDB System, IEEE Transaction on Broadcasting, Vol.42, No.3, September 1996

Chapter 4.5

(54) Shigeki Moriyama, Kennichi Tsuchida, Shunji Nakahara and Masanori Saitou : OFDM Henchouhoushiki Digital FPU no Densou Tokusei (in

Japanese),
---Describing the outline of an outdoor FPU of the OFDM modulation system.
The meeting of The Institute of Image Information and Television Engineers (ITE), 19-2 July 1995

(55) Masayuki Takada, Toru Kuroda and Nobuyuki Miki : Chijo Digital Housou no Daikibo Jishoujikken to Tokyo Pilot Jiken no Gaiyou (in Japanese),
---On the experiment carried out for confirming the service coverage area by transmitting TV signals from a pilot station of digital terrestrial TV broadcasting set at the Tokyo Tower.
The Institute of Image Information and Television Engineers (ITE), Vol.53, No.11, November 1999

(56) Tuchiya Junji : Chijou Digital Housou no Enkatuna Dounyu ni Mukete (inJapanese),
---Describing the process of introduction of digital terrestrial TV broadcasting in Japan.
The Research Center of the Ministry of Internal Affairs and Communications (MIC), August 1999

(57) ARIB : Chijo Digital Television Housou Unyou Kitei (in Japanese),
---On the operation guidance for digital terrestrial TV broadcasting prescribed by broadcasting stations and manufacturers.
TR-B14, May 2004

Chapter 4.6

(58) ITU-R Recommendation BT.1306, Error-correction, data framing, modulation and emission methods for digital terrestrial television broadcasting, May 2000

(59) Kenichi Tsuchida : Kokusai Hyoujunka Katudou (in Japanese),
---Describing the current international standardization activities in Japan for ITU-R.
The Institute of Image Information Television Engineeres (ITE) Vol.62, No.11, November 2006

(60) Yasuji Sakaguchi : Nannbei Peru niokeru Chideji ISDB-T Jituyouka

REFERENCE

Sienkatudou (in Japanese),
---Describing the technical assistance in Peru, which decided adoption of ISDB-T, and the situation of practical use of ISDB-T in Peru.
Radio Engineering & Electronics Association, FORM, No.301, December 2014

Chapter 5

(61) ARIB : ARIB Standard STD-B31, March 2014

(62) ITU-R Recommendation BT177 4-1 : Use of Satellite and Terrestrial Broadcast Infrastructure for Public Warning, Disaster Mitigation and Relief, 2007

(63) ITU-R RecommendationBT.1368-12 : Planning criteria, including protection ratios, for digital terrestrial television services in the VHF/UHF bands, February 2015

(64) Michihiro Uehara, Masayuki Takada, Toru Kuroda and Takesi Kimura : Chijou ISDB Housouhousiki no Kentou ~ BST-OFDM Housiki to Tajuhousiki ~ (in Japan),
---Describing the signal flows to multiplex each data group.
TV Gakujutuhou, Vol.20, No.22, March 1996

(65) ITU-R Recommendation BT.1306, Error-correction, data framing, modulation and emission methods for digital terrestrial television broadcasting, December 2011

(66) Eduardo Santos Bueno, Gunnar Bedicks Jr, Cristiano Akamine, Edson Lemos Horta : Resuts of Field Tests of the ISDB-TB System a 8MHz in Botswana, Revista de Radiodifusao, Vol.07, No.08, 2013

Chapter 6

(67) Osamu Yamada : Chijou Digital Housou no Kaigai Fukyuukatudou wo Furikaette (in Japanese),
---Describing the overseas diffusion activities for digital terrestrial TV broadcasting.
Radio Engineering & Electronics Association, FORN No.288, September 2011

(68) ITU-R Recommendation BT.709-5 : Parameters Values for the HDTV Standards for Production and International Program Exchange, April 2002

(69) Noburo Takada and Naohiro Yosikawa : Daisan no Kaikoku wo Toshita Nihon no Saiseisenryaku (in Japanese),
---Claiming that Japan is not good at conducting overseas diffusion activities for a system developed in Japan, so that the system will not be diffused overseas to be used only in Japan, and that the system of digital terrestrial TV broadcasting will take the same course.
Chiteki Sisan Souzou, 2008

Chapter 6.1

(70) IBC Daily News : You say ATSC, I say DVB, September 1999

(71) IBC Daily News : The IBC Tutorials, What are they and are they for me ? September 1999

(72) Hideo Fuseda : ICT Kokusai Kyousouryoku notameno ISDB-T Kokusai Tenkai (in Japanese),
---Describing the international expansion of ISDB-T by the Ministry of Internal Affairs and Communications, to strengthen the international competiveness of ICT.
The Institute of Image Information Television Engineers (ITE), Vol.62, No.11, November 2006

(73) Osamu Yamada : ICT Kokusai Fukyu Katudou eno Kitai (in Japanese),
---Describing the international expansion of ICT through diffusion of ISDB-T.
The Institute of Image Information Television Engineers (ITE), Vol.62, No.11, November 2006

(74) Yoshiki Maruyama : Asia Shokoku deno Fukyu Katudou (in Japanese) ,
---Describing the diffusion activities of ISDB-T in Asian countries.
The Institute of Image Information Television Engineers (ITE), Vol.62, No.11, November 2006

(75) Tay Joo Thong : Digital TV Field Trials in Singapore, The Singapore Broadcasting Authority (SBA), 1997

Chapter 6.3

(76) Osamu Yamada : Development of Japanese Terrestrial Digital Digital Broadcasting, Brazil SET'98 Technical Meeting, August 1998

(77) NAB2000 : Conference Speech, NHK BST, No.11, June 2000

(78) SET-ABERT Group Brazil : Brazilian Digital Television Tests, NAB'2000, April 2000

(79) FACTA : Chijou Digital Housou Nihonkikaku Yumedenai Kaigai Seiha (inJapanese),
---News article reporting that Brazil decided to adopt Japanese ISDB-T. September 2006

(80) Kenichi Kobayashi : Nannbei niokeru Chijou Digital Housou Nihon Hoshiki no Fukyu ~Subete ha Brazil no Ketudan kara Hajimatta~ (inJapanese),
---Report on situations of South-American countries, which subsequently decided to adopt ISDB-T after the adoption of ISDB-T in Brazil.
The NHK Monthly Report on Broadcast Research, March 2010

(81) Fernando Bittencourt : Brazil niokeru Digital Television (in Japanese),
---Describing the background of adoption of ISDB-T and the current broadcasting situation in Brazil, by Mr. Bittencourt as a leader in promoting digital broadcasting in Brazil.
The Institute of Image Information Television Engineers (ITE), Vol. 61, No.11, November 2007

(82) Yasuo Takahashi : Nanbei Shokoku deno Fukyu Katudou (in Japanese),
---Report on the outline of diffusion activities of ISDB-T in South-American countries by Mr. Takahashi who had been engaged in the activities.
The Institute of Image Information Television Engineers (ITE), Vol.62, No.11, November 2006

Chapter 6.4

(83) Tomohito Ikegami : Chile/Peru Deno Hosiki Hikaku Jikken (in Japanese),
---Describing comparative experiments of digital terrestrial TV broadcasting in Chili and Peru.
The Institute of Image Information Television Engineers (ITE), Vol.62, No.11, November 2006

(84) Masayuki Takada : Internationalization of the Japanese Digital Terrestrial Television System, ISDB-T, Broadcasting Technology, No.33, NHK STR, Winter 2008

(85) Denpa Publication : Flexibility, Expandability, Mobility Give ISDB-T Edge, BET 2009, April 2009

(86) DiBEG : Results of Comparative Test for Fixed reception Carried out by ABSCBN & TSI in Philippines, January 2010

Chapter 7

(87) Fernando Bittencourt : Brazil Niokeru Digital TV (in Japanese), Eizoujouhou Medhia Gakkai,
---Describing the process of decision to adopt the digital terrestrial TV broadcasting in Brazil, and the future of the broadcasting in Brazil.
The Institute of Image Information and Television Engineers (ITE), Vol.61, No.11, November 2007

(88) Takao Shimizu, etc. : Panel Discussion ~IT Kakumei to Digital Hoso~(in Japanese),
---Report on a panel discussion on the future of digital broadcasting.
The Institute of Image Information and Television Engineers (ITE), Vol.56, No.1, January 2002

(89) SET-ABERT Group Brazil : Brazilian Digital Television Tests, NAB'2000, April 2000

(90) Ana Eliza Faria e Silva et. al., "BRAZILIAN DIGITAL TELEVISION TEST RESULTS," ABU Technical Review, No.190, pp.14-26 (September - October issue 2000)

(91) Olimpio J. Franco : Brazil ni Okeru Digital TV Dounyu Shousi, FORM, N0.294, September, 2013

(92) G. Bedicks, F. Yamada ; F. Sukys ; C. E. S. Dantas ; L. T. M. Raunheitte ; C. Akamine, Results of the ISDB-T system tests, as part of digital TV study carried out in Brazil
IEEE Transactions on Broadcasting, Vol.52, No.1, March 2006

Chapter 8

(93) Osamu Yamada : Watakusino Kenkyu Management Ron ~Digital Houso no Kenkyu Kaihatu wo toosite~Densi Jouho Tuusingakkashi (in Japanese),
---Opinion on the R&D in general, learned through the R&D of digital broadcasting.
The Institute of Electronics Information Communication Engineers (IEICE), Vol.93, No.6, June 2010

(94) Osamu Yamada : Seichou Senryaku mazu Sosiki Inobeshon (in Japanese),
---Claiming that the transparency of an organization (organization innovation) is indispensable to maximize the capability of a researcher required for the technical innovation.
FACTA, May 2013

(95) Osamu Yamada : Digital TV Housou Housiki no Kenkyu Kaihatsu to Kaigai Tenkai ~ Kenkyu Kaihatsu Management to Gijutsu Rikkoku Nippon heno Teigen ~ (inJapanese),
---Opinion on the revival of Japan as a technology-intensive nation based on the R&D management learned through the R&D of digital broadcasting.
The Tokyo Branch Meeting of the Institute of Electronics Information Communication Engineers (IEICE), February 2009

(96) Clayton M. Christensen : The innovator's Dilemma, Harvard business school press, 1997

(97) ITU-R Recommendation BT-2020-1 : Parameter values for ultra-high definition television systems for production and international programme exchange, June 2014

(98) Kenji Tanioka : 8k Super-Hivisin Gijutu to Sono Iryou Ouyou(in Japanese),
--Opinion on the medical applications of 8k ultra-high-definition TV developed by Mr. Tanioka, Director General of NHK STRL in the 2000's.
The Institute of Image Information and Television Engineers (ITE), Vol.70, No.7, July, 2016

(99) Kosei Yamashita : Super Hivision 8K Gijutu no Iryuoyo, Eizoujoho Industrial, 46, July, 2014

ABOUT THE AUTHORS

OSAMU YAMADA graduated from the department of Electrical Engineering of Waseda University in 1967. He joined NHK as an engineer and started to work for NHK Aomori broadcasting station (the northernmost prefecture of the mainland) until 1971.

In 1971, he was dispatched to NHK Science & Technology Research Laboratories (NHK STRL). His first research item given was still picture broadcasting, which was not realized, but he experienced a lot of technologies, digital, recording, computer, one-chp CPU, circuit & software design, etc.. In 1979, he was given the research item of Teletext, and he proposed the research of error correcting codes as the most important technology of Teletext. He succeeded in the realization of Teletext digital terrestrial transmission technology without bit errors for the first time in the world by using the new error correcting code, the (272,190) code. Teletex services actually started in 1985. He got a doctor's degree in the error correcting code for Teletext from Tokyo University.

In 1985, he started the research of FM multiplexed broadcasting aiming at mobile reception broadcasting. Though NHK didn't have a plan to serve FM multiplex broadcasting at that time, he was especially interested in the realization of mobile reception broadcasting. In 1995, his group completed and realized high capacity mobile reception FM multiplex broadcasting as VICS.

In 1986, he started the research of digital terrestrial TV broadcasting (DTTB) having mobile reception and all TV broadcasting stations in Japan started DTTB in 2003.

In the late of 1980's, he stared to develop the optical card system using the (272,190) code with the manufacture and in 1990's the optical card system called DELA was adopted as the Green Card which have been used in the U.S.A.

In 1991, he was promoted to the Director of Digital Broadcasting Research Group, and started the research of Digital Satellite Broadcasting and his group realized it in 2000.

In 1990's-2000's, he had been engaged in the diffusion activities of ISDB-T in the world.

In 2000, as Director General of STRL, he started the research of Super Hivision (4,000 scanning TV system), 8K TV as a future TV system.

In 2002, he left NHK and joined Pioneer and had been leading the Pioneer engineer group as a Senior Managing Director.

In 2009, he left Pioneer, joined Waseda University and taught young students "Broadcasting Technologies and Media Argument" as a honorary professor.

In 2009, Dr. Yamada established his own company named International Technology Consulting Corporation and has been working as an entrepreneur.

He had been contributing to the broadcasting technology area for more than forty years, and through its experiences established a philosophy of the research management. He has been making presentations it at the related societies. He has won a lot of awards including C&C Award in 2012. He is a honorary member of IEICE (the Institute of Electronics, Information and communication Engineers) and ITE (The Institute of Television Engineers), and a life member of IEEE. He lives in Tokyo with his wife, Emi Yamada.

FERNANDO MATTOSO BITTENCOURT FILHO

graduated from the faculty of Electronic Engineering of the Federal University of Rio de Janeiro in 1971.

He started his career in TV Globo in 1969 as a trainee in the the Support and Maintenance at the Engineer Division area in Rio de Janeiro followed by Engineer General manager in TV Globo Station in Recife and Sao Paulo.

He came to Rio de janeiro as Entertainment Engineer Director on 1984 when he had the opportunity to participate in the project of the new Studio Production facilities inaugurated in 1995. This facility is today considered one of the biggest and most modern TV production facilities in the world.

In 1992 he was promoted as the CTO of TV Globo responsible for all operation, engineering project and support for the whole Engineer and technology activities, managing more than 2500 engineers and technicians in the whole company until 2014.

Since 1990's, he had been playing a role to lead Brazilian Digital TV Group to study and plan the introduction of Digital TV in Brazil. In 1999/2000, he carried out the first evaluation of the three existing Digital TV Systems in the world (ATSC-DVB-ISDB-T) under the SET (Brazilian Society of Television Engineering) / ABERT (the Association of the Brazilian Broadcasters) Group.

As conclusion, the group handed a complete report to the Ministry of Communication with a deep analysis and the performance of the three systems both in the field and lab with a recommendation for adopting the ISDB-T as the Brazilian Digital TV System.

After a long and exhaustive debate, the Brazilian Government finally decide in 2006 to adopt the ISDB-T with some kind of modification, mainly the adoption of H264 instead of MPEG2 which is used in ISDB-T. The Terrestrial Digital Brazilian System has been nominated ISDTV (International System for Digital Television).

He had been having a wide sphere of activity as follows.
(1) Active Member of SMPTE

   Latin Governor for two Terms.

   As Latin governor was responsible for the SMPTE activities in the region.
(2) Member of IEEE (International of Electrical and Electronics Engineers)
(3) SET President – 1994-1996 (Brazilian Society of Television Engineering)
(4) SET Vice-President – 2014-2016
(5) Commissioner of SCAC (the Social Communication Advisory Committee of the Congress Upper House in

Brazil. The SCAC is responsible to study and advise the Brazilian Congress Upper House in all matters concerning Telecommunication, Television, Radio, New Media. Regulatory and technological issues.

(6) Council Member of IBC (International Broadcasting Convention)

The Council is responsible for the IBC Congress. We discuss and indicate the themes and people to participate in the panels.

Also, the prizes and awards are managed by the Council.

(7) Council Member of the ISDB-Tb (Brazilian DTV System) - Forum

Created by the Brazilian Government to finalize the ISDB technical specification and harmonize the introduction of Digital TV in Brazil. The Forum have the participation of broadcasters, consumer electronics manufactures, universities and members of Government.

During his career he has received the following awards:

(1) Set 2004 Award for the contribution to the evolution of TV in Brazil

(2) ITE Award 2007 (Japanese Institute of Image and Television Engineering)

(3) SMPTE Fellow (Society of Motion Picture e Television Engineers) 2016

(4) ABERT 2012 Award for great contribution to the Brazilian Broadcasters growth.

(5) Japanese Government 2013

The Order of the Rising Sun, Gold Rays with Neck Ribbon.

For his contribution in the introduction and dissemination of Digital TV in South America .

(6) Set Award for the contribution to the introduction of Digital TV in Brazil

INDEX

INDEX	**Page**
[A]	
a ten-year saga	122
ABC in Hong Kong	106
ABERT/SET, ABERT and SET	131, 133, 135, 137, 145
ABU	51, 102, 103, 106
Technical Director General of ABU	51
academic	78, 154, 155
Adaptive Difference Pulse Coded Modulation (ADPCM)	46
adjacent	72, 73, 84, 85, 87, 88, 92, 137, 147
Advanced TV System Committee (ATSC)	10, 58, 64, 78, 80, 92, 103, 107, 111, 114, 122, 123, 125, 139, 143, 144, 147, 148
ATSC and DVB-T	125,126
ATSC, DVB-T and ISDB-T	96, 109, 117, 122, 123, 131, 138
Africa	18, 99
analog	
analog and digital circuit	28
analog broadcasing	10, 67, 69, 72, 83, 85, 86, 88, 103, 116
analog FM multiplex broadcasting	46
analog HDTV	64
analog picture	27
analog switch off	69
analog technologies	73
analog television (TV)	46, 57, 74, 77, 123
analog TV screen	45
analog-analog conversion	74
anntena	54
antenna effective length (m =λ/π)	87
antenna gain	87

appendix	93
Argentina	111
Association of Radio Industries and Businesses (ARIB)	18, 78, 99, 125
Asia Broadcasting Union (ABU)	51
assembly meeting of the ITU-R	76
Association of Radio Industries and Businesses (ARIB)	13
ATSC	64, 78, 92, 138. 139, 143, 144
ATSC and (or) DVB	79, 126
ATSC, DVB-T and ISDB-T	122, 131, 144
Austria	59
[B]	
Band Segmaented –OFDM (BST-OFDM)	73
BBC	31
BCH codes	35
block	
block error rate	37
block length	37
Botswana	99
Brazil	11, 12, 14, 102, 104, 107-115, 119, 125, 123, 125-128, 130-135, 144, 145, 149, 167
Brazil's decision 112,	112
Brazilian Broadcaster 130, 132, 149	130, 132, 149
Brazilian Broadcasting 125	125
Brazilian city 148	148
Brazilian Communications Minister	127
Brazilian digital TV	123
Brazilian DTTB 135	135
Brazilian Federal Government's Telecommunications Agency (ANATEL)	137
Brazilian government	12, 123, 127, 150
Brazilian law 135,	135
Brazilian President 123,	123
Brazilian researcher 11	11
Brazilian senario 135	135
Brazilian standard 128, 135	128, 135
Brazilian System Requirement 132	132
Brazilian TV 124,	124

INDEX

Brazilian TVGlobo 102, 108,	102, 108
Brazilian University 127,	127
Broadcast	
Broadcast Asia	103
Broadcasting Center	67
broadcasting equipment	23
Broadcasting Olympics	26
BS	
BS analog HDTV	64
BS digital broadcasting	22, 156
Band Segmented-OFDM (BST-OFDM)	89
burst errors	35, 45, 47, 96, 140

[C]

C/N	95
Cable loss	87
Cable TV (CATV)	57
The Argentine Chamber of Providers and Manufacturers of Radio-diffusion Equipment (CAPER)	119
Carrier-to-noise ratio threshold vs. Signal level	136
CCIR (previous name of ITU-R)	47, 59
CD	39
Ceefax	31
Central America	18
Centre Commun d'Etudes de Television et Telecommunications (CCETT)	59
channel plan.	88
Characteristics of transmission performance	137
Chile	79, 111
cliff effect	58
coded tramsmission Teletext	33
COFDM modulation	132
colloquium	32, 155
Colombia	12
colorization of the TV broadcasting system	23, 24
Columbia	18, 111
Comité Consultatif Internationale des Radiocommunications (CCIR)	31
commercial television stations	78
common technologies DTTB	70
Commonality	72
Comparative studies	11
COMPATIBILITY	89
convolution code	36

correctable bit number　37

[D]
Digital Audio Broadcasting (DAB)　59
Data Radio Channel (DARC)　51, 100
dark horse　51
DBPSK　97
deep space communication　59
desired
    Desired to Undesired signal ratio (D/U)　62
    desired wave　87, 88
    desired wave is for digital broadcasting　88
Digital Broadcating Expert Group (DiBEG)　18. 105, 108, 110, 112, 118, 121
difference set cyclic codes　36
Diffusion activities　100. 112
digital
    digital audio broadcasting　70
    Digital Audio Visual Council (DAVIC)　10
    Digital Broadcasting Expert Group (DiBEG)　18
    digital cable TV　70
    digital FPU　51
    Digital Marriage　129
    digital modulation technologies　155
    digital radio　57
    digital satellite broadcasting　70
    digital terrestrial audio broadcasting　72
    Digital Terrestrial TV Broadcasting (DTTB)　13
    Digital Terrestrial Television Expert Group (DigiTAG)　105
    digital TV　57, 137
    Digital TV Laboratory (DTVL)　75
    Digital Video Broadcasting (DAB)　10
    digitalization of broadcasting　104
    DTTB for mobile/portable reception　42
    DTTB System Development Committee　70
dilemma of the innovation　156, 157
dojikyo　137
doppler Effect　98
DQPSK　111
Digital Video Broadcasting (DVB)
    DVB handheld (DVB-H)　80
    DVB-T　78, 80, 105, 111, 112, 119, 120, 133, 141, 144, 148, 149

INDEX

DVB-T and ISDB-T	111, 132, 138, 146, 147, 149
DVB-T2	80

[E]

8-bit single-chip CPU	28
800 MHz band relay equipment	74
8 Vestigial Side-Band (8VSB)	
8VSB modulation	131
8VSB system	136
Eb/No	39, 92
European Broadcasting Union (EBU)	47, 59
educational programs	27
effective symbol length	91
Electric Communication Council of MPT	70
emergency	
emergency information	84
emergency warning function	84
Emergency Warning System (EWS)	79
error	
error correcting codes	32, 155
error correcting rate of 7/8	87
error rate vs. carrier-to-noise ratio	136
error rate vs. signal level	136
Eureka	
Eureka 147	62
Eureka 1197	53

[F]

14 segments	84, 99
4,000 scanning lines	22
429 kHz	84
5.7 MHz	84
Fast Fourier Transform (FFT)	61
Field Pickup Unit (FPU)	73
field strength	86, 87
final decision	125
fixed reception.	133
flexible system	84
FM	
FM broadcasting	62
FM multiplex broadcasting	11, 17, 21, 22, 46, 56, 100, 167
foot-note	48

forward/backward guarding	35
frame	
frame memory	27, 28, 29
frame structure	97
framing errors	35
free-of-charge	126
frequency	38, 52, 61, 67, 87, 99, 119, 140, 148
frequencies of 130MHz	69
frequency allocation plan	74
frequency axis	61, 97
frequency band	74, 98
frequency band width	99
frequency interleaving	92, 96
frequency interval	61
frequency spectrum	134
frequncy reuse	134

[G]

Galapagosized	100
gen-lock circuit	23
Germany	49, 59
ghost	62, 91, 92
ghost data	63
ghost interferences	40, 45, 46, 54, 59, 61, 62, 63, 67, 91
Ginga	128
Goddess of Serendipity	38
ground	
ground clearance of 4m	86
ground-breaking results	163
group delay	45
guard	
guard interval	91
guard interval ratios	93

[H]

High-Definition TV (HDTV)	10, 26
HDTV signals	132
hierarchical transmission	92
high-definition broadcasting	147
Hitachi	20
Hokkaido to Okinawa	76

INDEX

home electric appliances	45
Honda Motor Co., Ltd	163

[I]

I-axis	94
IBC '99	104
Ichiro's game-winning hit	79
ideograph characters	100
Institute of Electrical and Electronics Engineers (IEEE)	42
IEEE Communication Society	43
IEEE Global Communications Conference (GLOBECOM)	43
IEEE Transaction on Broadcasting	150
Immigrants	130
Impulse noise	45, 136
inner codes	92, 93
Institut fur Rundfunktechnik (IRT)	59
Institute of image inforamtion and Television Engineers (ITE)	29, 36
Integrated	
integrated Internet services	84
Integrated Services Digital Broadcating- Terrestrial (ISDB-T)	11-14, 16-18, 43, 51, 56, 70, 77, 79, 82-85, 87 89-91, 93, 96, 98, 100-124,126-129 132-134 139, 140, 144, 148, 149, 160, 166, 167, 169
Intel 8080	28
interference behavior	135
interfering wave	88
interleave length	92
International	
International Broadcasting Convention (IBC)	103
International standards	72
International Telecommunication Union-Radio Sector (ITU-R)	11, 77, 82, 84, 99
International Telecommunication Union-Radio Sector/ Task Group 11-3 (ITU-R-TG11/3)	10, 108
Inverse Fast Fourier Transform (IFFT)	93
ISDB-T for 7 and 8MHz	98
ITU-R standardization	50

[J]
Japanese Kanji characters	31
Japanese Ministry of Communications	125

[L]
laboratory and field tests	135
Lake Biwako Marathon	74
Large Scale Integrated Circuit (LSI)	10
large-scale transmission experiments	74
Latin-America	121
lengths of ghost interferences	67
Level controlled MSK (LMSK)	51
low UHF channels	74

[M]
Mackenzie	
Mackenzie lab	126
Mackenzie Presbyterian University	150
major electric-appliance manufacturers	20
majority logic error-correcting codes	36
manufactures	78
marathon relay	74
maximum capacity of information transmission	92
Medical Imaging Consortium (MIC*)	161
Metropolitan Police Department	49
microcomputers	28
minimum signal power	137
Minister of Communications	127
Ministry of Construction (MC)	52
Ministry of Internal Affairs and Communications (MIC)	12, 13, 78
Ministry of Posts and Telecommunications (MPT)	52, 70, 77
mobile broadcasting services	71
Mobile Pedestrian Handheld (MPH)	79
mobile reception	11, 56, 125, 144
mobile/portable receiving functions	22
mobile/portable reception	57, 77
MODE	90
Mode 1	90
Mode 2	90
Mode 3	90
modylation and error correction	95
Moore's law	45
Motorola 6800	28
Moving Picture Expert Group (MPEG)	10
MPEG-2	83, 110, 127, 128

INDEX

MPEG-4	83, 110, 127, 128
multi-	
multi-carrier segmentation	89
multi-channel broadcasting	11
multi-channel satellite broadcasting	27
multi-channel standard TV services	71
multi-information technology	27
multi-SDTV vs HDTV	122
multipath	143, 146, 149
multipath Interference	85, 136, 138
Multiple Sub-nyquist Sampling Encoding (MUSE)	10, 64

[N]

1998 World Cup	123
North American Broadcasters (NAB)	103, 109, 124
narrow MUSE system	64
national budget	76
National Convention of the Institute of Japanese TV Engineers	36
National Police Agency (NPA)	52
NEC	20, 60
network of personal relations	21
Nippon Hosou Kyoukai : Public Broadcaster (NHK)	10, 16, 21, 22, 24, 78, 125,
NHK Aomori	16, 21
NHK Broadcasting Center	24
NHK broadcasting stations	24
NHK Kofu broadcasting station	85
NHK Science & Technology Research Laboratories (STRL)	10, 17, 18, 22, 25, 129, 156, 159-161, 166, 168
NHK Technology Group	50
nightmares	167
NTSC	113, 118, 127

[O]

1/7 MHz	92
130MHz frequency band	85
188-byte	95
188-byte information	94
OFDM system	91
Okinawa Summit meeting	76
omnidirectional antennas.	54

one-chip LSI	38
One-Segment Broadcasting (One-Seg)	11, 77, 78, 83
operation guide	76
optical cards	43
Orthogonal Frequency Division Multiplexing (OFDM)	59
Osaka University	33
outer code	94
over-the-air reception	126

[P]

Pal-M. (US NTSC 525 lines, European Pal color system)	135
patterned Teletext	32
penguins in the second line	103
perseverance and vision for the future	130
Peru	111
Peter Principle	153
phase continuity of clock signals	35
Philippines	111, 113, 119
Pioneer Corporation.	17
positions and the tasks	156
power cables	45
protection ratio	86, 87
provisional system	75
public broadcasting station	46
Public Information (PI)	47

[Q]

Q-axis	94
Quadrature Phase Shift keying (QPSK)	51, 63

[R]

rabbit ear antennas,	123
radio broadcasting	17
Radio Data Service (RDS)	47-49, 52, 53
receiver input voltage	87
Reed-Solomon (RS)	38, 92, 94
relay braodcasting stations	85
research	
research management	152
research manager	158
researcher	154

[S]

60dBµv/m	86

INDEX

64 Quadrature Amplitude Modulation (64QAM)	87
70dBμv/m	86
sample frequency	93
satellite broadcasting	57
Satellite Digital Broadcasting	17
segmentation	84
service area for analog broadcasting	86
same frequency	85, 87
same frequency band	67
Santiago	114
segment	92
service areas	67
SET'98	107
shortened cyclic codes	35
signal	
signal distortion	45
signal generation	93
Signal Noise Ratio (S/N)	58
signal shut-off	48
Singapore	105
single frequency network (SFN)	67, 90, 147
single-segment	97
Sistem Brasileiro de Televisao Terrestre (SBTVD)	123, 128
slump at the Japanese companies.	163
Society of Moving Picture Technical Engineers (SMPTE)	103
Sony Corporation	164
South American countries	18, 111
South-east Asia	18
spare operation manuals	23
Spread Spectrum (SS)	58
standardization	70
state-of-the art technologies	153
stationary reception	11, 56
Still- Picture Broadcasting	27
Studio Equipment Division	24
Subsidiary Communications Authorization (SCA)	46
Sumatora Andaman earthquake	84
super-high definition TV	22
Super-Hivision camera	162
Super-Hivision medical applications	161
Swedish Telecom	47
Swift project	53
Switzerland	59
symbol period (Ts)	90
synchronized signal generator	23

[T]

(204,188) RS code.	94, 95
(255,239) RS code	94
(26,16) shortened cyclic code	47
(272,190) code	36
(272,190) X (272,190) code	39
(273,191) code	36
10dB lower signal level	86
13 data segments	73, 84, 92, 126, 156
taboo	
Task Group 11-3 of the ITU-R	77
Telediffusion de France (TDF)	62
Teleterminals	49
Teletex	11, 17, 27, 31, 33, 56, 100, 166
television marathon relay system	73
TERACOM	51
three hierarchies	92
TIME AXIS INTERLEAVING	96
time-axial interleave length	93
time-axis interleaving	117
Tokyo	
Tokyo FM	46
Tokyo Olympics	26
Tokyo Tower	21, 76
Tokyo University	33
Toshiba	20
trafic information	49
transmission	
Transmission and Multiplexing Configuration and Control (TMCC)	90, 97
transmission method	89
transmission power	67
transparency	163
Transport Stream (TS)	93, 94, 95
Tsunami	84
TV	
TV blanking periods	11
TV kit	23
TVGlobo	11, 107, 108, 167

[U]

Ultra High Frequency (UHF)	58
university of UTEM,	113

INDEX

uplink 84

[V]
Vehicle Information Communication System (VICS) 21, 52
Very High Frequency (VHF) 58

[W]
Working Group (WG) 51
World Baseball Classic (WBC) 79
WST 100

[Y]
yes-men or flatterers 156

Name	Page, Fig. Table
[A]	
Akamine, Cristiano	Fig.35
Alfonso, Aurin Palacin Junior	Fig.35
Almeida, Valderez de Donzelli	Fig.35
Aono, Roberto Tamotsu	Fig.35
Arellano, James Martin Madrid	117
Aurin, Alfons Palacin Junior	Fig.35
Avoc, Mac	103, 107, 167
[B]	
Baiadori, Fábio	Fig.35
Baron, Stan	77
Bittencourt, Ferenando	11, 12, 14, 107, 115, 129, 167, Fig.34
Brito, Carlos de Nogueira	108, Fig.35
Bedicks, Gunnar	150
[C]	
Castro, Paulo Henrique Corona Viveiros de	Fig.35
Chaves de Oliveira, Vitor	13
Chiba, Toshio	161
Cipriano, Manuel Pirgo	117
[D]	
Dantas, Carlos Eduardo	Fig.35
Diniz, Daniel da Costa	Fig.35
Dodria, J	121
Durney, Hugo W. ,	113, 121
[E]	
Ebisawa, Katuji	161
[F]	
Faria, Ana Eliza e Silva	13, 102, Fig.35
Filho, Sizenando José Ferreira	107, Fig.35
Franco, Olímpio José	Fig.35
Franco, Roberto	Fig.35
Franzen, Ricardo	Fig.35
Furukawa, Yasushi	112, Table 6
Fuseda, Hideo	112, 118, Table 6

INDEX

[G]
Gallegos, Cesar	117, 121
Geraldo, Edson Benedito	Fig.35
Gorett,i Maria Romeiro	Fig.35
Graves, Robert	103, 107, 111

[H]
Hasegawa, Toyoaki	106, 109, 161, 168
Hatori, Mitutoshi	43, 168
Herriquez, Daniel Ilic	113, 121
Hirosaki, Boutaro	60
Honda, Soichiro	163

[I]
Ibuka, Masaru	164
Ikeda, Tetsuomi	75,
Ikegami, Tomohito	Table 6
Imai, Hideki	43, 168
Isobe, Tadashi	49
Ito, Susumu	Fig.15
Izumi, Takehiro	168

[J]
Jose, Franco Olimpio	115

[K]
Kasami, Tadao	47
Karlson, Tore	51
Kenichi, Tanioka	161
Khushu, Om. P.	51, 106
Kodama, Hiroaki	114, 121
Kuroda, Toru	44, 49, 50, 62, 65, 76, 110, 168

[L]
Lin, Shu	44
Long, Tery	77
Lourenço, Daniel Domingos	Fig.35
Lula, Luiz Inácio da Silva	123

[M]
Makitalo. Osten	47
Martins, Ana Cecília Munhoz	Fig.35
Maruyama, Yoshiki	Table 6

Massey. James L.	36
Masuko, Yutaka	48
Merburg, Perter	51
Mondino, Tereza	Fig.35
Mondria, Jaime V.	113
Morikawa, Shuichi	50
Moriyama, Shigeki	51, 62, 65, 73, 106, 169

[N]

Nakagawa, Masao	Fig.15
Nakahara, Shunji	66, 67, 72, 106, 169
Nakamura, Yoshiro	168
Nakonechnyj, Liliana	107, Fig.35
Ng, Lin Sang	106
Nio, Koichi	25, 168
Nogueira, Sidnei Pinto	Fig.35
Numaguch,i Yasutaka	168
Nunez-Pacheco, Cristian Rodrigo	112

[O]

Ogawa, Hajime	121
Ohkubo, Akira	110
Oliveira, Eduardo de e Silva Bicudo	Fig.35

[P]

Pederneiras, Murilo Henrique Filho	111
Peterson William	32, 43
Plass, Roberto Gerstmann	113, 121

[R]

Raunheitte, Luís Tadeu	Fig.35
Rodney, James Santigo	120
Romero, Carlos	118, 121
Roppongi, Eiji	118, 121, Table 6

[S]

Saito, Masanori	62, 65, 75, 168
Saito, Tomohiro	50
Sakakibara, Seikichi	64
Sakashita, Hirohiko	Table 6
Sakauch,i Masao	Fig.15
Sakuma, Seiji	Table 6

INDEX

Sasaki, Seiichi	75
Sawabe, Eiichi	168
Sekiguchi, Kiyoshi	116
Sergio, Francisco Husni Ribeiro	Fig.35
Shigeta, Noriyuki	110
Shimizu, Masao	106
Shinagawa, Masato	106
Silva, Luis Tapia	113, 121
Silva, Sandro Rodrigues da	Fig.35
Sugimoto, Atsushi	105, 106, 110
Sukys, Francisco	Fig.35

[T]

Takada, Masayuki	49, 62, 65, 86, 114, 118, 169, Table 6
Takahashi, Yasuo	106
Takahashi, Yasuo	Table 6
Takahata, Fumio	Fig.15
Takeda, Yoshiyuki	110
Tanaka, Muneyuki	42
Teixeira, Miro	135
Terasaki, Akira	112
Terasaki, Akira	112
Torres, Rodrigo Pena	113

[V]

Valle, Luis	119

[W]

Wictor, Fernando Pietrukoviz Quinttela	Fig.35
Weldom, E.J	32, 43

[Y]

Yabashi, Takashi	Table 6
Yamada, Osamu	14, 78, 129, 161, Table 6
Yamane, Hisakichi	30, 158, 168
Yasuda, Yasuhiko	70
Yoshida, Noboru	105

APPENDIX

ARIB STD-B31
Version 2.2-E1

ENGLISH TRANSLATION

TRANSMISSION SYSTEM FOR DIGITAL
TERRESTRIAL TELEVISION BROADCASTING

ARIB STANDARD

ARIB STD-B31 Version 2.2

Version 1.0	May	31st 2001
Version 1.1	November	15th 2002
Version 1.2	January	24th 2002
Version 1.3	February	6th 2003
Version 1.4	June	5th 2003
Version 1.5	July	29th 2003
Version 1.6	November	30th 2005
Version 1.7	September	26th 2007
Version 1.8	December	16th 2009
Version 1.9	July	15th 2010
Version 2.0	March	28th 2011
Version 2.1	December	18th 2012
Version 2.2	March	18th 2014

Association of Radio Industries and Businesses

General Notes to the English Translation of ARIB Standards and Technical Reports

1. Notes on Copyright

- The copyright of this document is ascribed to the Association of Radio Industries and Businesses (ARIB).

- All rights reserved. No part of this document may be reproduced, stored in a retrieval system or transmitted, in any form or by any means, without the prior written permission of ARIB.

2. Notes on English Translation

- ARIB Standards and Technical Reports are usually written in Japanese. This document is a translation into English of the original document for the purpose of convenience of users. If there are any discrepancies in the content, expressions, etc. between the original document and this translated document, the original document shall prevail.

- ARIB Standards and Technical Reports, in the original language, are made publicly available through web posting. The original document of this translation may have been further revised and therefore users are encouraged to check the latest version at an appropriate page under the following URL:
http://www.arib.or.jp/english/index.html.

ARIB STD-B31

Foreword

The Association of Radio Industries and Businesses (ARIB) investigates and summarizes the basic technical requirements for various radio systems in the form of "ARIB Standards". These standards are developed with the participation of and through discussions amongst radio equipment manufacturers, telecommunication operators, broadcasting equipment manufacturers, broadcasters and users.

ARIB Standards include "government technical regulations" (mandatory standard) that are set for the purpose of encouraging effective use of frequency and preventing interference with other spectrum users, and "private technical standards" (voluntary standards) that are defined in order to ensure compatibility and adequate quality of radio equipment and broadcasting equipment as well as to offer greater convenience to radio equipment manufacturers, telecommunication operators, broadcasting equipment manufacturers, broadcasters and users.

This ARIB Standard is developed for transmission system for digital terrestrial television broadcasting. In order to ensure fairness and transparency in the defining stage, the standard was set by consensus at the ARIB Standard Assembly with the participation of both domestic and foreign interested parties from radio equipment manufacturers, telecommunication operators, broadcasting equipment manufacturers, broadcasters and users.

ARIB sincerely hopes that this ARIB Standard will be widely used by radio equipment manufacturers, telecommunication operators, broadcasting equipment manufacturers, broadcasters and users.

NOTE:
Although this ARIB Standard contains no specific reference to any Essential Industrial Property Rights relating thereto, the holders of such Essential Industrial Property Rights state to the effect that the rights listed in the Attachment 1 and 2, which are the Industrial Property Rights relating to this standard, are held by the parties also listed therein, and that to the users of this standard, in the case of Attachment 1, such holders shall not assert any rights and shall unconditionally grant a license to practice such Industrial Property Rights contained therein, and in the case of Attachment 2, the holders shall grant, under reasonable terms and conditions, a non-exclusive and non-discriminatory license to practice the Industrial Property Rights contained therein. However, this does not apply to anyone who uses this ARIB Standard and also owns and lays claim to any other Essential Industrial Property Rights of which is covered in whole or part in the contents of the provisions of this ARIB Standard.

ARIB STD-B31

Attachment 1 (Selection of Option 1)
(N/A)

Attachment 2 (Selection of Option 2)

Patent Applicant/ Holder	Name of Patent	Registration No./ Application No.	Remarks
Japan Broadcasting Corporation (NHK)	誤り訂正復号回路	特許 1585258	Japan
	誤り訂正復号方式	特許 1587162	Japan, United States, Canada, Korea
	誤り検出回路	特許 1587174	Japan, United States
	誤り訂正復号方式	特許 1707686	Japan, United States, Canada, Korea
	直交周波数分割多重ディジタル信号送信装置および受信装置	特許 2904986	Japan
	Method and apparatus for digital transmission using orthogonal frequency division multiplexing	5406551	United States
		0553841	United Kingdom
		0553841	Germany
		0553841	France
	符号化変調装置および復調装置	特許 2883238	Japan
	直交周波数分割多重変調信号伝送方式	特許 3110244	Japan
	放送方式および送受信機	特開平 8-294098	Japan
	ディジタル信号の送信方法、受信方法、送信装置および受信装置	特開平 9-46307	Japan
	ディジタル信号伝送方法および受信機	特開平 10-93521	Japan
	デジタル信号伝送方法、およびデジタル信号伝送装置	特開平 10-322388	Japan
	デジタル信号伝送装置	特許 3133958	Japan
	ＯＦＤＭ波伝送装置	特許 3133960	Japan
	デジタル信号送信装置、およびデジタル信号受信装置	特開平 10-336158	Japan
	送信装置および受信装置	特開 2000-101543	Japan
	OFDM 伝送システムの AC 送受信装置方法および送信装置、受信装置 Note1	特開 2002-9727	Japan
Japan Broadcasting Corporation (NHK) Advanced Digital Television Broadcasting Laboratory	デジタル信号受信装置	特許 2975932	Japan

214

Patent Applicant/ Holder	Name of Patent	Registration No./ Application No.	Remarks
Japan Broadcasting Corporation (NHK)	直交周波数分割多重伝送方式とその送信装置及び受信装置	特許 3083159	Japan
	Orthogonal Frequency-division Multiplex Transmission System, and its Transmitter and Receiver	98800917.X	China
		1999-7001638	Korea
Advanced Digital Television Broadcasting Laboratory		087110598	Taiwan
Matsushita Electric Industrial Co., Ltd.	直交周波数分割多重伝送方式とその送信装置及び受信装置	特開 2000-236313	Japan
Advanced Digital Television Broadcasting Laboratory	Submitted comprehensive confirmation of patents for ARIB STD-B31 Ver1.0 Note b		
Victor Company of Japan, Ltd.	直交周波数分割多重信号送受信装置	特許 2790239	Japan, United States, Germany, France, United Kingdom
	直交周波数分割多重信号送受信装置	特許 2874729	Japan, United States
	直交周波数分割多重信号送受信装置	特許 3055540	Japan
	直交周波数分割多重信号送受信装置	特許 3055541	Japan
	直交周波数分割多重信号の送受信システム	特開 2000-224142	Japan
Sony Corporation	Submitted comprehensive confirmation of patents for ARIB STD-B31 Ver1.0 Note a		
	Submitted comprehensive confirmation of patents for ARIB STD-B31 Ver1.1*		
	Submitted comprehensive confirmation of patents for ARIB STD-B31 Ver2.2*8		
Mitsubishi Electric Corporation*	再多重化装置および再多重化方法	特許 3216531	Japan
TOSHIBA Corporation* TOSHIBA AVE Corporation*	デジタル放送システム、デジタル放送演奏所装置、デジタル放送用送信所装置	特開 2000-32410	Japan
Motorola Japan Ltd.*1	Submitted comprehensive confirmation of patents for ARIB STD-B31 Ver1.3		

ARIB STD-B31

Patent Applicant/ Holder	Name of Patent	Registration No./ Application No.	Remarks
Motorola Japan Ltd.*2	Submitted comprehensive confirmation of patents for ARIB STD-B31 Ver1.5		
Matsushita Electric Industrial Co., Ltd.*2	Submitted comprehensive confirmation of patents for ARIB STD-B31 Ver1.5		
NEC Corporation	直交周波数分割多重復調装置、及び直交周波数分割多重復調におけるシンボルの位相誤差の補正方法*3	特許第3090137号	Japan
Japan Broadcasting Corporation (NHK)	地上デジタルテレビジョン放送における緊急速報を受信する受信機、及び緊急速報を送信する送信装置*4	特開2009-213105	Japan
NHK Engineering Services Inc.	地上デジタルテレビジョン放送における緊急速報を受信する受信機、及び緊急速報を送信する送信装置*4	特開2009-272954	Japan
QUALCOMM Incorporated	Submitted comprehensive confirmation of patents for ARIB STD-B31 Ver1.9 *5		
	Submitted comprehensive confirmation of patents for ARIB STD-B31 Ver2.0*7		
QUALCOMM Incorporated	Broadcast and multicast services in wireless communication systems*6	JP 2010-502124	US 20080056387, CN, HK, EP, IN, KR, TW

Note a : Valid for ARIB STD-B31 Ver1.0 (received on May 17, 2001)
Note b : Valid for ARIB STD-B31 Ver1.0 (received on May 24, 2001)
* : Valid for the revised parts of ARIB STD-B31 Ver1.1 (received on November 8, 2001)
*1 : Valid for the revised parts of ARIB STD-B31 Ver1.3 (received on January 22, 2003)
Note 1 : those received at the time of ARIB STD-B31 revision to Ver1.4 (May 14, 2003)
*2 : Valid for the revised parts of ARIB STD-B31 Ver1.5 (received on July 22, 2003)
*3 : Valid for ARIB STD-B31 Ver1.0 (received on September 18, 2007)
*4 : Valid for the revised parts of ARIB STD-B31 Ver1.8 (received on December 7, 2009)
*5 : Valid for the revised parts of ARIB STD-B31 Ver1.9 (received on July 8, 2010)
*6 : Valid for the revised parts of ARIB STD-B31 Ver1.9 (received on January 20, 2011)
*7 : Valid for the revised parts of ARIB STD-B31 Ver2.0 (received on March 18, 2011)
*8 : Valid for the revised parts of ARIB STD-B31 Ver2.2 (received on March 11, 2014)

ARIB STD-B31

TOTAL CONTENTS

Foreword

Transmission System for Digital Terrestrial Television Broadcasting 1

Attachment
Operational Guidelines for Digital Terrestrial Television Broadcasting 89

Appendix 139

ARIB STD-B31

Transmission System for Digital Terrestrial Television Broadcasting

ARIB STD-B31

Transmission System for Digital Terrestrial Television Broadcasting

Contents

Chapter 1: General Terms 5
  1.1 Objective 5
  1.2 Scope 5
  1.3 References 5
    1.3.1 Normative References 5
    1.3.2 Informative References 5
  1.4 Terminology 7
    1.4.1 Definitions 7
    1.4.2 Abbreviations 8
Chapter 2: ISDB-T Overview 10
  2.1 Hierarchical transmission 10
  2.2 Partial reception 11
  2.3 Modes 11
Chapter 3: Channel-Coding Scheme 12
  3.1 Basic configuration of the channel coding 17
  3.2 TS re-multiplexing 18
    3.2.1 Multiplex-frame configuration 18
    3.2.2 Model receiver for forming multiplex frame patterns 20
      3.2.2.1 Input signals to the hierarchical divider 20
      3.2.2.2 Operation of the model receiver from the hierarchical divider to the Viterbi decoding input 21
  3.3 Outer code 22
  3.4 Division of TS into hierarchical layers 23
  3.5 Energy dispersal 24
  3.6 Delay adjustment 25
  3.7 Byte interleaving 26
  3.8 Inner code 27
  3.9 Carrier modulation 28
    3.9.1 Configuration of the carrier modulator 28
    3.9.2 Delay adjustment 28
    3.9.3 Bit interleaving and mapping 29
      3.9.3.1 DQPSK 29
      3.9.3.2 QPSK 30
      3.9.3.3 16QAM 31
      3.9.3.4 64QAM 32
    3.9.4 Modulation-level normalization 33
    3.9.5 Data-segment configuration 33
  3.10 Combining hierarchical layers 35

3.11 Time and frequency interleaving 36
    3.11.1 Time interleaving 36
    3.11.2 Frequency interleaving 38
        3.11.2.1 Inter-segment interleaving 39
        3.11.2.2 Intra-segment interleaving 40
3.12 Frame structure 44
    3.12.1 OFDM-segment configuration for the differential modulation 44
    3.12.2 OFDM-segment configuration for the coherent modulation 48
3.13 Pilot signals 50
    3.13.1 Scattered pilot (SP) 50
    3.13.2 Continual pilot (CP) 51
    3.13.3 TMCC 51
    3.13.4 AC (Auxiliary Channel) 51
3.14 Transmission spectrum configuration 53
    3.14.1 RF-signal format 54
    3.14.2 Insertion of a guard interval 55
3.15 TMCC signal (Transmission and Multiplexing Configuration Control) 55
    3.15.1 Overview 55
    3.15.2 Assignment of TMCC carrier bits 55
    3.15.3 References signal for demodulation of TMCC symbols 56
    3.15.4 Synchronizing signal 56
    3.15.5 Segment type identification 56
    3.15.6 TMCC information 57
        3.15.6.1 System identification 58
        3.15.6.2 Indicator of transmission-parameter switching 59
        3.15.6.3 Startup control signal (Start flag for emergency-alarm broadcasting) 60
        3.15.6.4 Partial-reception flag 60
        3.15.6.5 Carrier modulation mapping scheme 61
        3.15.6.6 Convolutional-coding rate 62
        3.15.6.7 Time interleaving length 62
        3.15.6.8 Number of segments 63
        3.15.6.9 Channel-coding scheme 63
        3.15.6.10 Modulation scheme 64
3.16 AC (auxiliary channel) signals 64
    3.16.1 Overview 64
    3.16.2 AC signal bit assignment 64
    3.16.3 Reference signal for demodulation of AC symbols 65
    3.16.4 Configuration identification 65
    3.16.5 Additional information on the transmission control of modulating waves 65
    3.16.6 Seismic motion warning information 66
        3.16.6.1 Synchronizing signal 67
        3.16.6.2 Start and ending flag 67
        3.16.6.3 Update flag 68

ARIB STD-B31

    3.16.6.4 Signal identification 69
    3.16.6.5 Detailed seismic motion warning information 70
    3.16.6.6 CRC 74
    3.16.6.7 Parity Bit 75
  3.16.7 Modulation scheme 75
Chapter 4: Frequency Utilization Requirements 76
  4.1 Frequency bandwidth and others 76
  4.2 Permissible transmission-frequency deviation 76
  4.3 IFFT sampling frequency and permissible deviation 76
  4.4 Transmission-spectrum mask 77
  4.5 Maximum permitted power level of spurious emission or unwanted emission 78
Annex A: Transmission Parameters and Data Rates for 7MHz and 8MHz Bandwidth Systems 79

ARIB STD-B31

<Blank Page>

ARIB STD-B31

Chapter 1: General Terms

1.1 Objective

The purpose of this standard is to define the transmission system for digital terrestrial television broadcasting among several schemes of standard television broadcasting handled by using terrestrial basic broadcasting stations.

1.2 Scope

This standard applies to digital terrestrial television broadcasting using UHF and VHF bands. For details on the source coding-scheme and multiplexing-scheme standards among those related to digital terrestrial television broadcasting, see relevant standards.

1.3 References

1.3.1 Normative References

The following documents are those from which excerpts included in this standard were taken:

- "Ministerial ordinance for amending the entire standard transmission system for digital broadcasting among standard television broadcasting and the like (Ordinance No. 87 of the Ministry of Internal Affairs and Communications, 2011)" (hereinafter referred to as "Ordinance")
- "The definition of the arrangement of TMCC symbol and AC symbol and the configuration of time interleave and frequency interleave (relevant to Section 11 and Section 12 of Ordinance)" (Notification No. 303 of the Ministry of Internal Affairs and Communications, 2011)" (hereinafter referred to as "Notification No. 303")
- "The definition of the configuration of TMCC information (relevant to Section 13 of Ordinance)" (Notification No. 304 of the Ministry of Internal Affairs and Communications, 2011)" (hereinafter referred to as "Notification No. 304")
- "The definition of the configuration of seismic motion warning information (relevant to the Annexed Table 18 of Ordinance)" (Notification No. 306 of the Ministry of Internal Affairs and Communications, 2011)" (hereinafter referred to as "Notification No. 306")
- "Radio Equipment Regulations (Radio Regulatory Commission Rules No.18, 1950)" (Ministerial Ordinance of the Ministry of Internal Affairs and Communications)
- "Transmission equipment for terrestrial basic broadcasting stations that the Minister of Internal Affairs and Communications shall announce separately as prescribed in the Radio Equipment Regulations and their technical requirements" (Notification No. 68 of the Ministry of Internal Affairs and Communications, 2013)" (hereinafter referred to as "Notification No. 68")

1.3.2 Informative References

The following are the standards and other documents related to the transmission of digital terrestrial television broadcasting based on this standard:

- ARIB STD-B10, "Service Information for Digital Broadcasting System", ARIB Standard
- ARIB STD-B21, "Receiver for Digital Broadcasting", ARIB Standard (desirable specifications)
- ARIB STD-B24, "Data Coding and Transmission Specification for Digital Broadcasting", ARIB Standard

ARIB STD-B31

- ARIB STD-B25, "Access Control System Specifications for Digital Broadcasting", ARIB Standard
- ARIB STD-B29, "Transmission System for Digital Terrestrial Sound Broadcasting", ARIB Standard
- ARIB STD-B32, "Video Coding, Audio Coding and Multiplexing Specifications for Digital Broadcasting", ARIB Standard
- ARIB STD-B46, "Transmission System for Terrestrial Mobile Multimedia Broadcasting based on Connected Segment Transmission", ARIB Standard
- ARIB STD-B53, "Receiver for Terrestrial Mobile Multimedia Broadcasting based on Connected Segment Transmission", ARIB Standard (desirable specifications)
- ARIB STD-B55, "Transmission System for Area Broadcasting", ARIB Standard

ARIB STD-B31

1.4 Terminology

1.4.1 Definitions

Digital terrestrial broadcasting	Digital broadcasting and high-definition television broadcasting from among the various standard television broadcasting systems using the terrestrial basic broadcasting stations stipulated in Chapter 3, Ordinance
Digital terrestrial sound broadcasting	Digital broadcasting among various types of ultra-high-frequency-wave broadcasting carried out with terrestrial basic broadcasting stations as defined in Chapter 2, Ordinance
Terrestrial multimedia broadcasting	Multimedia broadcasting carried out with terrestrial basic broadcasting stations as defined in Chapter 4, Ordinance
Data segment	Data group that corresponds to the effective carrier. This is an elementary block for channel coding.
OFDM segment	Basic band (1/14 of television-channel bandwidth) for transmission signals, generated by adding control-signal carriers to data carriers. OFDM segment also means signal processed to make up a frame.
Partial reception	Reception of only one OFDM segment at the center of a group of segments
Mode	Identification of transmission mode based on the spacings between OFDM carrier frequencies
IFFT sampling frequency	IFFT sampling frequency for OFDM modulation on the transmission side
FFT sampling frequency	FFT sampling frequency for model receivers used to form multiple frame patterns
ISDB-T	Digital terrestrial television broadcasting system in which transmission bands consist of 13 OFDM segments
ISDB-T_{SB}	Digital terrestrial sound broadcasting system in which transmission bands consist of one or three OFDM segments
OFDM symbol	Transmission symbol for the OFDM transmission signal
OFDM frame	Transmission frame consisting of 204 OFDM symbols
Multiplex frame	Frame that is provided for signal-processing purposes and is used to re-multiplex MPEG-2 TSs to create a single TS. This frame is identical to an OFDM frame in terms of duration.
Model receiver	Virtual receiver used to arrange transmission TSPs on a multiplex frame
Carrier symbol	A symbol per OFDM carrier
Segment number	Number used to identify 13 OFDM segments and their corresponding data segments
Subchannel number	ISDB-T_{SB} tuning step with a virtual bandwidth of 1/7 MHz
Connected signal transmission	A type of transmission of ISDB-T_{SB} signals arranged without a guard band
Constraint length	Number obtained by adding 1 to the number of delay elements in a convolutional coder
Hierarchical transmission	Simultaneous transmission of multiple OFDM segments that are channel-coded differently
Hierarchical layer information	Channel-coding parameter information on each layer in hierarchical transmission
Control information	Information other than MPEG-2 TS that assists the receiver in demodulation and decoding operations
Additional information	Information that is transmitted using part of the control

ARIB STD-B31

	information carrier
Seismic motion warning Information	The information regarding seismic motion warning conducted based on the regulation of Clause 1 of Article 13, the *Meteorological Service Act* (Act No. 165 of 1952) Although seismic motion warning is generally called "Earthquake Early Warning," this standard uses the term "Seismic Motion Warning," as is the case with the Ordinance and Notifications referred to.
Transmission TSP	204-byte packet formed by adding 16-byte parity to 188-byte MPEG-2 TSP
Spurious emission	Emission on a frequency or frequencies which are outside the necessary bandwidth and the level of which may be reduced without affecting the corresponding transmission of information. Spurious emissions include harmonic emissions, parasitic emissions, intermodulation products and frequency conversion products, but exclude out-of-band emissions.
Out-of-band emission	Emission on a frequency or frequencies immediately outside the necessary bandwidth resulting from the modulation process, but excluding spurious emissions.
Unwanted emissions	Consist of spurious emission and out-of-band emissions.
Spurious domain	The frequency range beyond the out-of-band domain in which spurious emissions generally predominate.
Out-of-band domain	The frequency range, immediately outside the necessary bandwidth but excluding the spurious domain, in which out-of-band emissions generally predominate. In the case of digital terrestrial television broadcasting, the out-of-band domain is within +/-15 MHz from the center frequency of the necessary bandwidth (the frequency of the boundary between the out-of-band and spurious domain is included in the spurious domain).
Necessary bandwidth	A 6-MHz-wide frequency band in the case of digital terrestrial television broadcasting.

1.4.2 Abbreviations

AC	Auxiliary Channel
CP	Continual Pilot
DBPSK	Differential Binary Phase Shift Keying
DQPSK	Differential Quadrature Phase Shift Keying
FFT	Fast Fourier Transform
IF	Intermediate frequency
IFFT	Inverse Fast Fourier Transform
ISDB	Integrated Services Digital Broadcasting
ISDB-T	ISDB for Terrestrial Television Broadcasting
ISDB-T_{SB}	ISDB for Terrestrial Sound Broadcasting
MPEG	Moving Picture Experts Group
OCT	Octal notation
OFDM	Orthogonal Frequency Division Multiplexing
PRBS	Pseudo-Random Binary Sequence
QAM	Quadrature Amplitude Modulation
QPSK	Quadrature Phase Shift Keying
RF	Radio frequency
RS	Reed-Solomon

SP	Scattered Pilot
SFN	Single Frequency Network
TMCC	Transmission and Multiplexing Configuration Control
TSP	Transport Stream Packet

Chapter 2: ISDB-T Overview

With transmission system for digital terrestrial television broadcasting (ISDB-T), one or more transport stream (TS) inputs, defined in "MPEG-2 Systems," are re-multiplexed to create a single TS. This TS is then subjected to multiple channel-coding steps in accordance with the intentions of the service, and is finally sent as a single OFDM signal. ISDB-T also offers time interleaving to provide powerful channel coding for mobile-reception in which variations in field strength are inevitable.

The transmission spectrum of ISDB-T consists of 13 successive OFDM blocks (hereinafter referred to as "OFDM segments"), each bandwidth of which is equal to one fourteenth of a digital terrestrial television-broadcasting channel bandwidth. An OFDM-segment carrier configuration that allows connection of multiple segments makes it possible to provide a transmission bandwidth appropriate in terms of units of segment width for the target media, while at the same time enabling use of the same receiver for both ISDB-T and ISDB-T$_{SB}$ (see "Transmission System for Digital Terrestrial Sound Broadcasting," ARIB Standard, ARIB STD-B29).

2.1 Hierarchical transmission

Channel coding of ISDB-T is conducted in units of OFDM segments. Therefore, part of a single television channel can be used for fixed-reception service and the rest for mobile-reception service. Such signal transmission is defined as hierarchical transmission. Each hierarchical layer consists of one or more OFDM segments, and parameters such as the carrier modulation scheme, inner-code coding rate, and time interleaving length can be specified for each hierarchical layer. Note that up to three hierarchical layers can be provided and that the segment used for partial reception, which will be discussed later, is also counted as one hierarchical layer.

The number of segments and the set of channel-coding parameters for each hierarchical layer are determined in accordance with the organization information. Note that TMCC signals convey control information that assists in receiver operations.

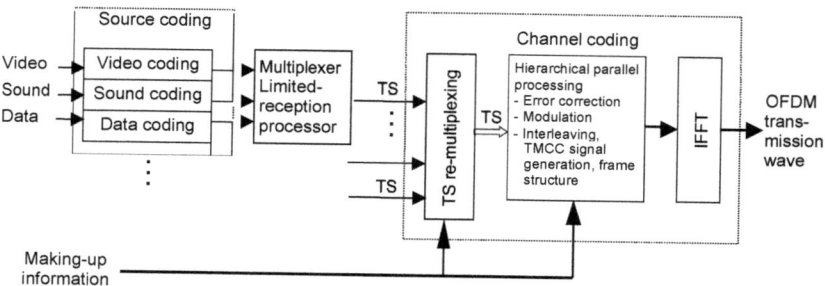

Fig. 2-1: ISDB-T Overview

2.2 Partial reception

As for an OFDM segment at the center of an ISDB-T transmission signal consisting of 13 segments, it is possible to conduct channel coding such that the range of frequency interleaving is limited within the segment. This configuration enables an ISDB-T_{SB} receiver to receive one-segment service embedded in a hierarchical television signal (see "Channel Coding Scheme" in Chapter 3).

2.3 Modes

In consideration of the suitability of the distance between SFN stations and the robustness to Doppler shift during mobile-reception, ISDB-T offers three different spacings between OFDM carrier frequencies. These spacings are identified as system modes. The available spacings between OFDM carrier frequencies are approximately 4 kHz, 2 kHz, and 1 kHz in modes 1, 2, and 3, respectively.

The number of carriers used varies depending on the mode, but the information bit rate that can be transmitted remains the same in all modes.

Chapter 3: Channel-Coding Scheme

Data transmitted through ISDB-T consists of a group of data (hereinafter referred to as "data segments") that includes multiple TSPs (transport-stream packets) defined in "MPEG-2 Systems." These data segments are subjected to required channel coding. Further, pilot signals are added to data segments in the OFDM framing section to form an OFDM segment (with a bandwidth of 6/14 MHz). A total of 13 OFDM segments are converted to OFDM transmission signals collectively by IFFT.

This channel-coding scheme allows hierarchical transmission in which multiple hierarchical layers with different transmission parameters can be transmitted simultaneously. Each hierarchical layer consists of one or more OFDM segments. Parameters such as the carrier modulation scheme, inner-code coding rate, and time interleaving length can be specified for each hierarchical layer.

In the configuration that contains one-segment service, a center OFDM segment of TV signal can be also received by a digital sound broadcasting receiver.

Note that up to three hierarchical layers can be transmitted.

Fig. 3-1 shows conceptual drawings of hierarchical transmission and partial reception. In addition, Tables 3-1 and 3-2 present OFDM segment transmission parameters identified as system modes and transmission signal parameters, respectively.

Note also that Table 3-3 shows the data rate per segment, while Table 3-4 presents the total data rate for all 13 segments.

Note also that the effective symbol length and guard interval ratio are stipulated by Article 20-4 and Article 20-5 of Ordinance, along with the data rate by Annexed Table 9 of Ordinance.

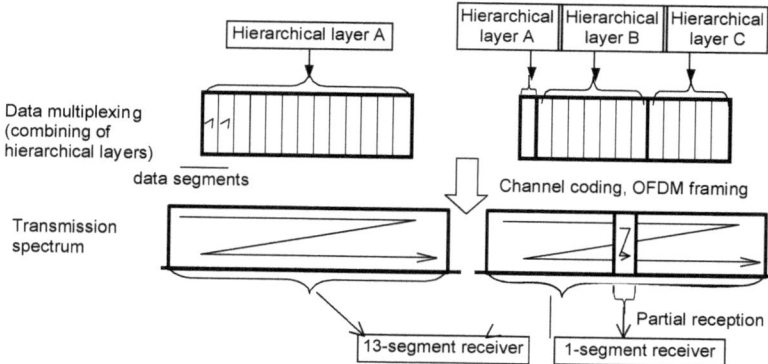

Fig. 3-1: Hierarchical Transmission and Partial Reception in Digital Terrestrial Television Broadcasting

ARIB STD-B31

Table 3-1: OFDM-Segment Parameters

Mode		Mode 1		Mode 2		Mode 3	
Segment Bandwidth (Bws)		6000/14 = 428.571... kHz					
Spacing between carrier frequencies (Cs)		Bws/108 = 3.968... kHz		Bws/216 = 1.984... kHz		Bws/432 = 0.992... kHz	
Number of carriers	Total count	108	108	216	216	432	432
	Data	96	96	192	192	384	384
	SP*1	9	0	18	0	36	0
	CP*1	0	1	0	1	0	1
	TMCC*2	1	5	2	10	4	20
	AC1*3	2	2	4	4	8	8
	AC2*3	0	4	0	9	0	19
Carrier modulation scheme		QPSK 16QAM 64QAM	DQPSK	QPSK 16QAM 64QAM	DQPSK	QPSK 16QAM 64QAM	DQPSK
Symbols per frame		204					
Effective symbol length		252 μs		504 μs		1008 μs	
Guard interval		63 μs (1/4), 31.5 μs (1/8), 15.75 μs (1/16), 7.875 μs (1/32)		126 μs (1/4), 63 μs (1/8), 31.5 μs (1/16), 15.75 μs (1/32)		252 μs (1/4), 126 μs (1/8), 63 μs (1/16), 31.5 μs (1/32)	
Symbol length		315 μs (1/4), 283.5 μs (1/8), 267.75 μs (1/16), 259.875 μs (1/32)		630 μs (1/4), 567 μs (1/8), 535.5 μs (1/16), 519.75 μs (1/32)		1260 μs (1/4), 1134 μs (1/8), 1071 μs (1/16), 1039.5 μs (1/32)	
Frame length		64.26 ms (1/4), 57.834 ms (1/8), 54.621 ms (1/16), 53.0145 ms (1/32)		128.52 ms (1/4), 115.668 ms (1/8), 109.242 ms (1/16), 106.029 ms (1/32)		257.04 ms (1/4), 231.336 ms (1/8), 218.484 ms (1/16), 212.058 ms (1/32)	
FFT sampling frequency		2048/252 = 8.126984... MHz					
Inner code		Convolutional code (1/2, 2/3, 3/4, 5/6, 7/8)					
Outer code		RS (204,188)					

*1: SP (Scattered Pilot) and CP (Continual Pilot) are used by the receiver for synchronization and demodulation purposes.
*2: TMCC (Transmission and Multiplexing Configuration Control) is control information.
*3: AC (Auxiliary Channel) is used to transmit additional information on broadcasting. AC1 is available in an equal number in all segments, while AC2 is available only in differential modulated segments.

ARIB STD-B31

Table 3-2: Transmission-Signal Parameters

Mode		Mode 1	Mode 2	Mode 3
Number of OFDM segments (Ns)		13		
Bandwidth (Bw)		$B_{ws} \times N_s + C_s$ = 5.575... MHz	$B_{ws} \times N_s + C_s$ = 5.573... MHz	$B_{ws} \times N_s + C_s$ = 5.572... MHz
Number of segments of differential modulations		n_d		
Number of segments of coherent modulations		n_s ($n_s + n_d = N_s$)		
Spacings between carrier frequencies (Cs)		$B_{ws}/108$ = 3.968... kHz	$B_{ws}/216$ = 1.984... kHz	$B_{ws}/432$ = 0.992... kHz
Number of carriers	Total count	$108 \times N_s + 1 = 1405$	$216 \times N_s + 1 = 2809$	$432 \times N_s + 1 = 5617$
	Data	$96 \times N_s = 1248$	$192 \times N_s = 2496$	$384 \times N_s = 4992$
	SP	$9 \times n_s$	$18 \times n_s$	$36 \times n_s$
	CP*1	$n_d + 1$	$n_d + 1$	$n_d + 1$
	TMCC	$n_s + 5 \times n_d$	$2 \times n_s + 10 \times n_d$	$4 \times n_s + 20 \times n_d$
	AC1	$2 \times N_s = 26$	$4 \times N_s = 52$	$8 \times N_s = 104$
	AC2	$4 \times n_d$	$9 \times n_d$	$19 \times n_d$
Carrier modulation scheme		QPSK, 16QAM, 64QAM, DQPSK		
Symbols per frame		204		
Effective symbol length		252 µs	504 µs	1008 µs
Guard interval		63 µs (1/4), 31.5 µs (1/8), 15.75 µs (1/16), 7.875 µs (1/32)	126 µs (1/4), 63 µs (1/8), 31.5 µs (1/16), 15.75 µs (1/32)	252 µs (1/4), 126 µs (1/8), 63 µs (1/16), 31.5 µs (1/32)
Symbol length		315 µs (1/4), 283.5 µs (1/8), 267.75 µs (1/16), 259.875 µs (1/32)	630 µs (1/4), 567 µs (1/8), 535.5 µs (1/16), 519.75 µs (1/32)	1260 µs (1/4), 1134 µs (1/8), 1071 µs (1/16), 1039.5 µs (1/32)
Frame length		64.26 ms (1/4), 57.834 ms (1/8), 54.621 ms (1/16), 53.0145 ms (1/32)	128.52 ms (1/4), 115.668 ms (1/8), 109.242 ms (1/16), 106.029 ms (1/32)	257.04 ms (1/4), 231.336 ms (1/8), 218.484 ms (1/16), 212.058 ms (1/32)
Interleave	Frequency	Inter-segment and intra-segment frequency interleave		
	Time	I=0 (0 symbols), I=4 (380 symbols), I=8 (760 symbols), I=16 (1,520 symbols)	I=0 (0 symbols), I=2 (190 symbols), I=4 (380 symbols), I=8 (760 symbols)	I=0 (0 symbols), I=1 (95 symbols), I=2 (190 symbols), I=4 (380 symbols)
Inner code*2		Convolutional code (1/2, 2/3, 3/4, 5/6, 7/8)		
Byte interleave		Convolutional-byte interleave per 12 bytes		
Outer code		RS (204,188)		

*1: The number of CPs represents the sum of those CPs in segments, plus one CP added to the right of the entire bandwidth.

*2: The inner code is taken as a convolutional code in which the mother-code with a constraint length of 7 (number of states: 64) and a coding rate of 1/2 is punctured.

ARIB STD-B31

Table 3-3: Data Rate of a Single Segment

Carrier modulation	Convolutional code	Number of TSPs transmitted *1 (Mode 1/2/3)	Data rate (kbps) *2			
			Guard interval ratio: 1/4	Guard interval ratio: 1/8	Guard interval ratio: 1/16	Guard interval ratio: 1/32
DQPSK QPSK	1/2	12/24/48	280.85	312.06	330.42	340.43
	2/3	16/32/64	374.47	416.08	440.56	453.91
	3/4	18/36/72	421.28	468.09	495.63	510.65
	5/6	20/40/80	468.09	520.10	550.70	567.39
	7/8	21/42/84	491.50	546.11	578.23	595.76
16QAM	1/2	24/48/96	561.71	624.13	660.84	680.87
	2/3	32/64/128	748.95	832.17	881.12	907.82
	3/4	36/72/144	842.57	936.19	991.26	1021.30
	5/6	40/80/160	936.19	1040.21	1101.40	1134.78
	7/8	42/84/168	983.00	1092.22	1156.47	1191.52
64QAM	1/2	36/72/144	842.57	936.19	991.26	1021.30
	2/3	48/96/192	1123.43	1248.26	1321.68	1361.74
	3/4	54/108/216	1263.86	1404.29	1486.90	1531.95
	5/6	60/120/240	1404.29	1560.32	1652.11	1702.17
	7/8	63/126/252	1474.50	1638.34	1734.71	1787.28

*1: Represents the number of TSPs transmitted per frame
*2: Represents the data rate (bits) per segment for transmission parameters
Data rate (bits): Number of TSPs transmitted × 188 (bytes/TSP) × 8 (bits/byte) × (1/frame length)

Table 3-4: Total Data Rate [*1]

Carrier modulation	Convolutional code	Number of TSPs transmitted (Mode 1/2/3)	Data rate (Mbps)			
			Guard interval ratio: 1/4	Guard interval ratio: 1/8	Guard interval ratio: 1/16	Guard interval ratio: 1/32
DQPSK QPSK	1/2	156/312/624	3.651	4.056	4.295	4.425
	2/3	208/416/832	4.868	5.409	5.727	5.900
	3/4	234/468/936	5.476	6.085	6.443	6.638
	5/6	260/520/1040	6.085	6.761	7.159	7.376
	7/8	273/546/1092	6.389	7.099	7.517	7.744
16QAM	1/2	312/624/1248	7.302	8.113	8.590	8.851
	2/3	416/832/1664	9.736	10.818	11.454	11.801
	3/4	468/936/1872	10.953	12.170	12.886	13.276
	5/6	520/1040/2080	12.170	13.522	14.318	14.752
	7/8	546/1092/2184	12.779	14.198	15.034	15.489
64QAM	1/2	468/936/1872	10.953	12.170	12.886	13.276
	2/3	624/1248/2496	14.604	16.227	17.181	17.702
	3/4	702/1404/2808	16.430	18.255	19.329	19.915
	5/6	780/1560/3120	18.255	20.284	21.477	22.128
	7/8	819/1638/3276	19.168	21.298	22.551	23.234

*1: This table shows an example of the total data rate in which the same parameters are specified for all 13 segments.

Note that the total data rate during hierarchical transmission varies depending on the hierarchical parameter configuration. In the case shown above, the data volume transmitted by all 13 segments is equal to the sum of all data volumes transmitted by these segments that can be determined based on Table 3-3.

ARIB STD-B31

3.1 Basic configuration of the channel coding

Multiple TSs output by the MPEG-2 multiplexer are fed to the TS re-multiplexer such that TSPs can be properly arranged for signal processing one data segment at a time. In the re-multiplexer, each TS is first converted into 188-byte burst-signal form by means of a clock having a rate four times higher than that of the FFT sample clock. An outer code is then applied, and these TSs are converted into a single TS.

When hierarchical transmission is performed, the TS is divided into multiple hierarchical layers in accordance with the hierarchy information. These layers are then fed to a maximum of three parallel-processor blocks.

In the parallel processor, digital data-processing steps including error-correction coding, interleaving, and carrier modulation are primarily conducted. Note also that the difference in delay time (generated in byte-interleaving and bit-interleaving signal processes) between hierarchical layers is adjusted in advance to adjust timing. Error correction, interleaving length, and the carrier modulation scheme are specified for one hierarchical layer independently.

Following parallel processing, hierarchical layer signals are combined and then fed to the time and frequency interleaving sections to ensure the improvement of error-correction effectively against both the variation of field strength and multipath interference in mobile-reception.

Convolutional interleaving is used as the time-interleaving scheme to reduce both transmission and reception delay times and minimize the receiver memory size. As for frequency interleaving, both inter-segment and intra-segment interleaving are employed to ensure the appropriate segment structure and proper interleaving.

To ensure that the receiver properly performs demodulation and decoding in hierarchical transmission in which multiple sets of transmission parameters are used, a TMCC (Transmission and Multiplexing Configuration Control) signal is also transmitted using specific carriers. And also AC (Auxiliary Channel) signal assigned to specific carriers is used to transmit additional information on broadcasting.

OFDM frame consists of information data, pilot signals for synchronization and reproduction, TMCC signal, and AC signal. Once formation of a frame is complete, all signals are converted to OFDM transmission signals by IFFT process.

Note that the basic configuration and others of the transmission signals are stipulated in Article 20-1, Article 21, Article 11-2, Article 11-6, Article 12-2, Article 15, and so on of Ordinance.

ARIB STD-B31

Fig. 3-2 shows the basic configuration of the channel coding.

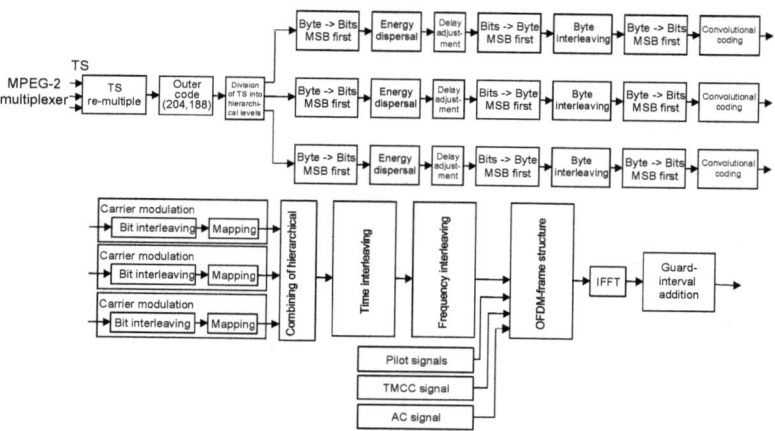

Fig. 3-2: Blocks Available in the Channel Coding

3.2 TS re-multiplexing

3.2.1 Multiplex-frame configuration

A re-multiplexed transport stream (TS) is formed by multiplex frames as elementary units, each of which consists of n pieces of transport-stream packets (TSPs). Table 3-5 shows the numbers of TSPs used for different transmission modes and guard-interval ratios.

Each of the TSPs comprising a multiplex frame is 204 bytes in length, consisting of 188-byte program data and 16-byte null data. This TSP is referred to as "transmission TSP." The multiplex-frame length matches that of the OFDM frame when the clock rate for sending transmission TSP is increased to four times that of the FFT sample clock rate.

As shown in Fig. 3-3, each of the transmission TSPs within a multiplex frame is transmitted by hierarchical layer X of an OFDM signal (layer X designates either layer A, B, or C) or belongs to a null packet (TSP$_{null}$) that is not transmitted as an OFDM signal. The arrangement of transmission TSPs within a multiplex frame is determined in advance to ensure that it is identical to that of the TSs that will be reproduced by the model receiver shown in Fig. 3-4.

ARIB STD-B31

Table 3-5: Multiplex-Frame Configuration

Mode	Number of transmission TSPs included in one multiplex frame			
	Guard-interval ratio 1/4	Guard-interval ratio 1/8	Guard-interval ratio 1/16	Guard-interval ratio 1/32
Mode 1	1280	1152	1088	1056
Mode 2	2560	2304	2176	2112
Mode 3	5120	4608	4352	4224

(Ordinance Annexed Table 15, Item 1)

Because the number of transport-stream packets that can be transmitted per unit time varies substantially depending on the parameters specified for each hierarchical layer, it is generally not possible to achieve consistency between TSs input to the re-multiplexer and a single TS output from it. However, the addition of an appropriate number of null packets allows interfacing between the re-multiplexer and modulator during transmission of transport streams at a constant clock rate, regardless of which transmission parameters are specified.

Because multiplex-frame length is the same as OFDM-frame length, the receiver can reproduce transport-stream synchronization based on OFDM-signal synchronization, thus ensuring improved synchronization performance.

Correlating TSP arrangement within a multiplex frame with "division of TS into multiple hierarchical layers and combining of these layers" allows the receiving side to select the same single TS as the one transmitted from among multiple signals of different layers, and to reproduce that TS.

For this reason, we define the model receiver operation on the transmitting side to indirectly stipulate TSP arrangement. The receiving side can reproduce TS without any TSP position information when it operates in the same manner as the model receiver.

Fig. 3-3 shows an example of a re-multiplexed transport stream.

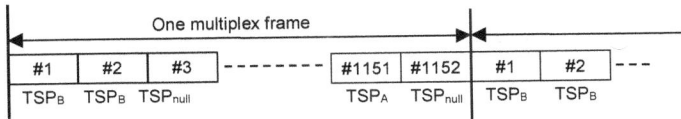

Fig. 3-3: Example of a Re-Multiplexed Transport Stream
(Mode 1, Guard Interval of 1/8)

ARIB STD-
B31

3.2.2 Model receiver for forming multiplex frame patterns

TSPs are arranged on a multiplex frame in accordance with the configuration of TS reproduced by the model receiver shown in Fig. 3-4. Note that a clock written in this section means an FFT sampling clock.

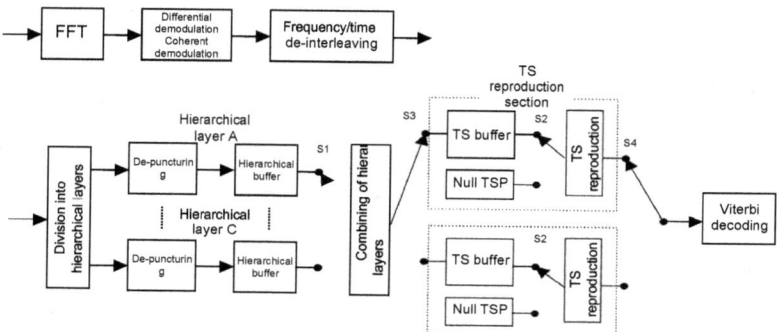

Fig. 3-4: Model Receiver for Forming Multiplex Frame Patterns

3.2.2.1 Input signals to the hierarchical divider

Upon completion of processing such as carrier demodulation and de-interleaving, input signals to the hierarchical divider are arranged in ascending order of segment number, and also in ascending order of the carrier frequency of information symbol within a segment (obtained by excluding the carriers of control symbol). Fig. 3-5 shows an example in which two hierarchical layers are available (one layer modulated through DQPSK 1/2 with 5 segments, and the other modulated through 64QAM 7/8 with 8 segments), and a guard interval of 1/8 and Mode 1 are selected.

During the period of one OFDM symbol, data the size of 480 (96 × 5) carriers is input to hierarchical layer A, followed by the input of data the size of 768 (96 × 8) carriers to hierarchical layer B and a null signal the size of 1056 carriers.

The null signal corresponds to the sum of samplings which are equivalent to pilot signals inserted by the OFDM framing section, FFT sampling in excess of the net signal band, and guard-interval duration. This operation is repeated as many times as 204 symbols for the duration of one OFDM frame.

Note that delays are adjusted such that the periods of time required for differential or coherent demodulation become the same.

ARIB STD-B31

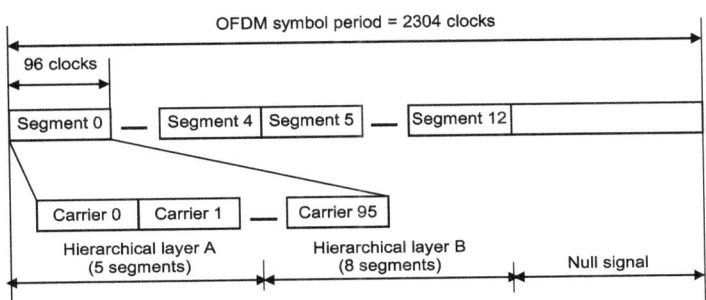

Fig. 3-5: Time Arrangement for Input Signals to Hierarchical Layers

3.2.2.2 Operation of the model receiver from the hierarchical divider to the Viterbi decoding input

Signal, divided into multiple hierarchical layers, is then subjected to de-puncturing before being stored in the hierarchical buffer. In this case, we assume that the processing delay time is the same for all layers, and that there is no delay time for the model receiver.

At this time, the number of bits $B_{X,k}$ that are input to and stored in the hierarchical buffer upon input of the kth datum to hierarchical layer X in a single multiplex frame can be determined by the following formula:

$$B_{X,k} = 2 \times ([k \times S_x \times R_x] - [(k-1) \times S_x \times R_x])$$

where [ ] indicates that all digits to the right of the decimal point are discarded. Note that R_X represents the convolutional-code coding rate at hierarchical layer X. Note also that S_X takes one of the values given in Table 3-6, depending on the modulation scheme selected for hierarchical layer X.

Table 3-6: S_x Value

Modulation scheme	S_X
DQPSK/QPSK	2
16QAM	4
64QAM	6

Switch S1 is switched over to another hierarchical buffer when data the size of one TS packet (408 bytes*) is input to the hierarchical buffer. This data is transferred to the TS buffer provided in the TS reproduction section. In this case, we assume that data transfer is instantaneous.

　　* Convolutional coding of a single TS packet (204 bytes) of data produces 408 bytes, as the coding rate of the mother code of the convolutional code is 1/2.

ARIB STD-B31

The TS reproduction section checks the TS buffer every TS packet period (408 clocks). If there is more data than the size of one TS packet, this section switches S2 over to the TS buffer position and reads out one TS packet of data. When there is no data in the TS buffer, the TS reproduction section switches S2 over to the null TSP position and transmits a null packet.

Switch S3 is used to alternately switch between two TS reproduction sections for inputting a hierarchical combiner output signal. In Mode 1, switching is performed at the beginning of an OFDM frame. Switch S4 is used to switch between TS reproduction-section signal outputs. This switch is switched over to the same position as S3 in three TS packet period (408 × 3 clocks) following the switching of S3, that is, at the beginning of an OFDM frame.

In Modes 2 and 3, switching of S3 and S4 is performed at 1/2 OFDM-frame intervals (102 OFDM-symbol intervals) and 1/4 OFDM-frame intervals (51 OFDM-symbol intervals), respectively.

3.3 Outer code

A shortened (204,188) Reed-Solomon code is used in every TSP as an outer code. The shortened (204,188) Reed-Solomon code is generated by adding 51-byte 00HEX at the beginning of the 188-byte input data bytes, processing with the (255,239) Reed-Solomon code, and then removing these 51 bytes.

The GF (2^8) element is used as the Reed-Solomon code element. The following primitive polynomial p (x) is used to define GF (2^8):

$$p\ (x) = x^8 + x^4 + x^3 + x^2 + 1$$

Note also that the following polynomial g (x) is used to generate (204,188) shortened Reed-Solomon code:

$$g\ (x) = (x - \lambda^0)\ (x - \lambda^1)\ (x - \lambda^2)\ \cdots\ (x - \lambda^{15})\ provided\ that\ \lambda = 02\ HEX$$

(Ordinance Annexed Table 12, Item 1)

[Description]

Shortened (204,188) Reed-Solomon code is the same as the outer code used for digital satellite broadcasting, and can correct up to 8 random bytes in error among 204 bytes.

Fig. 3-6 shows MPEG2 TSP and TSP that is error-protected by RS code. Note that the error-protected 204-byte packet is also called "transmission TSP."

ARIB STD-B31

3.5 Energy dispersal

Energy dispersal is conducted at each hierarchical layer using a circuit, shown in Fig. 3-8, that is generated by a PRBS (Pseudo Random Bit Sequence). All signals other than the synchronization byte in each of the transmission TSPs at different hierarchical layers are EXCLUSIVE ORed using PRBSs, on a bit-by-bit basis.

The initial value of the register in the PRBS-generating circuit must be "100101010000000" (arranged in ascending order of bits, from left to right), and this value must be initialized every OFDM frame. At this time, the beginning of an OFDM frame must be the MSB of the byte next to the transmission TSP's synchronization byte. Note also that the shift register must also perform shifting during the synchronization byte.

$$g(x) = X^{15} + X^{14} + 1$$

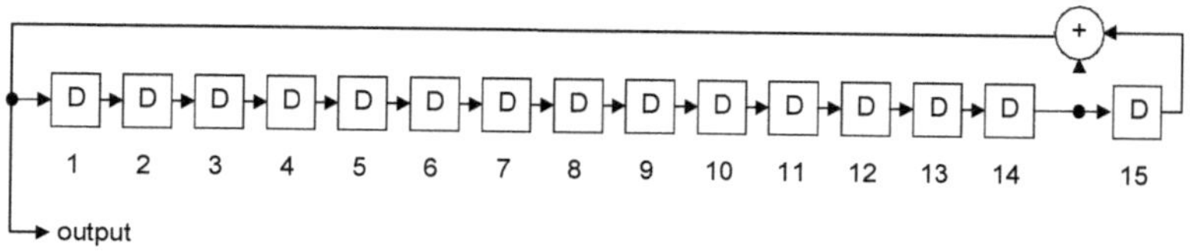

Fig. 3-8: PRBS-Generating Polynomial and Circuit

(Ordinance Annexed Table 15, Annexed Statement 1)

ARIB STD-B31

3.6 Delay adjustment

Delay adjustment associated with byte interleaving, intended to provide identical transmission and reception delay times for all hierarchical layers, is conducted on the transmitting side.

An appropriate adjustment value must be selected and specified for each hierarchical layer from among those (equivalent to the number of transmission TSPs) shown below, such that all delays, including transmission and reception delays caused by byte interleaving (11 transmission TSPs), are one frame in length.

Table 3-7: Delay-Adjustment Values Required as a Result of Byte Interleaving

Carrier modulation	Convolutional code	Delay-adjustment value (number of transmission TSPs)		
		Mode 1	Mode 2	Mode 3
DQPSK QPSK	1/2	12 × N·11	24 × N·11	48 × N·11
	2/3	16 × N·11	32 × N·11	64 × N·11
	3/4	18 × N·11	36 × N·11	72 × N·11
	5/6	20 × N·11	40 × N·11	80 × N·11
	7/8	21 × N·11	42 × N·11	84 × N·11
16QAM	1/2	24 × N·11	48 × N·11	96 × N·11
	2/3	32 × N·11	64 × N·11	128 × N·11
	3/4	36 × N·11	72 × N·11	144 × N·11
	5/6	40 × N·11	80 × N·11	160 × N·11
	7/8	42 × N·11	84 × N·11	168 × N·11
64QAM	1/2	36 × N·11	72 × N·11	144 × N·11
	2/3	48 × N·11	96 × N·11	192 × N·11
	3/4	54 × N·11	108 × N·11	216 × N·11
	5/6	60 × N·11	120 × N·11	240 × N·11
	7/8	63 × N·11	126 × N·11	252 × N·11

N represents the number of segments used by that hierarchical layer.
(Ordinance Annexed Table 15, Annexed Statement 2, Item 2)

With hierarchical transmission, it is possible to specify different sets of transmission parameters (number of segments, inner-code coding rate, and modulation scheme) for different hierarchical layers. In this case, however, the transmission bit rate for one layer differs from that for another layer, resulting in different transmission capacities calculated as the time periods from coding of the inner code on the transmitting side to decoding on the receiving side.

Therefore, the amount of transmission TSP delay (11 TSPs) caused by byte interleaving (discussed later) for one layer differs from that for another layer when it is converted to delay time.

To compensate for this relative difference in delay time between hierarchical layers, delay adjustment is conducted at each layer prior to byte interleaving, in accordance with the transmission bit rate.

ARIB STD-B31

3.7 Byte interleaving

The 204-byte transmission TSP, which is error-protected by means of RS code and energy-dispersed, undergoes convolutional byte interleaving. Interleaving must be 12 bytes in depth. Note, however, that the byte next to the synchronization byte must pass through a reference path that causes no delay.

Fig. 3-9 shows the byte interleaving circuit.

In the inter-code interleaving circuit, path 0 has no delay. The memory size for path 1 must be 17 bytes, that for path 2 be 17 × 2 = 34 bytes, and so on. Input and output must be switched over to a different path every byte, in a sequential and cyclic manner, in ascending order of path number (path 0 -> path 1 -> path 2 ···· path 11 -> path 0 -> path 1 -> path 2).

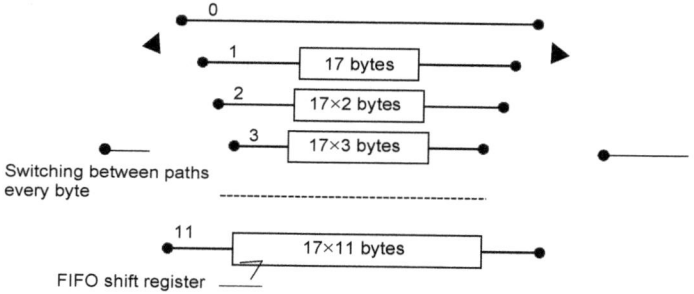

Fig. 3-9: Byte Interleaving Circuit

(Ordinance Annexed Table 15, Annexed Statement 2, Item 1)

ARIB STD-B31

3.8 Inner code

The inner code is a punctured convolutional code with a mother code having a constraint length k of 7, and a coding rate of 1/2. The generating polynomial of the mother code must be G1 = 171OCT and G2 = 133OCT. Fig. 3·10 shows the coding circuit of the mother code with constraint length k of 7, and a coding rate of 1/2.

Table 3·8 shows the selectable inner-code coding rates and transmission signal sequence that are punctured at that time. Note that the puncturing pattern must be reset such that the patterns shown in Table 3·8 are initiated by frame synchronization. This is intended to ensure improved receiver reliability in compensating for synchronization between puncturing patterns.

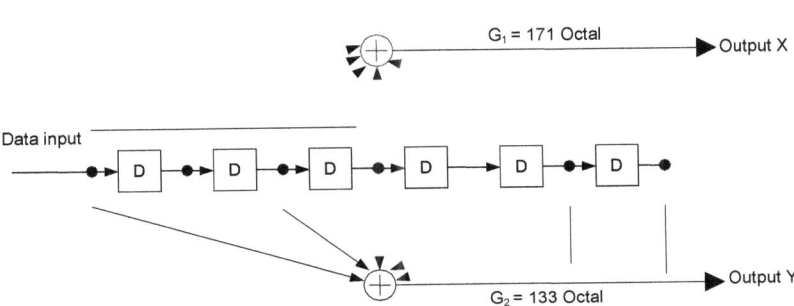

Fig. 3-10: Coding Circuit of a Convolutional Code with Constraint Length k of 7 and a Coding Rate of 1/2

Table 3-8: Inner-Code Coding Rates and Transmission-Signal Sequence

Coding rate	Puncturing pattern	Transmission-signal sequence
1/2	X : 1 Y : 1	X1, Y1
2/3	X : 1 0 Y : 1 1	X1, Y1, Y2
3/4	X : 1 0 1 Y : 1 1 0	X1, Y1, Y2, X3
5/6	X : 1 0 1 0 1 Y : 1 1 0 1 0	X1, Y1, Y2, X3 Y4, X5
7/8	X : 1 0 0 0 1 0 1 Y : 1 1 1 1 0 1 0	X1, Y1, Y2, Y3, Y4, X5, Y6, X7

(Ordinance Annex Table 12, Item 3 and Item 4)

ARIB STD-B31

3.9 Carrier modulation

3.9.1 Configuration of the carrier modulator

In the carrier modulation process, the input signal is bit-interleaved and mapped through the schemes specified for each hierarchical layer. Fig. 3-11 shows the carrier-modulator configuration.

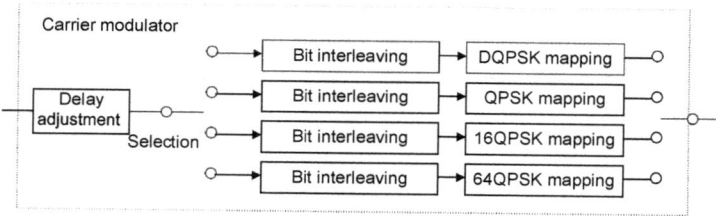

Fig. 3-11: Carrier-Modulator Configuration

3.9.2 Delay adjustment

Transmission and reception delays equivalent to 120 carrier symbols occur as a result of bit interleaving of the carrier modulator. The delay time varies depending on the carrier modulation scheme, that is, the number of bits comprising the carrier symbol.

This difference in delay time is corrected at the bit interleaving input side through the addition of the delay-adjustment value shown in Table 3-9 such that the total transmission and reception delays are equal to 2 OFDM symbols.

Table 3-9: Delay-Adjustment Values Required as a Result of Bit Interleaving

Carrier modulation	Delay-adjustment value (number of bits)		
	Mode 1	Mode 2	Mode 3
DQPSK QPSK	384 × N-240	768 × N-240	1536 × N-240
16QAM	768 × N-480	1536 × N-480	3072 × N-480
64QAM	1152 × N-720	2304 × N-720	4608 × N-720

N represents the number of segments used by that hierarchical layer.
(Ordinance Annexed Table 10, Annexed Statement 1 Note 2)

ARIB STD-B31

3.9.3 Bit interleaving and mapping

3.9.3.1 DQPSK

The input signal must be 2 bits per symbol and p/4-shift DQPSK-mapped to output multi-bit I- and Q-axes data. Upon completion of serial-parallel conversion, the 120-bit delay element shown in Fig. 3-12 is inserted into the phase-calculator input for bit interleaving. Figs. 3-12 and 3-13 show the system diagram and mapping constellation, respectively.

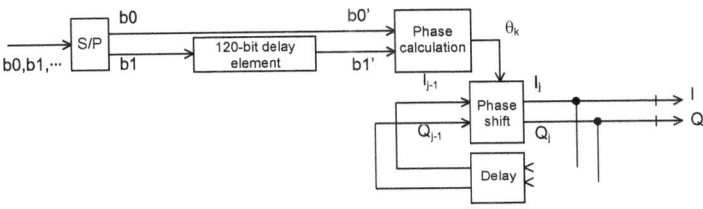

Fig. 3-12: π/4-Shift DQPSK Modulation System Diagram

Table 3-10: Phase Calculation

input b0' b1'	output θ_j
0 0	$\pi/4$
0 1	$-\pi/4$
1 0	$3\pi/4$
1 1	$-3\pi/4$

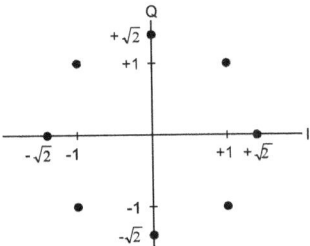

Fig. 3-13: π/4-Shift DQPSK Constellation

The following shows the phase shift:

$$\begin{pmatrix} I_j \\ Q_j \end{pmatrix} = \begin{pmatrix} \cos\theta_j & -\sin\theta_j \\ \sin\theta_j & \cos\theta_j \end{pmatrix} \begin{pmatrix} I_{j-1} \\ Q_{j-1} \end{pmatrix}$$

Provided that (I_j, Q_j) and (I_{j-1}, Q_{j-1}) represent the output symbol and the OFDM symbol immediately preceding the output symbol, respectively

(Ordinance Annexed Table 10, Annexed Statement 1, Item 1)

3.9.3.2 QPSK

The input signal must be 2 bits per symbol and QPSK-mapped to output multi-bit I- and Q-axes data. To conduct mapping, the 120-bit delay element shown in Fig. 3-14 is inserted into the mapping input for bit interleaving.

Figs. 3-14 and 3-15 show the system diagram and mapping constellation, respectively.

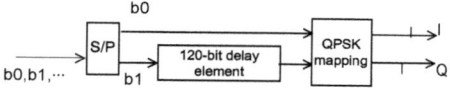

Fig. 3-14: QPSK Modulation System Diagram

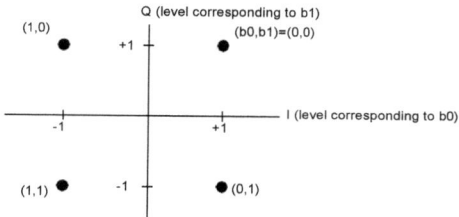

Fig. 3-15: QPSK Constellation

(Ordinance Annexed Table 10, Annexed Statement 1, Item 2)

ARIB STD-B31

3.9.3.3 16QAM

The input signal must be 4 bits per symbol and 16QAM-mapped to output multi-bit I- and Q-axes data. To conduct mapping, the delay elements shown in Fig. 3-16 are inserted into b1 to b3 for bit interleaving.

Figs. 3-16 and 3-17 show the system diagram and mapping constellation, respectively.

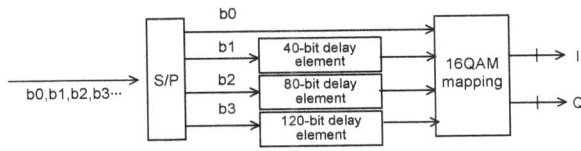

Fig. 3-16: 16QAM Modulation System Diagram

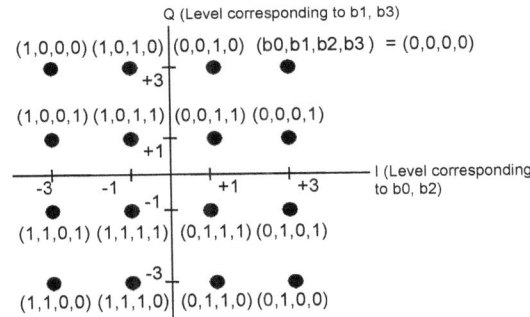

Fig. 3-17: 16QAM Constellation

(Ordinance Annexed Table 10, Annexed Statement 1, Item 3)

3.9.3.4 64QAM

The input signal must be 6 bits per symbol and 64QAM-mapped to output multi-bit I- and Q-axes data. To conduct mapping, the delay elements shown in Fig. 3-18 are inserted into b1 to b5 for bit interleaving.

Figs. 3-18 and 3-19 show the system diagram and mapping constellation, respectively.

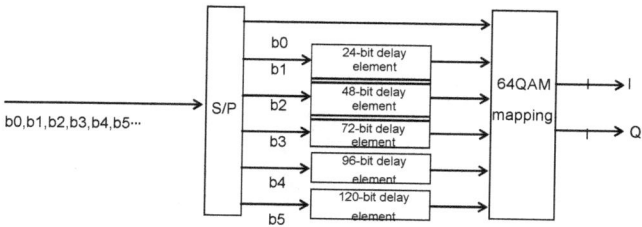

Fig. 3-18: 64QAM Modulation System Diagram

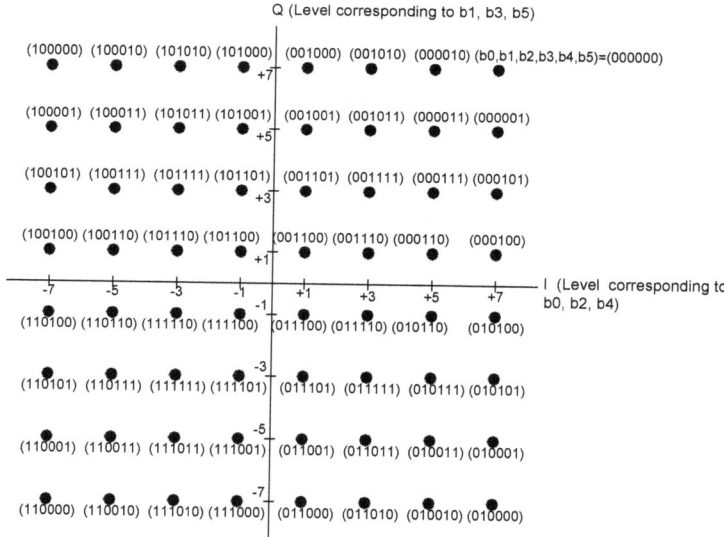

Fig. 3-19: 64QAM Constellation

(Ordinance Annexed Table 10, Annexed Statement 1, Item 4)

ARIB STD-B31

3.9.4 Modulation-level normalization

When we let the points in the constellations shown in Figs. 3-13, 3-15, 3-17, and 3-19 be expressed as Z (= I + jQ), the transmission-signal level must be normalized by multiplying each of these points by the corresponding normalization factor shown in Table 3-11.

As a result, the average OFDM symbol power becomes 1 regardless of which modulation scheme is used.

Table 3-11: Modulation Level Normalization

Carrier modulation scheme	Normalization factor
π/4-shift DQPSK	$Z/\sqrt{2}$
QPSK	$Z/\sqrt{2}$
16QAM	$Z/\sqrt{10}$
64QAM	$Z/\sqrt{42}$

(Ordinance Annexed Table 10, Annexed Statement 1, Note 4)

3.9.5 Data-segment configuration

A data segment is equivalent to data part in an OFDM segment shown in Section 3-12. Data segments consist of 96, 192, and 384 carrier symbols in Modes 1, 2, and 3, respectively. Note that $S_{i,j,k}$ in the figure represents the kth segment carrier symbol. Note also that "i" must be equivalent to the carrier direction in the OFDM segment, while "j" must be equivalent to the symbol direction in the OFDM segment. Fig. 3-20 shows the data-segment configuration.

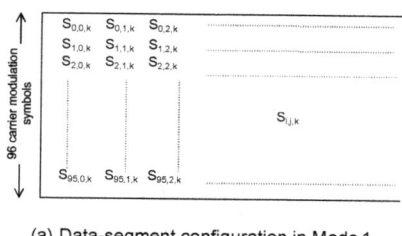

(a) Data-segment configuration in Mode 1

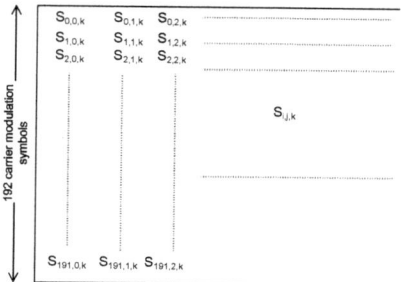

(b) Data-segment configuration in Mode 2

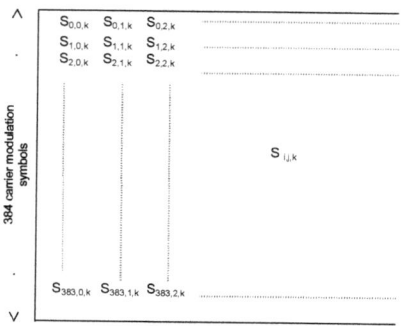

(c) Data-segment configuration in Mode 3

Fig. 3-20: Data-Segment Configurations

ARIB STD-B31

3.10 Combining hierarchical layers

Signals of different hierarchical layers, subjected to channel coding and carrier modulation by the specified parameters, must be combined and inserted into data segments and undergo speed conversion.

Fig. 3-21 shows the configuration of the hierarchical combiner.

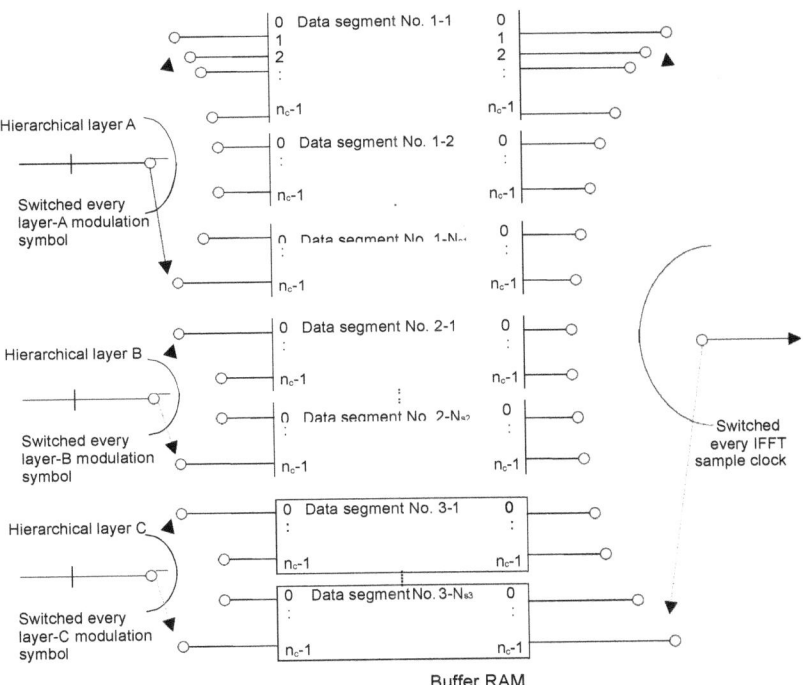

Fig. 3-21: Configuration of the Layer Combiner

In the figure shown above, n_c is 96, 192, and 384 in Modes 1, 2, and 3, respectively. Note also that $N_{s1} + N_{s2} + N_{s3} = 13$.

(Ordinance Annexed Table 10, Annexed Statement 2)

ARIB STD-B31

3.11 Time and frequency interleaving

3.11.1 Time interleaving

Once signals of different hierarchical layers are combined, they must be time-interleaved in units of modulation symbols (for each of the I and Q axes), as shown in Fig. 3-22.

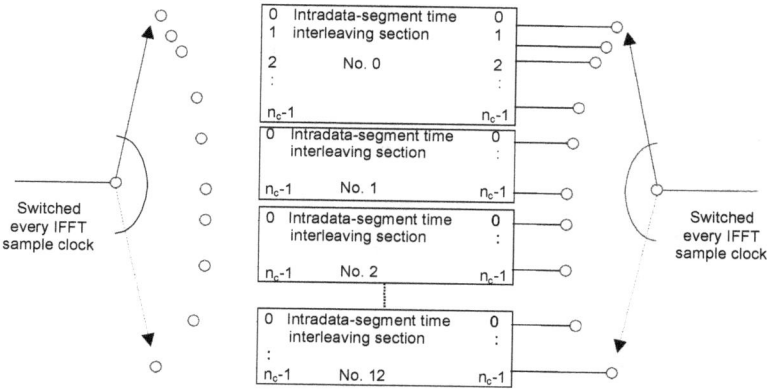

n_c is 96, 192, and 384 in Modes 1, 2, and 3, respectively.
Fig. 3-22: Configuration of the Time Interleaving Section

(Notification No. 303, Annexed Table 2, Annexed Statement 1)

Fig. 3-23 shows the configuration of one of the intra-data segment time interleaving sections presented in Fig. 3-22. Note that "I" in the figure is a parameter related to interleaving length that can be specified for each hierarchical layer. This parameter is shown in Table 3-12.

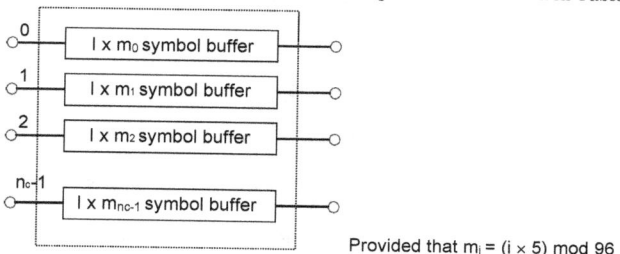

Provided that $m_i = (i \times 5) \bmod 96$

n_c is 96, 192, and 384 in Modes 1, 2, and 3, respectively.
Fig. 3-23: Configuration of the Intra-segment Time Interleaving Section

(Notification No. 303, Annexed Table 2, Annexed Statement 2)

256

The time interleaving length must be specified as I for each hierarchical layer, independently of other layers. The resulting difference in delay time must be corrected on the transmitting side using the number of symbols or the delay appropriate for each layer shown in Table 3·12, such that the total number of transmission and reception delays is a multiple of the number of frames.

Table 3-12: Time Interleaving Lengths and Delay Adjustment Values

Mode 1			Mode 2			Mode 3		
Length (I)	Number of delay-adjustment symbols	Number of delayed frames in transmission and reception	Length (I)	Number of delay-adjustment symbols	Number of delayed frames in transmission and reception	Length (I)	Number of delay-adjustment symbols	Number of delayed frames in transmission and reception
0	0	0	0	0	0	0	0	0
4	28	2	2	14	1	1	109	1
8	56	4	4	28	2	2	14	1
16	112	8	8	56	4	4	28	2

(Notification No. 303, Annexed Table 2, Annexed Statement 3(2))

Note that this delay adjustment must be conducted on signals prior to time interleaving.

[Description]
The number of transmission and reception delay frames that are time interleaved after delay adjustment is shown in Table 3·12 for each hierarchical layer. The same applies to a single hierarchical layer.

Time interleaving is intended to ensure improved the robustness against fading interference by randomizing symbol data in terms of the time after modulation. Specification of the interleaving length for each hierarchical layer allows the optimal interleaving length to be specified for the target channel if each layer employs a different channel, that is, a type of reception that differs from that of other layers.

Fig. 3·24 shows the arrangement of carriers following time interleaving.

The purpose of using convolutional interleaving as the time interleaving method is to reduce the total transmission and reception delay time and decrease the amount of receiver memory taken up.

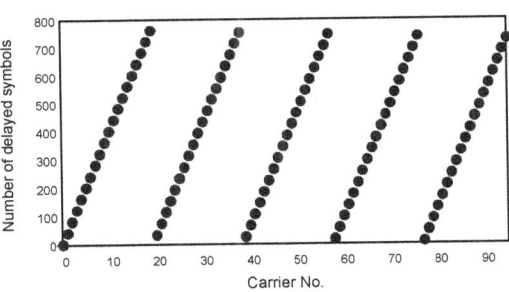

Fig. 3-24: Arrangement of Carriers Following Time Interleaving (Mode 1, I=8)

ARIB STD-B31

3.11.2 Frequency interleaving

Fig. 3-25 shows the configuration of the frequency interleaving section.

During segment division, data-segment numbers 0 to 12 are assigned sequentially to the partial-reception portion, differential modulations (segments for which DQPSK is specified for modulating carriers), and coherent modulation (segments for which QPSK, 16QAM, or 64QAM is specified for modulating carriers).

As for the relationship between the hierarchical configuration and data segments, data segments of the same hierarchical level must be successively arranged, and hierarchical layers must be named layer A, B, and C sequentially, in ascending order of data-segment number (that is, from smaller to larger segment numbers).

Inter-segment interleaving must be conducted on two or more data segments when they belong to the same type of modulated portion, even if their hierarchical levels differ.

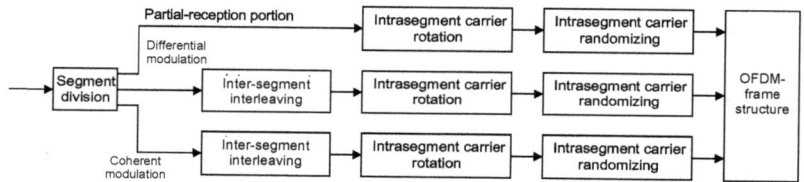

Fig. 3-25: Configuration of the Frequency Interleaving Section

(Notification No. 303, Annexed Table 2, Annexed Statement 4)

[Description]
Inter-segment interleaving is not conducted on the partial-reception portion, as it is assumed that the receiver designed to receive only that segment will be used.

Note also that because the differential and coherent modulations differ in terms of frame structure, as shown in Section 3-12 ("Frame structure"), inter-segment interleaving is performed in each group.

Inter-segment interleaving conducted across layer boundaries is intended to maximize the frequency interleaving effect.

ARIB STD-B31

3.11.2.1 Inter-segment interleaving

Inter-segment interleaving must be conducted on each of the differential modulation (DQPSK) and coherent modulation (QPSK, 16QAM, 64QAM), as shown in Figs. 3-26 (a), 3-26 (b), and 3-26 (c).

Note that $S_{i,j,k}$, and n in the figures represent carrier symbols in the data-segment configuration (Fig. 3-20) and the number of segments assigned to the differential and coherent modulation, respectively.

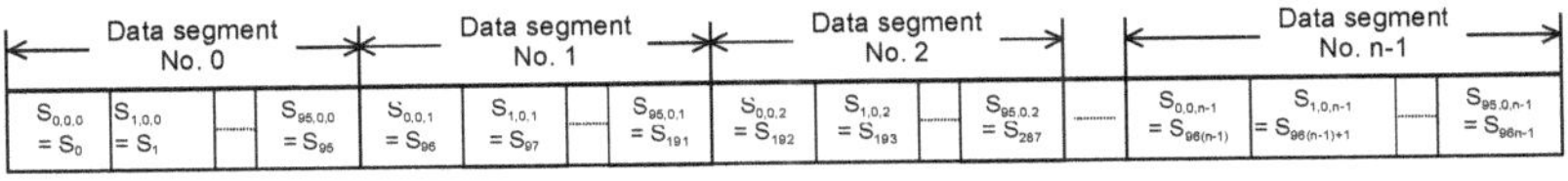

Data segment No. 0	Data segment No. 1	Data segment No. 2	Data segment No. n-1
$S_{0,0,0}=S_0$ $S_{1,0,0}=S_1$ $\cdots$ $S_{95,0,0}=S_{95}$	$S_{0,0,1}=S_{96}$ $S_{1,0,1}=S_{97}$ $\cdots$ $S_{95,0,1}=S_{191}$	$S_{0,0,2}=S_{192}$ $S_{1,0,2}=S_{193}$ $\cdots$ $S_{95,0,2}=S_{287}$	$S_{0,0,n-1}=S_{96(n-1)}$ $S_{1,0,n-1}=S_{96(n-1)+1}$ $\cdots$ $S_{95,0,n-1}=S_{96n-1}$

Arrangement of symbols before interleaving

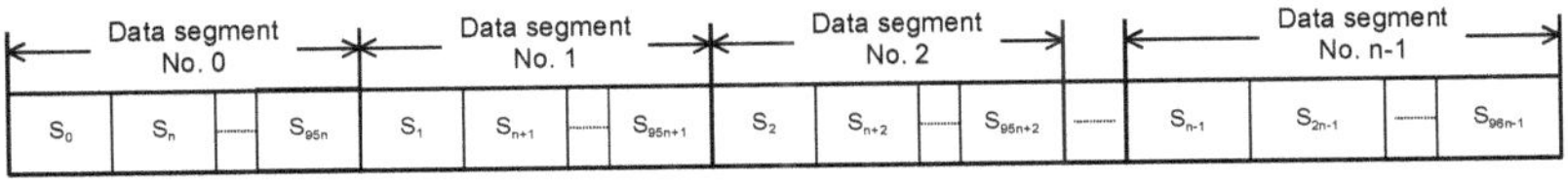

Data segment No. 0	Data segment No. 1	Data segment No. 2	Data segment No. n-1
S_0 S_n $\cdots$ S_{95n}	S_1 S_{n+1} $\cdots$ S_{95n+1}	S_2 S_{n+2} $\cdots$ S_{95n+2}	S_{n-1} S_{2n-1} $\cdots$ S_{96n-1}

Arrangement of symbols after interleaving

Fig. 3-26 (a): Inter-segment Interleaving in Mode 1

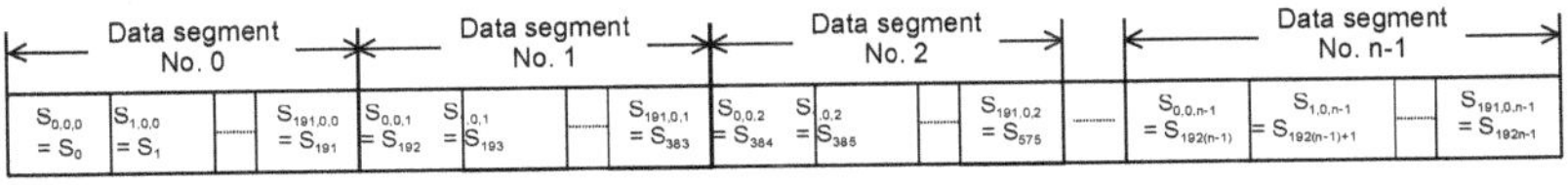

Data segment No. 0	Data segment No. 1	Data segment No. 2	Data segment No. n-1
$S_{0,0,0}=S_0$ $S_{1,0,0}=S_1$ $\cdots$ $S_{191,0,0}=S_{191}$	$S_{0,0,1}=S_{192}$ $S_{1,0,1}=S_{193}$ $\cdots$ $S_{191,0,1}=S_{383}$	$S_{0,0,2}=S_{384}$ $S_{1,0,2}=S_{385}$ $\cdots$ $S_{191,0,2}=S_{575}$	$S_{0,0,n-1}=S_{192(n-1)}$ $S_{1,0,n-1}=S_{192(n-1)+1}$ $\cdots$ $S_{191,0,n-1}=S_{192n-1}$

Arrangement of symbols before interleaving

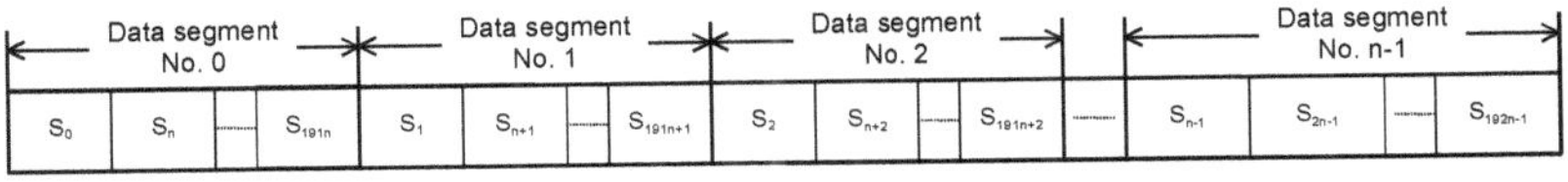

Data segment No. 0	Data segment No. 1	Data segment No. 2	Data segment No. n-1
S_0 S_n $\cdots$ S_{191n}	S_1 S_{n+1} $\cdots$ S_{191n+1}	S_2 S_{n+2} $\cdots$ S_{191n+2}	S_{n-1} S_{2n-1} $\cdots$ S_{192n-1}

Arrangement of symbols after interleaving

Fig. 3-26 (b): Inter-segment Interleaving in Mode 2

(Notification No. 303, Annexed Table 2, Annexed Statement 5)

ARIB STD-B31

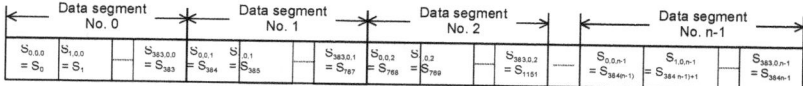

Arrangement of symbols before interleaving

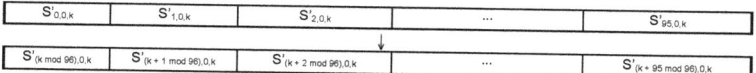

Arrangement of symbols after interleaving

Fig. 3-26 (c): Inter-segment Interleaving in Mode 3

(Notification No. 303, Annexed Table 2, Annexed Statement 5)

3.11.2.2 Intra-segment interleaving

Intra-segment interleaving must be conducted in two steps: carrier rotation by segment number, followed by carrier randomizing.

In the carrier rotation, carrier changes are carried out as shown in Figs. 3-27 (a), 3-27 (b), and 3-27 (c). Here, $S'_{i,j,k}$ represents the carrier symbol of the kth segment following inter-segment interleaving.

$S'_{0,0,k}$	$S'_{1,0,k}$	$S'_{2,0,k}$	...	$S'_{95,0,k}$
$S'_{(k \bmod 96),0,k}$	$S'_{(k+1 \bmod 96),0,k}$	$S'_{(k+2 \bmod 96),0,k}$	...	$S'_{(k+95 \bmod 96),0,k}$

Fig. 3-27 (a): Carrier Rotation in Mode 1

$S'_{0,0,k}$	$S'_{1,0,k}$	$S'_{2,0,k}$	...	$S'_{191,0,k}$
$S'_{(k \bmod 192),0,k}$	$S'_{(k+1 \bmod 192),0,k}$	$S'_{(k+2 \bmod 192),0,k}$	...	$S'_{(k+191 \bmod 192),0,k}$

Fig. 3-27 (b): Carrier Rotation in Mode 2

$S'_{0,0,k}$	$S'_{1,0,k}$	$S'_{2,0,k}$	...	$S'_{383,0,k}$
$S'_{(k \bmod 384),0,k}$	$S'_{(k+1 \bmod 384),0,k}$	$S'_{(k+2 \bmod 384),0,k}$	...	$S'_{(k+383 \bmod 384),0,k}$

Fig. 3-27 (c): Carrier Rotation in Mode 3

(Notification No. 303, Annexed Table 2, Annexed Statement 6)

ARIB STD-B31

Next, carrier randomizing in Mode 1, 2, and 3 is shown in Table 3-13 (a), (b), and (c), respectively.

These tables show which carriers are assigned, as a result of carrier randomizing, to carrier-rotated data arranged in ascending order of carrier number.

Table 3-13 (a): Intra-Segment Carrier Randomizing in Mode 1

Before	0	1	2	3	4	5	6	7	8	9	10	11	12	13	14	15	16	17	18	19	20	21	22	23
After	80	93	63	92	94	55	17	81	6	51	9	85	89	65	52	15	73	66	46	71	12	70	18	13

Before	24	25	26	27	28	29	30	31	32	33	34	35	36	37	38	39	40	41	42	43	44	45	46	47
After	95	34	1	38	78	59	91	64	0	28	11	4	45	35	16	7	48	22	23	77	56	19	8	36

Before	48	49	50	51	52	53	54	55	56	57	58	59	60	61	62	63	64	65	66	67	68	69	70	71
After	39	61	21	3	26	69	67	20	74	86	72	25	31	5	49	42	54	87	43	60	29	2	76	84

Before	72	73	74	75	76	77	78	79	80	81	82	83	84	85	86	87	88	89	90	91	92	93	94	95
After	83	40	14	79	27	57	44	37	30	68	47	88	75	41	90	10	33	32	62	50	58	82	53	24

Table 3-13 (b): Intra-Segment Carrier Randomizing in Mode 2

Before	0	1	2	3	4	5	6	7	8	9	10	11	12	13	14	15	16	17	18	19	20	21	22	23
After	98	35	67	116	135	17	5	93	73	168	54	143	43	74	165	48	37	69	154	150	107	76	176	79

Before	24	25	26	27	28	29	30	31	32	33	34	35	36	37	38	39	40	41	42	43	44	45	46	47
After	175	36	28	78	47	128	94	163	184	72	142	2	86	14	130	151	114	68	46	183	122	112	180	42

Before	48	49	50	51	52	53	54	55	56	57	58	59	60	61	62	63	64	65	66	67	68	69	70	71
After	105	97	33	134	177	84	170	45	187	38	167	10	189	51	117	156	161	25	89	125	139	24	19	57

Before	72	73	74	75	76	77	78	79	80	81	82	83	84	85	86	87	88	89	90	91	92	93	94	95
After	71	39	77	191	88	85	0	162	181	113	140	61	75	82	101	174	118	20	136	3	121	190	120	92

Before	96	97	98	99	100	101	102	103	104	105	106	107	108	109	110	111	112	113	114	115	116	117	118	119
After	160	52	153	127	65	60	133	147	131	87	22	58	100	111	141	83	49	132	12	155	146	102	164	66

Before	120	121	122	123	124	125	126	127	128	129	130	131	132	133	134	135	136	137	138	139	140	141	142	143
After	1	62	178	15	182	96	80	119	23	6	166	56	99	123	138	137	21	145	185	18	70	129	95	90

Before	144	145	146	147	148	149	150	151	152	153	154	155	156	157	158	159	160	161	162	163	164	165	166	167
After	149	109	124	50	11	152	4	31	172	40	13	32	55	159	41	8	7	144	16	26	173	81	44	103

Before	168	169	170	171	172	173	174	175	176	177	178	179	180	181	182	183	184	185	186	187	188	189	190	191
After	64	9	30	157	126	179	148	63	188	171	106	104	158	115	34	186	29	108	53	91	169	110	27	59

(Notification No. 303, Annexed Table 2, Annexed Statement 7)

ARIB STD-B31

Table 3-13 (c): Intra-Segment Carrier Randomizing in Mode 3

Before	0	1	2	3	4	5	6	7	8	9	10	11	12	13	14	15	16	17	18	19	20	21	22	23
After	62	13	371	11	285	336	365	220	226	92	56	46	120	175	298	352	172	235	53	164	368	187	125	82

Before	24	25	26	27	28	29	30	31	32	33	34	35	36	37	38	39	40	41	42	43	44	45	46	47
After	5	45	173	258	135	182	141	273	126	264	286	88	233	61	249	367	310	179	155	57	123	208	14	227

Before	48	49	50	51	52	53	54	55	56	57	58	59	60	61	62	63	64	65	66	67	68	69	70	71
After	100	311	205	79	184	185	328	77	115	277	112	20	199	178	143	152	215	204	139	234	358	192	309	183

Before	72	73	74	75	76	77	78	79	80	81	82	83	84	85	86	87	88	89	90	91	92	93	94	95
After	81	129	256	314	101	43	97	324	142	157	90	214	102	29	303	363	261	31	22	52	305	301	293	177

Before	96	97	98	99	100	101	102	103	104	105	106	107	108	109	110	111	112	113	114	115	116	117	118	119
After	116	296	85	196	191	114	58	198	16	167	145	119	245	113	295	193	232	17	108	283	246	64	237	189

Before	120	121	122	123	124	125	126	127	128	129	130	131	132	133	134	135	136	137	138	139	140	141	142	143
After	128	373	302	320	239	335	356	39	347	351	73	158	276	243	99	38	287	3	330	153	315	117	289	213

Before	144	145	146	147	148	149	150	151	152	153	154	155	156	157	158	159	160	161	162	163	164	165	166	167
After	210	149	383	337	339	151	241	321	217	30	334	161	322	49	176	359	12	346	60	28	229	265	288	225

Before	168	169	170	171	172	173	174	175	176	177	178	179	180	181	182	183	184	185	186	187	188	189	190	191
After	382	59	181	170	319	341	86	251	133	344	361	109	44	369	268	257	323	55	317	381	121	360	260	275

Before	192	193	194	195	196	197	198	199	200	201	202	203	204	205	206	207	208	209	210	211	212	213	214	215
After	190	19	63	18	248	9	240	211	150	230	332	231	71	255	350	355	83	87	154	218	138	269	348	130

Before	216	217	218	219	220	221	222	223	224	225	226	227	228	229	230	231	232	233	234	235	236	237	238	239
After	160	278	377	216	236	308	223	254	25	98	300	201	137	219	36	325	124	66	353	169	21	35	107	50

Before	240	241	242	243	244	245	246	247	248	249	250	251	252	253	254	255	256	257	258	259	260	261	262	263
After	106	333	326	262	252	271	263	372	136	0	366	206	159	122	188	6	284	96	26	200	197	186	345	340

Before	264	265	266	267	268	269	270	271	272	273	274	275	276	277	278	279	280	281	282	283	284	285	286	287
After	349	103	84	228	212	2	67	318	1	74	342	166	194	33	68	267	111	118	140	195	105	202	291	259

Before	288	289	290	291	292	293	294	295	296	297	298	299	300	301	302	303	304	305	306	307	308	309	310	311
After	23	171	65	281	24	165	8	94	222	331	34	238	364	376	266	89	80	253	163	280	247	4	362	379

Before	312	313	314	315	316	317	318	319	320	321	322	323	324	325	326	327	328	329	330	331	332	333	334	335
After	290	279	54	78	180	72	316	282	131	207	343	370	306	221	132	7	148	299	168	224	48	47	357	313

Before	336	337	338	339	340	341	342	343	344	345	346	347	348	349	350	351	352	353	354	355	356	357	358	359
After	75	104	70	147	40	110	374	69	146	37	375	354	174	41	32	304	307	312	15	272	134	242	203	209

Before	360	361	362	363	364	365	366	367	368	369	370	371	372	373	374	375	376	377	378	379	380	381	382	383
After	380	162	297	327	10	93	42	250	156	338	292	144	378	294	329	127	270	76	95	91	244	274	27	51

(Notification No. 303, Annexed Table 2, Annexed Statement 7)

ARIB STD-B31

[Description]
Carrier rotation and carrier randomizing are intended to eliminate periodicity in carrier arrangement. These operations make it possible to prevent burst errors of a specific segment's carrier, which may occur if the carrier arrangement period matches the frequency-selective fading after inter-segment interleaving.

Figs. 3-28 (a) and (b) show examples of carrier randomizing in Mode 1 and carrier randomizing including time interleaving, respectively.

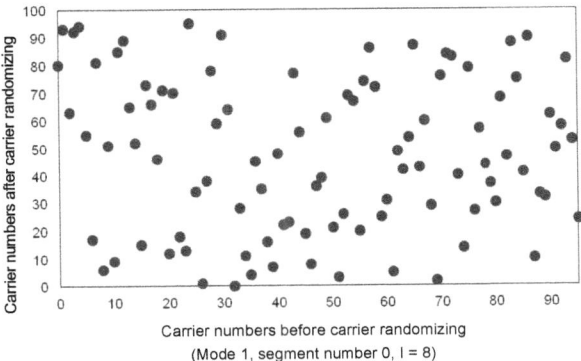

Fig. 3-28 (a): Example of Carrier Arrangement before and after Carrier Randomizing

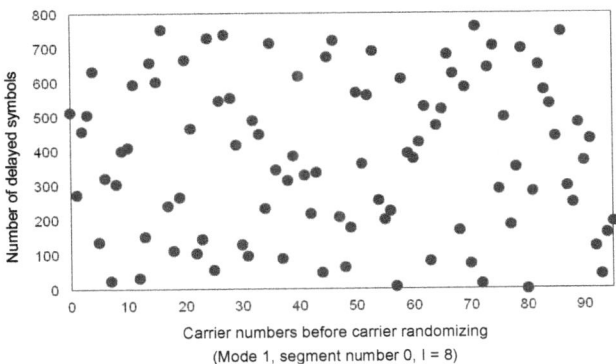

Fig. 3-28 (b): Example of Carrier Arrangement after Time Interleaving and Carrier Randomizing

ARIB STD-B31

3.12 Frame structure

All data-processing tasks in data segments required for channel coding are complete when the steps discussed up to Section 3.11 are performed. This section stipulates OFDM-frame structure achieved through the addition of various pilot signals to data segments.

3.12.1 OFDM-segment configuration for the differential modulation

Fig. 3-29 shows the OFDM-segment configuration for a differential modulation (DQPSK) (Mode 1).

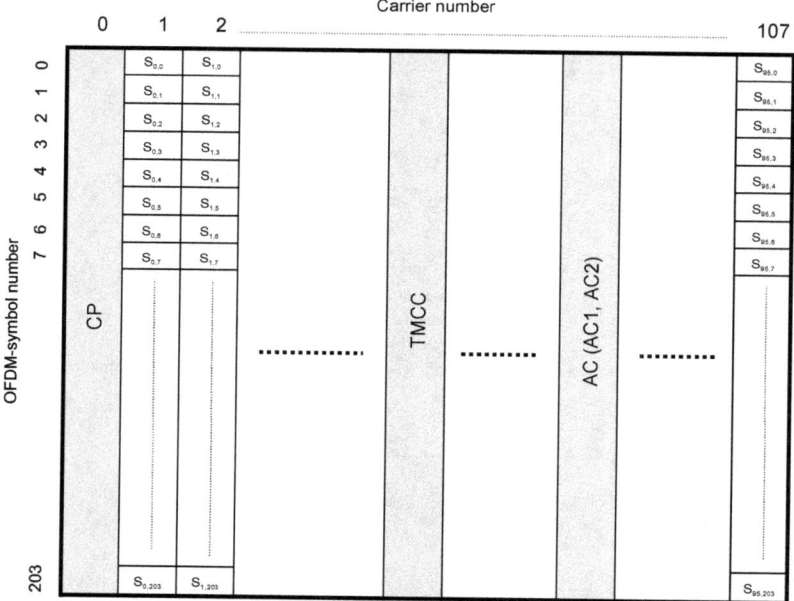

Fig. 3-29: OFDM-Segment Configuration for the Differential Modulation

(Ordinance Annexed Table 7, Item 1)

Note, however, that $S_{i,j}$ represents carrier symbols within data segments following interleaving.

Note also that the CP (Continual Pilot), the TMCC (Transmission and Multiplexing Configuration Control), and the AC (Auxiliary Channel) are the continuous carrier, the signal for conveying control information, and the extension signal for conveying additional information on broadcasting, respectively.

In Mode 1, carrier numbers 0 to 107 are available, while in Modes 2 and 3, carrier numbers 0 to 215 and 0 to 431 are assigned, respectively.

ARIB STD-B31

The arrangement of various control signals (represented by carrier numbers) that are added by the OFDM-frame structure section in each mode is shown in Tables 3·14 (a), (b), and (c).

Table 3-14: Arrangement of the CP, TMCC, and AC Carriers for the Differential Modulation

(a) Arrangement of the CP, AC, and TMCC Carriers in Mode 1

Segment No.	11	9	7	5	3	1	0	2	4	6	8	10	12
CP	0	0	0	0	0	0	0	0	0	0	0	0	0
AC1_1	10	53	61	11	20	74	35	76	4	40	8	7	98
AC1_2	28	83	100	101	40	100	79	97	89	89	64	89	101
AC2_1	3	3	29	28	23	30	3	5	13	72	36	25	10
AC2_2	45	15	41	45	63	81	72	18	93	95	48	30	30
AC2_3	59	40	84	81	85	92	85	57	98	100	52	42	55
AC2_4	77	58	93	91	105	103	89	92	102	105	74	104	81
TMCC 1	13	25	4	36	10	7	49	31	16	5	78	34	23
TMCC 2	50	63	7	48	28	25	61	39	30	10	82	48	37
TMCC 3	70	73	17	55	44	47	96	47	37	21	85	54	51
TMCC 4	83	80	51	59	47	60	99	65	74	44	98	70	68
TMCC 5	87	93	71	86	54	87	104	72	83	61	102	101	105

Segment numbers are arranged in ascending order of frequency along the frequency axis (see Section 3.14).

(Notification No. 303, Annexed Table 1, Annexed Statement 1)

ARIB STD-B31

(b) Arrangement of the CP, AC, and TMCC Carriers in Mode 2

Segment No.	11	9	7	5	3	1	0	2	4	6	8	10	12
CP	0	0	0	0	0	0	0	0	0	0	0	0	0
AC1_1	10	61	20	35	4	8	98	53	11	74	76	40	7
AC1_2	28	100	40	79	89	64	101	83	101	100	97	89	89
AC1_3	161	119	182	184	148	115	118	169	128	143	112	116	206
AC1_4	191	209	208	205	197	197	136	208	148	187	197	172	209
AC2_1	3	29	23	3	13	36	10	3	28	30	5	72	25
AC2_2	45	41	63	72	93	48	30	15	45	81	18	95	30
AC2_3	59	84	85	85	98	52	55	40	81	92	57	100	42
AC2_4	77	93	105	89	102	74	81	58	91	103	92	105	104
AC2_5	108	108	108	108	108	108	108	108	108	108	108	108	108
AC2_6	111	136	138	113	180	133	111	137	131	111	121	144	118
AC2_7	123	153	189	126	203	138	153	149	171	180	201	156	138
AC2_8	148	189	200	165	208	150	167	192	193	193	206	160	163
AC2_9	166	199	211	200	213	212	185	201	213	197	210	182	189
TMCC 1	13	4	10	49	16	78	23	25	36	7	31	5	34
TMCC 2	50	7	28	61	30	82	37	63	48	25	39	10	48
TMCC 3	70	17	44	96	37	85	51	73	55	47	47	21	54
TMCC 4	83	51	47	99	74	98	68	80	59	60	65	44	70
TMCC 5	87	71	54	104	83	102	105	93	86	87	72	61	101
TMCC 6	133	144	115	139	113	142	121	112	118	157	124	186	131
TMCC 7	171	156	133	147	118	156	158	115	136	169	138	190	145
TMCC 8	181	163	155	155	129	162	178	125	152	204	145	193	159
TMCC 9	188	167	168	173	152	178	191	159	155	207	182	206	176
TMCC 10	201	194	195	180	169	209	195	179	162	212	191	210	213

(Notification No. 303, Annexed Table 1, Annexed Statement 2)

ARIB STD-B31

(c) Arrangement of the CP, AC, and TMCC Carriers in Mode 3

Segment No.	11	9	7	5	3	1	0	2	4	6	8	10	12
CP	0	0	0	0	0	0	0	0	0	0	0	0	0
AC1_1	10	20	4	98	11	76	7	61	35	8	53	74	40
AC1_2	28	40	89	101	101	97	89	100	79	64	83	100	89
AC1_3	161	182	148	118	128	112	206	119	184	115	169	143	116
AC1_4	191	208	197	136	148	197	209	209	205	197	208	187	172
AC1_5	277	251	224	269	290	256	226	236	220	314	227	292	223
AC1_6	316	295	280	299	316	305	244	256	305	317	317	313	305
AC1_7	335	400	331	385	359	332	377	398	364	334	344	328	422
AC1_8	425	421	413	424	403	388	407	424	413	352	364	413	425
AC2_1	3	23	13	10	28	5	25	29	3	36	3	30	72
AC2_2	45	63	93	30	45	18	30	41	72	48	15	81	95
AC2_3	59	85	98	55	81	57	42	84	85	52	40	92	100
AC2_4	77	105	102	81	91	92	104	93	89	74	58	103	105
AC2_5	108	108	108	108	108	108	108	108	108	108	108	108	108
AC2_6	111	138	180	111	131	121	118	136	113	133	137	111	144
AC2_7	123	189	203	153	171	201	138	153	126	138	149	180	156
AC2_8	148	200	208	167	193	206	163	189	165	150	192	193	160
AC2_9	166	211	213	185	213	210	189	199	200	212	201	197	182
AC2_10	216	216	216	216	216	216	216	216	216	216	216	216	216
AC2_11	245	219	252	219	246	288	219	239	229	226	244	221	241
AC2_12	257	288	264	231	297	311	261	279	309	246	261	234	246
AC2_13	300	301	268	256	308	316	275	301	314	271	297	273	258
AC2_14	309	305	290	274	319	321	293	321	318	297	307	308	320
AC2_15	324	324	324	324	324	324	324	324	324	324	324	324	324
AC2_16	352	329	349	353	327	360	327	354	396	327	347	337	334
AC2_17	369	342	354	365	396	372	339	405	419	369	387	417	354
AC2_18	405	381	366	408	409	376	364	416	424	383	409	422	379
AC2_19	415	416	428	417	413	398	382	427	429	401	429	426	405
TMCC 1	13	10	16	23	36	31	34	4	49	78	25	7	5
TMCC 2	50	28	30	37	48	39	48	7	61	82	63	25	10
TMCC 3	70	44	37	51	55	47	54	17	96	85	73	47	21
TMCC 4	83	47	74	68	59	65	70	51	99	98	80	60	44
TMCC 5	87	54	83	105	86	72	101	71	104	102	93	87	61
TMCC 6	133	115	113	121	118	124	131	144	139	142	112	157	186
TMCC 7	171	133	118	158	136	138	145	156	147	156	115	169	190
TMCC 8	181	155	129	178	152	145	159	163	155	162	125	204	193
TMCC 9	188	168	152	191	155	182	176	167	173	178	159	207	206
TMCC 10	201	195	169	195	162	191	213	194	180	209	179	212	210
TMCC 11	220	265	294	241	223	221	229	226	232	239	252	247	250
TMCC 12	223	277	298	279	241	226	266	244	246	253	264	255	264
TMCC 13	233	312	301	289	263	237	286	260	253	267	271	263	270
TMCC 14	267	315	314	296	276	260	299	263	290	284	275	281	286
TMCC 15	287	320	318	309	303	277	303	270	299	321	302	288	317
TMCC 16	360	355	358	328	373	402	349	331	329	337	334	340	347
TMCC 17	372	363	372	331	385	406	387	349	334	374	352	354	361
TMCC 18	379	371	378	341	420	409	397	371	345	394	368	361	375
TMCC 19	383	389	394	375	423	422	404	384	368	407	371	398	392
TMCC 20	410	396	425	395	428	426	417	411	385	411	378	407	429

(Notification No. 303, Annexed Table 1, Annexed Statement 3)

ARIB STD-B31

The CP of a differential modulation's segment serves as the SP of a coherent modulation's segment when the differential modulation's segment at the lowermost frequency is adjacent to one of the coherent modulation's segments. The CP is thus provided at this low-frequency end. The receiver uses this CP as the high-frequency end SP for coherent detection in the coherent modulation's segment.

The TMCC and AC (AC1, AC2) carriers are arranged randomly with respect to the frequency in order to reduce the degradation caused by periodic dips on channel characteristics under multi-path environment.

Note that AC1 carriers for the differential modulation's segments are arranged at the same positions as those for the coherent modulation's segments.

3.12.2 OFDM-segment configuration for the coherent modulation

Fig. 3-30 shows an example of OFDM-segment configuration for a coherent modulation (QPSK, 16QAM, 64QAM) in Mode 1. $S_{i,j}$ represents carrier symbols within data segments following interleaving.

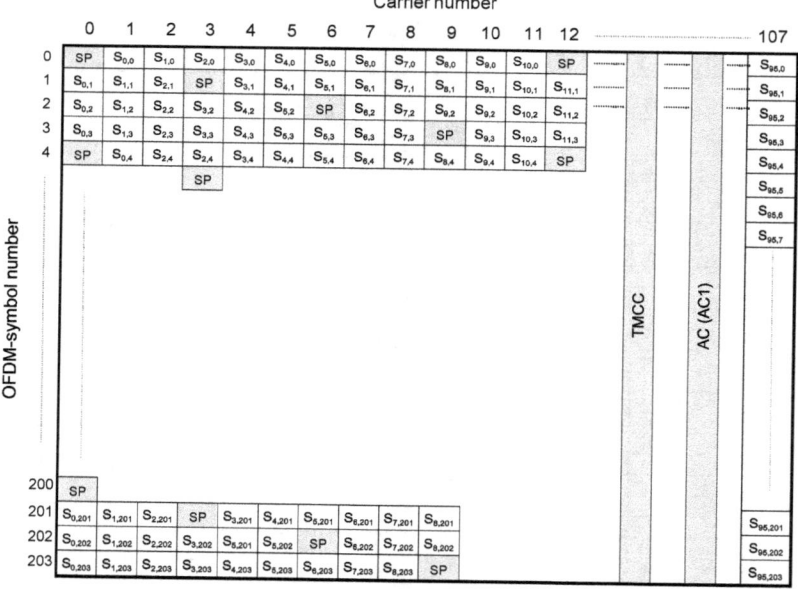

Fig. 3-30: OFDM-Segment Configuration for the Coherent Modulation

(Ordinance Annexed Table 7, Item 2)

ARIB STD-B31

The SP (Scattered Pilot) is inserted into a segment once every 12 carriers in the carrier direction, and once every 4 symbols in the symbol direction, as shown in the figure. Table 3·15 shows the AC and TMCC carrier arrangements.

The AC1 carrier arrangement for the coherent modulation is the same as that for the differential modulation. Note that AC2 is available only for the differential modulation. Therefore, the coherent modulation does not have any AC2.

Table 3-15: AC and TMCC Carrier Arrangements for the Coherent modulation

(a) AC and TMCC Carrier Arrangements in Mode 1

Segment No.	11	9	7	5	3	1	0	2	4	6	8	10	12
AC1_1	10	53	61	11	20	74	35	76	4	40	8	7	98
AC1_2	28	83	100	101	40	100	79	97	89	89	64	89	101
TMCC 1	70	25	17	86	44	47	49	31	83	61	85	101	23

(b) AC and TMCC Carrier Arrangements in Mode 2

Segment No.	11	9	7	5	3	1	0	2	4	6	8	10	12
AC1_1	10	61	20	35	4	8	98	53	11	74	76	40	7
AC1_2	28	100	40	79	89	64	101	83	101	100	97	89	89
AC1_3	161	119	182	184	148	115	118	169	128	143	112	116	206
AC1_4	191	209	208	205	197	197	136	208	148	187	197	172	209
TMCC 1	70	17	44	49	83	85	23	25	86	47	31	61	101
TMCC 2	133	194	155	139	169	209	178	125	152	157	191	193	131

(c) AC and TMCC Carrier Arrangements in Mode 3

Segment No.	11	9	7	5	3	1	0	2	4	6	8	10	12
AC1_1	10	20	4	98	11	76	7	61	35	8	53	74	40
AC1_2	28	40	89	101	101	97	89	100	79	64	83	100	89
AC1_3	161	182	148	118	128	112	206	119	184	115	169	143	116
AC1_4	191	208	197	136	148	197	209	209	205	197	208	187	172
AC1_5	277	251	224	269	290	256	226	236	220	314	227	292	223
AC1_6	316	295	280	299	316	305	244	256	305	317	317	313	305
AC1_7	335	400	331	385	359	332	377	398	364	334	344	328	422
AC1_8	425	421	413	424	403	388	407	424	413	352	364	413	425
TMCC 1	70	44	83	23	86	31	101	17	49	85	25	47	61
TMCC 2	133	155	169	178	152	191	131	194	139	209	125	157	193
TMCC 3	233	265	301	241	263	277	286	260	299	239	302	247	317
TMCC 4	410	355	425	341	373	409	349	371	385	394	368	407	347

(Notification No. 303, Annexed Table 1, Annexed Statement 4, 5, and 6)

The TMCC and AC (AC1) carriers are arranged randomly with respect to the frequency direction in order to reduce the periodic impact of dip on channel characteristics caused by multipath. Note that AC1 carriers for the differential modulation's segments are arranged at the same positions as those for the coherent modulation's segments.

ARIB STD-B31

3.13 Pilot signals

3.13.1 Scattered pilot (SP)

Scattered pilot is a BPSK signal that correlates output bit sequence W_i of the PRBS-generating circuit shown in Fig. 3-31, where the i of W_i is corresponds to the carrier number i of OFDM-segment. The initial value of the PRBS-generating circuit is defined for each segment.

The initial values are shown in Table 3-16, while the correspondence between W_i and the modulating signal is presented in Table 3-17.

$$g(x) = X^{11} + X^9 + 1$$

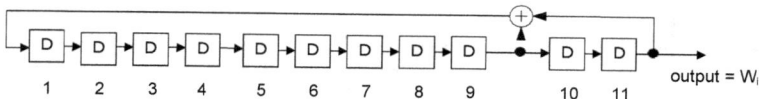

output = W_i

Fig. 3-31: PRBS-Generating Circuit

Table 3-16: Initial Value of the PRBS-Generating Circuit
(Arranged in Ascending Order of Bits from Left to Right)

Segment No.	Initial value in Mode 1	Initial value in Mode 2	Initial value in Mode 3
11	1 1 1 1 1 1 1 1 1 1 1	1 1 1 1 1 1 1 1 1 1 1	1 1 1 1 1 1 1 1 1 1 1
9	1 1 0 1 1 0 0 1 1 1 1	0 1 1 0 1 0 1 1 1 1 0	1 1 0 1 1 1 0 0 1 0 1
7	0 1 1 0 1 0 1 1 1 1 0	1 1 0 1 1 1 0 0 1 0 1	1 0 0 1 0 1 0 0 0 0 0
5	0 1 0 0 0 1 0 1 1 1 0	1 1 0 0 1 0 0 0 0 1 0	0 1 1 1 0 0 0 1 0 0 1
3	1 1 0 1 1 1 0 0 1 0 1	1 0 0 1 0 1 0 0 0 0 0	0 0 1 0 0 0 1 1 0 0 1
1	0 0 1 0 1 1 1 1 0 1 0	0 0 0 0 1 0 1 1 0 0 0	1 1 1 0 0 1 1 0 1 1 0
0	1 1 0 0 1 0 0 0 0 1 0	0 1 1 1 0 1 0 0 1	0 0 1 0 0 0 1 0 1 1
2	0 0 0 1 0 0 0 0 1 0 0	0 0 0 0 0 1 0 0 1 0 0	1 1 1 0 0 1 1 1 1 0 1
4	1 0 0 1 0 1 0 0 0 0 0	0 0 1 0 0 0 1 1 0 0 1	0 1 1 0 1 0 1 0 0 1 1
6	1 1 1 1 0 1 1 0 0 0 0	0 1 1 0 0 1 1 1 0 0 1	1 0 1 1 1 0 1 0 0 1 0
8	0 0 0 0 1 0 1 1 0 0 0	1 1 1 0 0 1 1 0 1 1 0	0 1 1 0 0 0 1 0 0 1 0
10	1 0 1 0 0 1 0 0 1 1 1	0 0 1 0 1 0 1 0 0 0 1	1 1 1 1 0 1 0 0 1 0 1
12	0 1 1 1 0 0 0 1 0 0 1	0 0 1 0 0 0 0 1 0 1 1	0 0 0 1 0 0 1 1 1 0 0

Note: Each of the initial values shown in Table 3-16 matches the value obtained by setting all bits to an initial value of 1s and continuously generating all carriers in the entire band, starting with the leftmost carrier (carrier 0 of segment 11) and ending with the rightmost carrier.

(Ordinance Annexed Table 14, Item 1, Note 1 (2))

Table 3-17: W_i and Modulating Signal

W_i value	Modulating-signal amplitude (I, Q)
1	(-4/3, 0)
0	(+4/3, 0)

(Ordinance Annexed Table 14, Item 2)

3.13.2 Continual pilot (CP)

As with the scattered pilot discussed in Section 3.13.1, CP is a BPSK signal modulated in accordance with the carrier position (carrier number within a segment) into which it is to be inserted, and also in accordance with the W_i value. The correspondence between W_i and the modulating signal is the same as that shown in Table 3-17. Note that the phase angle of CP determined with respect to carrier position is constant in every symbol.

3.13.3 TMCC

TMCC is transmitted by means of the DBPSK signal modulated in accordance with the information shown in Section 3.14. The reference for differential modulation B_0 is stipulated by Wi shown in Section 3.13.1. After differential coding, the TMCC modulating signal takes signal points (+4/3, 0) and (-4/3, 0) for information 0 and 1, respectively.

Information B'_0 to B'_{203} available following differential coding is stipulated in relation to information B_0 to B_{203} prior to differential coding, as follows:

$B'_0 = W_i$ (reference for differential modulation)

$B'_k = B'_{k-1} \oplus B_k$ (k = 1, 203, $\oplus$ represents EXCLUSIVE OR)

3.13.4 AC (Auxiliary Channel)

AC is a channel designed to convey additional information on broadcasting. The additional information on broadcasting refers to additional information on modulating signal-transmission control or information on seismic motion warning.

AC is transmitted by means of modulating the pilot carrier of a type similar to CP through DBPSK, and its reference for differential modulation is provided at the top frame symbol, and takes the signal point with its value corresponding to Wi stipulated in Section 3.13.1.

The AC modulating signal takes signal points (+4/3, 0) and (-4/3, 0) for information 0 and 1, respectively, available following differential coding. If there is no additional information on broadcasting, information 1 is inserted as stuffing bits.

ARIB STD-B31

Two channels are available as ACs: AC1 channel with which the same carrier position is employed for all segments, regardless of which modulation scheme is used; and AC2 channel, which is provided in the differential modulation's segments.

Table 3-18 shows examples of the transmission capacity per segment. Note that the transmission capacity for all television channels varies depending on the segment configuration.

Table 3-18: Examples of Transmission Capacities for AC Carriers (Mode 1, Guard Interval Ratio of 1/8)

Type	Coherent modulation's segment		Differential modulation's segment	
	1 carrier	13 carriers	1 carrier	13 carriers
AC1	7.0 (kbps)	91.3 (kbps)	7.0 (kbps)	91.3 (kbps)
AC2	—	—	14.0 (kbps)	182.5 (kbps)

(Without error-correction coding)

ARIB STD-B31

3.14 Transmission spectrum configuration

Fig. 3-32 stipulates the arrangement of OFDM segments. Segment No. 0 must be positioned at the center of the entire band, with successively numbered segments placed alternately above and below that segment.

For hierarchical transmission, segments of the differential modulation must be assigned alternately above and below segment No. 0, in ascending order of segment number, with segments of the coherent modulation assigned alternately above and below segments of the differential modulation.

("Partial-reception portion," "Differential modulation portion," and "Coherent modulation portion" in the figure are merely examples of segment usage.)

Note also that, for hierarchical transmission, the segment position assigned to partial reception must be always No. 0.

To make up the entire transmission spectrum, a continuous carrier with its phase stipulated by W_i is provided at the right-hand end of the band. The modulating signal used for the rightmost carrier is shown in Table 3-19.

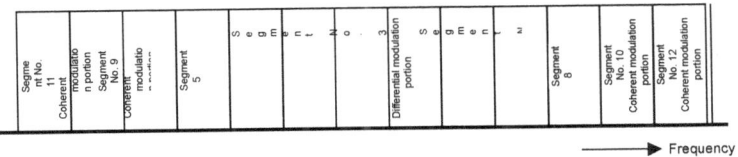

Fig. 3-32: OFDM-Segment Numbers on the Transmission Spectrum and Example of Usage

(Ordinance Annexed Table 17)

Table 3-19: Modulating Signal for the Rightmost Continuous Carrier

Mode	Modulating-signal amplitude (I, Q)
Mode 1	(-4/3, 0)
Mode 2	(+4/3, 0)
Mode 3	(+4/3, 0)

(Ordinance Annexed Table 14, Item 3)

ARIB STD-B31

The continuous carrier at the uppermost frequency of the television band is a pilot carrier required for demodulation when the adjacent segment is a synchronous modulation. This carrier is always provided with ISDB-T.

The partial-reception segment must be assigned to No. 0 in order to ensure easy tuning by the receiver.

3.14.1 RF-signal format

The signal format in the RF band is stipulated as follows:

Definition

- k: Carrier number that is successive across the entire band, with number 0 assigned to carrier 0 of segment 11
- n: Symbol number
- K: Carrier total count (Mode 1: 1405; Mode 2: 2809; Mode 3: 5617)
- T_s: Time duration of OFDM Symbol
- T_g: Time duration of guard-interval
- T_u: Time duration of useful part of a symbol
- f_c: RF-signal center frequency
- K_c: Carrier number corresponding to the RF-signal center frequency (Mode 1: 702; Mode 2: 1404; Mode 3: 2808)
- $c(n,k)$: Complex signal-point vector corresponding to symbol number n and carrier number k
- $s(t)$: RF signal

$$s(t) = \mathrm{Re}\left\{ e^{j 2\pi f_c t} \sum_{n=0}^{\infty} \sum_{k=0}^{K-1} c(n,k) \Psi(n,k,t) \right\}$$

Provided

$$\Psi(n,k,t) = \begin{cases} e^{j 2\pi \frac{k - K_c}{T_u}(t - T_g - nT_s)} & nT_s \le t < (n+1)T_s \\ 0 & t < nT_s,\ (n+1)T_s \le t \end{cases}$$

Note that the center frequency for digital terrestrial television broadcasting is stipulated by the RF frequency corresponding to Kc.

(Ordinance Annexed Table 16)

ARIB STD-B31

3.14.2 Insertion of a guard interval

A guard interval, the latter part of the IFFT (Inverse Fast Fourier Transform) data output for the specified duration, is added without any modification to the beginning of the effective symbol. This operation is shown in Fig. 3-33.

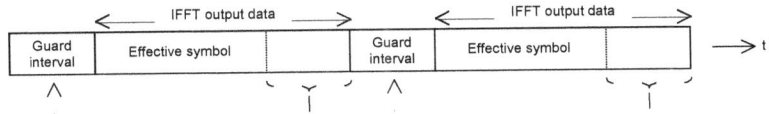

Fig. 3-33: Insertion of a Guard Interval

(Ordinance Annexed Table 5)

3.15 TMCC signal (Transmission and Multiplexing Configuration Control)

The information coding scheme and transmission system for the transmission and multiplexing configuration control signal (TMCC signal) are stipulated in this section.

3.15.1 Overview

The TMCC signal is used to convey information on how the receiver is to perform demodulation of information such as the hierarchical configuration and the OFDM-segment transmission parameters. The TMCC signal is transmitted by means of the TMCC carrier stipulated in Section 3.13.

3.15.2 Assignment of TMCC carrier bits

Table 3-20 shows the assignment of 204 TMCC carrier bits B_0 to B_{203}.

Table 3-20: Bit Assignment

B_0	Reference signal for differential demodulation of TMCC symbols
$B_1 - B_{16}$	Synchronizing signal (w0 = 0011010111101110, w1 = 1100101000010001)
$B_{17} - B_{19}$	Segment type identification (differential: 111; coherent: 000)
$B_{20} - B_{121}$	TMCC information (102 bits)
$B_{122} - B_{203}$	Parity bit

(Ordinance Annexed Table 11)

ARIB STD-B31

3.15.3 References signal for demodulation of TMCC symbols

The reference amplitude and phase of reference signal for demodulation of TMCC symbols is given by W_i in Table 3-17.

(Ordinance Annexed Table 11, Note 1)

3.15.4 Synchronizing signal

The synchronizing signal consists of a 16-bit word and takes one of two forms: one with w0 = 0011010111101110 and the other with w1 = 1100101000010001 obtained by inverting each bit of w0. One of w0 and w1 is transmitted alternately for each frame. The following shows an example of synchronizing signal transmission:

Table 3-21: Example of Synchronizing Signal

Frame No.	Synchronizing signal
1	0011010111101110
2	1100101000010001
3	0011010111101110
4	1100101000010001
:	:

Note: Frame numbers are assigned for convenience of description.

(Ordinance Annexed Table 11, Note 2)

[Description]

A synchronizing signal is designed to indicate frame start and use of for establishment of synchronization between transmission and reception of a TMCC signal and OFDM frame. To prevent false synchronization lock caused by the TMCC-information bit pattern matching that of the synchronizing signal, the polarity of the synchronizing signal is inverted every frame. Because TMCC information itself is not inverted every frame, it is possible to prevent false synchronization lock by means of inversion of the synchronizing-signal polarity.

3.15.5 Segment type identification

This signal is used to determine whether a segment is a differential or coherent modulation and consists of a 3-bit word. "111" and "000" are assigned to this signal for a differential and coherent modulation, respectively.

(Ordinance Annexed Table 11, Note 3)

[Description]

The number of TMCC carriers varies depending on the segment format. There is only one TMCC carrier if the partial-reception segment belongs to one of the synchronous modulations. Even in this case, to ensure reliable decoding, three bits are assigned to the identification signal such that the code-to-code distance becomes maximal when these bits are inverted.

3.15.6 TMCC information

TMCC information assists the receiver in demodulating and decoding various information including the system identification, the indicator of transmission-parameter switching, the startup control signal (the start flag for emergency-alarm broadcasting), the current information, the next information, etc.

The current information represents the current hierarchical configuration and transmission parameters, while the next information includes the transmission parameters following configuration switching. Prior to the countdown for switching (see Section 3.15.6.2), the next information can be specified or changed at the desired time. However, no changes can be made during countdown.

Tables 3-22 and 3-23 show the TMCC-information bit assignment and the transmission parameters included in current and next information, respectively.

The phase-shift-correction value for connected segment transmission is control information for digital terrestrial sound broadcasting (ISDB-T_{SB}) that uses the same transmission system as ISDB-T.

Of the 102 bits of TMCC information, 90 bits have been defined as of today. The remaining 12 bits are reserved for future expansion. For operation, all the reserved bits are stuffed with "1"s.

Table 3-22: TMCC Information

Bit assignment	Description		Remarks
$B_{20} - B_{21}$	System identification		See Table 3-24.
$B_{22} - B_{25}$	Indicator of transmission-parameter switching		See Table 3-25.
B_{26}	Startup control signal (Start flag for emergency-alarm broadcasting)		See Table 3-26.
B_{27}	Current information	Partial-reception flag	See Table 3-27.
$B_{28} - B_{40}$		Transmission-parameter information for hierarchical layer A	See Table 3-23.
$B_{41} - B_{53}$		Transmission-parameter information for hierarchical layer B	
$B_{54} - B_{66}$		Transmission-parameter information for hierarchical layer C	
B_{67}	Next information	Partial-reception flag	See Table 3-27.
$B_{68} - B_{80}$		Transmission-parameter information for hierarchical layer A	See Table 3-23.
$B_{81} - B_{93}$		Transmission-parameter information for hierarchical layer B	
$B_{94} - B_{106}$		Transmission-parameter information for hierarchical layer C	
$B_{107} - B_{109}$	Phase-shift-correction value for connected segment transmission (Note)		1 for all bits
$B_{110} - B_{121}$	Reserved		1 for all bits

Note: Used for digital terrestrial sound broadcasting or terrestrial multimedia broadcasting.

(Notification No. 304, Annexed Table 1)

ARIB STD-B31

Table 3-23: Contents of Transmission-Parameter Information

Description	Number of bits	Remarks
Carrier modulation mapping scheme	3	See Table 3-28.
Convolutional-coding rate	3	See Table 3-29.
Time interleaving length	3	See Table 3-30.
Number of segments	4	See Table 3-31.

(Notification No. 304, Annexed Table 1, Annexed Statement 5)

3.15.6.1 System identification

Two bits are assigned to the signal provided for system identification purposes. "00" is for digital terrestrial television broadcasting system and "01" is for digital terrestrial sound broadcasting system, respectively. The remaining values are reserved. Table 3-24 shows the contents of the system identification bits.

Table 3-24: System Identification

$B_{20} - B_{21}$	Meaning
00	Digital terrestrial television broadcasting system
01	Digital terrestrial sound broadcasting system
10, 11	Reserved

(Notification No. 304, Annexed Table 1, Annexed Statement 1)

ARIB STD-B31

3.15.6.2 Indicator of transmission-parameter switching

To switch between sets of transmission parameters, the contents of the indicator of transmission-parameter switching are counted down in order to inform the receiver of transmission-parameter switching and adjust the timing accordingly. These indicator bits are normally set to "1111." However, when it is necessary to switch parameters, the countdown starts 15 frames prior to switching, thus decrementing the contents of these bits by 1 every frame. Note that when the contents reach "0000," they must be set back to "1111."

Switching must be performed in synchronization with the next frame that outputs "0000." That is, a new set of transmission parameters apply, starting with the frame with which the contents of the bits are set back to "1111." Table 3-25 shows the meaning of each count of the indicator of transmission-parameter switching.

Table 3-25: Indicator of Transmission-Parameter Switching

$B_{22} - B_{25}$	Meaning
1111	Normal value
1110	15 frames prior to switching
1101	14 frames prior to switching
1100	13 frames prior to switching
:	:
0010	3 frames prior to switching
0001	2 frames prior to switching
0000	1 frame prior to switching

(Notification No. 304, Annexed Table 1, Annexed Statement 2)

[Description]

When switching any of the transmission parameters and flags contained in the current information and the next information in Table 3-22 (partial-reception flag, carrier modulation scheme, convolutional-coding rate, time interleaving length, and the number of segments), the contents of the 4-bit indicator of transmission parameter switching shown in Table 3-25 are counted down. When switching only the startup control signal (the start flag for emergency-alarm broadcasting), the contents of the indicator for transmission parameter switching are not counted down.

ARIB STD-B31

3.15.6.3 Startup control signal (Start flag for emergency-alarm broadcasting)

The content of the startup control signal must be "1" and "0" when the receiver startup is and is not controlled, respectively. Table 3-26 shows the meaning of the startup control signal (start flag for emergency-alarm broadcasting) in each case.

Table 3-26: Startup Control Signal (Start Flag for Emergency-Alarm Broadcasting)

B_{26}	Meaning
0	No startup control
1	Startup control available (When an emergency-alarm signal is transmitted)

(Notification No. 304, Annexed Table 1, Annexed Statement 3)

3.15.6.4 Partial-reception flag

The content of the partial-reception flag must be "1" and "0" when the segment at the center of the transmission band is and is not used for partial reception, respectively. Table 3-27 shows the meaning of the flag content in each case.

When segment No .0 is used for partial reception, hierarchical layer A in Table 3-22 must be assigned to that segment. Note that the content of this flag is set to "1" if there is no next information.

Table 3-27: Partial-Reception Flag

B_{27}/B_{67}	Meaning
0	No partial reception
1	Partial reception available

(Notification No. 304, Annexed Table 1, Annexed Statement 4)

ARIB STD-B31

3.15.6.5 Carrier modulation mapping scheme

Table 3-28 shows the meanings of carrier modulation mapping scheme bits.

Note that the content of these bits is "111" for an unused hierarchical layer, or when there is no next information.

Table 3-28: Carrier Modulation Mapping Scheme

B_{28}–B_{30}/B_{41}–B_{43}/B_{54}–B_{56} B_{68}–B_{70}/B_{81}–B_{83}/B_{94}–B_{96}	Meaning
000	DQPSK
001	QPSK
010	16QAM
011	64QAM
100–110	Reserved
111	Unused hierarchical layer

(Notification No. 304, Annexed Table 1, Annexed Statement 6)

With a TMCC signal, the meanings of all sets of bit contents are the same for all three hierarchical layers. When signals of two hierarchical layers or fewer are transmitted, the content of these bits for vacant hierarchical layer(s) must be "111". Note also that the content of these bits must be "111" if there is no next information, as when broadcasting ends.

3.15.6.6 Convolutional-coding rate

Table 3-29 shows the meanings of contents of convolutional-coding-rate bits.

Note that the content of these bits is "111" for an unused hierarchical layer or when there is no next information.

Table 3-29: Convolutional-Coding Rate

B_{31}–B_{33}/B_{44}–B_{46}/B_{57}–B_{59} B_{71}–B_{73}/B_{84}–B_{86}/B_{97}–B_{99}	Meaning
000	1/2
001	2/3
010	3/4
011	5/6
100	7/8
101–110	Reserved
111	Unused hierarchical layer

(Notification No. 304, Annexed Table 1, Annexed Statement 7)

3.15.6.7 Time interleaving length

Table 3-30 shows the meanings of contents of time-interleaving-length bits. This information represents time interleaving length I shown in Table 3-12.

Note that the content of these bits is "111" for an unused hierarchical layer or when there is no next information.

Table 3-30: Time Interleaving Length

B_{34}–B_{36}/B_{47}–B_{49}/B_{60}–B_{62} B_{74}–B_{76}/B_{87}–B_{89}/B_{100}–B_{102}	Meaning (value I)
000	0 (Mode 1), 0 (Mode 2), 0 (Mode 3)
001	4 (Mode 1), 2 (Mode 2), 1 (Mode 3)
010	8 (Mode 1), 4 (Mode 2), 2 (Mode 3)
011	16 (Mode 1), 8 (Mode 2), 4 (Mode 3)
100	Not used
101–110	Reserved
111	Unused hierarchical layer

(Notification No. 304, Annexed Table 1, Annexed Statement 8)

Note also that "100" in Table 3-30 are assigned to the use of digital terrestrial sound broadcasting system and are not used in this system.

3.15.6.8 Number of segments

Table 3-31 shows 4-bit binary code corresponding to the number of segments for each hierarchical layer. Note that the 4-bit binary code is "1111" for an unused hierarchical layer or when there is no next information.

Table 3-31: Number of Segments

B_{37}–B_{40}/B_{50}–B_{53}/B_{63}–B_{66} B_{77}–B_{80}/B_{90}–B_{93}/B_{103}–B_{106}	Meaning
0000	Reserved
0001	1 segment
0010	2 segments
0011	3 segments
0100	4 segments
0101	5 segments
0110	6 segments
0111	7 segments
1000	8 segments
1001	9 segments
1010	10 segments
1011	11 segments
1100	12 segments
1101	13 segments
1110	Reserved
1111	Unused hierarchical layer

(Notification No. 304, Annexed Table 1, Annexed Statement 9)

3.15.6.9 Channel-coding scheme

B_{20} to B_{121} of TMCC information are error-correction coded by means of the shortened code (184,102) of the difference-set cyclic code (273,191). The following shows the generating polynomial of the (273,191) code:

$$g(x) = x^{82} + x^{77} + x^{76} + x^{71} + x^{67} + x^{66} + x^{56} + x^{52} + x^{48} + x^{40} + x^{36} + x^{34} + x^{24} + x^{22} + x^{18} + x^{10} + x^4 + 1$$

(Ordinance Annexed Table 12, Item 2)

[Description]

Because TMCC information is used to specify transmission parameters and control the receiver operation, it must be transmitted with higher reliability than program signals. Due to the difficulties involved with a receiver using the same concatenated-code decoding circuit for TMCC information and program signals, and in consideration of the fact that the use of block code is advantageous due to its shorter processing time, the shortened code (184,102) of the difference-set cyclic code (273,191) is used as the error-correction code for TMCC information. Note also that the same TMCC signals are transmitted by means of multiple carriers. Therefore, it is possible to reduce the required C/N by simply adding these signals, thus ensuring improved reception performance. These error-correction techniques and the addition process make it possible to receive TMCC signals at a lower C/N than for program signals.

ARIB STD-B31

Note also that, by excluding the synchronizing signal and segment type identification from the group of bits checked for errors, the contents of all TMCC carrier bits are the same, which makes it possible to determine the content of each bit, including a parity bit, by determining the contents of the majority of the carriers.

3.15.6.10　Modulation scheme

TMCC carriers must be modulated through DBPSK (see Section 3.13.3).

3.16　AC (Auxiliary Channel) signals

This section stipulates the transmission system for AC signals.

3.16.1　Overview

AC signals are transmitted using the AC carriers stipulated in Section 3.13.

"AC signal" refers to an additional information signal on broadcasting.

The additional information on broadcasting means the additional information on the transmission control of modulating wave or the seismic motion warning (Earthquake Early Warning) information.

The seismic motion warning information is transmitted using the AC carriers of segment No. 0.

(Ordinance Article 22)

It is possible to transmit the additional information on the transmission control of modulating wave using arbitrary AC carriers.

3.16.2　AC signal bit assignment

Table 3-32 shows the bit assignment of B_0 to B_{203} for 204-bit AC signal arranged on segment No. 0.

Table 3-32: AC Signal Bit Assignment

B_0	Reference signal for demodulation of AC symbols
B_1–B_3	Configuration identification
B_4–B_{203}	Additional information on the transmission control of modulating wave or seismic motion warning information

(Ordinance Annexed Table 18)

ARIB STD-B31

3.16.3 Reference signal for demodulation of AC symbols

The reference amplitude and phase reference signal for demodulating of AC symbols is given by Wi in Table 3-17.

(Ordinance Annexed Table 18, Note 1)

3.16.4 Configuration identification

To identify the configuration of an AC signal, three bits are assigned as configuration identification. Table 3-33 shows the meanings of bit assignment for configuration identification.

Table 3-33: Configuration Identification

$B_1 - B_3$	Meaning
000	Transmits the additional information on the transmission control of modulating wave
010	
011	
100	
101	
111	
001	Transmits the seismic motion warning information
110	

(Ordinance Annexed Table 18, Note 2)

"001" and "110" representing the transmission of seismic motion warning information must be the same codes as those of the top three bits ($B_1 - B_3$) of a TMCC synchronizing signal, and their outputs are transmitted alternatively to each frame at the same timing as the TMCC signal.

3.16.5 Additional information on the transmission control of modulating waves

In consideration of versatile usage possibilities, no bit assignment is stipulated to the transmission means for the additional information on the transmission control of modulating waves.

ARIB STD-B31

3.16.6 Seismic motion warning information

Table 3-34 shows the bit assignment for seismic motion warning information.

Table 3-34: Seismic Motion Warning Information

Bit assignment	Explanation	Remarks
$B_4 - B_{16}$	Synchronizing signal	Refer to Table 3-35.
$B_{17} - B_{18}$	Start/ending flag	Refer to Table 3-36.
$B_{19} - B_{20}$	Update flag	
$B_{21} - B_{23}$	Signal identification	Refer to Table 3-37.
$B_{24} - B_{111}$	Detailed seismic motion warning information	Refer to Table 3-38.
$B_{112} - B_{121}$	CRC	Refer to Fig. 3-35.
$B_{122} - B_{203}$	Parity bit	

(Notification No. 306)

The seismic motion warning information is transmitted by the AC carriers of the segment No. 0. Note that the seismic motion warning information must be the same in all AC carriers within the segment No. 0.

[Description]

Letting the seismic motion warning information be the same in all AC carriers within the segment No. 0 enables the seismic motion warning information transmitted by different AC carriers to be added in analog on the receiver side, thus making reception possible even in lower CN ratios.

ARIB STD-B31

3.16.6.1 Synchronizing signal

When transmitting the seismic motion warning information, 13 bits are assigned as a synchronizing signal. The value identical to 13 bits (B_4–B_{16}) excluding the top three bits of the TMCC synchronizing signal must be taken.

Table 3-35: Example of Synchronizing Signal Transmission

Frame number	Synchronizing signal
1	1010111101110
2	0101000010001
3	1010111101110
4	0101000010001
:	:

Note: Frame numbers are assigned for the convenience of explanation.
(Notification No. 306, Note 3)

The code with the configuration identification and synchronizing signal combined must be the synchronizing word (w0=0011010111101110, w1=1100101000010001) with 16 bits identical to that for the TMCC synchronizing signal, and w0 and w1 are fed alternatively every frame at the same timing as the TMCC synchronizing signal.

[Description]
As it is possible to add TMCC and AC signal in analog, the reception sensibility for frame synchronization in receivers can be enhanced.

3.16.6.2 Start and ending flag

Two bits are assigned as the start and ending flag of seismic motion warning information. Table 3-36 shows the meanings of the start and ending flag bits.

Table 3-36: Start and Ending Flag

B_{17} – B_{18}	Meaning
00	Detailed seismic motion warning information available[Note]
11	Detailed seismic motion warning information not available
10, 01	Not used

Note: Includes a test signal for detailed seismic motion warning information
(Notification No. 306, Note 4)

ARIB STD-B31

When initiating to feed the seismic motion warning information, the start and ending flags are changed from "11" to "00." Furthermore, when completing to feed the seismic motion warning information, the start and ending flags are changed from "00" to "11."

[Description]
When there is no additional information on broadcasting, all bits of the AC signal are modulated to "1" as stipulated in Section 3.13.4. Therefore, the start and ending flags when indicating the detailed seismic motion warning information or its test signals must be set to "00." In addition, in order to enhance the reliability in start and ending flags, an inverse signal with its inter-code spacings set to the maximum must be employed using two bits for the start and ending flags. To ensure reliability in start and ending flags, "10" and "01" must not be used. The start and ending flags can be used as the startup signal of receivers.

3.16.6.3 Update flag

An update flag must be incremented by one every time there is a change in the content of a series of the detailed seismic motion warning information to be transmitted when the start and ending flags are "00," and its starting value must be set to "00" while it must return to "00" after "11." When the start and ending flag is "11," the update flag must be set to "11."

(Notification No. 306, Note 5)

[Description]
While the value of start and ending flags of the seismic motion warning information is maintained in the state of "00," and when the signal identification (B_{21}–B_{23}) or the content of the seismic motion warning information (B_{56}–B_{111}) shown in Table 3-38 is updated, the value of the update flag must be incremented by one as indicated in Fig. 3-34, and the fact that the signal identification or the seismic motion information is updated must be notified to receivers.

An example of the update flag outputs is shown in Fig. 3-34.

Start/ending flag	"11"	"00"					"11"
Update flag	"11"	"00"	"01"	"10"	"11"	"00"	"11"
Signal identification	"111"	"000"					"111"
Contents of seismic-motion information	None	No. 1 report	No. 2 report	No. 3 report	No. 4 report	No. 5 report	None

Fig. 3-34: Example of Update Flag Output

Note: No. 1 report, No. 2 report, etc., show the state of changes in the signal identification indicated in Table 3-37 or the content of seismic motion information indicated in Table 3-38. There must be no change in the value of the update flag even if the changes occur in the current time or the page classification indicated in Table 3-38.

ARIB STD-B31

Note that a variety of patterns are conceivable in the output configurations and the updating of contents, and the details of specific output methods and update flag operation methods are stipulated separately.

3.16.6.4 Signal identification

The signal identification of seismic motion warning information is a signal used to identify the types of the detailed seismic motion warning information. The meanings of signal identification bit values must be set as shown in Table 3-37.

Table 3-37: Signal Identification

B_{21}–B_{23}	Meaning
000	Detailed seismic motion warning information (with relevant area)(Note 1)
001	Detailed seismic motion warning information (without relevant area)(Note 2)
010	Test signal for detailed seismic motion warning information (with relevant area)(Note 1)
011	Test signal for detailed seismic motion warning information (without relevant area)(Note 2)
100	Reserved
101	
110	
111	No detailed seismic motion warning information available

Note 1: This means that there are target areas for a seismic motion warning within broadcasting areas.
Note 2: This means that there are no target areas for a seismic motion warning within broadcasting areas.
(Notification No. 306, Note 6, Annexed Table 1)

When the start and ending flags are "00" and "11," the signal identification "000"/"001"/"010"/"011" and "111" are fed, respectively.

The test signal for the detailed seismic motion warning information (with/without relevant areas) and the detailed seismic motion warning information (with/without relevant areas) are not fed simultaneously.

[Description]
As shown in Table 3-40, it is possible to feed a maximum of two pieces of seismic motion warning information, but it is not allowed to feed a test signal and a real signal simultaneously.

In addition, when the signal identification feeds the seismic motion information with relevant area and without

Relevant area simultaneously, either information is fed as the seismic motion information with relevant area. By doing so, it is possible to promptly notify receivers of at least one piece of seismic motion information as the information with the relevant area.

ARIB STD-B31

3.16.6.5 Detailed seismic motion warning information

The bit assignment for the detailed seismic motion warning information is stipulated on a signal identification basis.

3.16.6.5.1 Detailed seismic motion warning information for Signal Identification "000"/"001"/"010"/"011"

Table 3-38 shows the bit assignment of detailed seismic motion warning information for the signal identification "000"/"001"/"010"/"011" (when the signal identification represents the detailed seismic motion warning information or the test signal for detailed seismic motion warning information).

Table 3-38: Detailed Seismic Motion Warning Information for Signal Identification "000"/"001"/"010"/"011"

Bit assignment		Explanation
$B_{24} - B_{54}$	Current time	The information of current time information when the seismic motion warning information is fed.
B_{55}	Page classification	The code used to identify the types of information on seismic-motion, which is the target of seismic motion warning
$B_{56} - B_{111}$	Seismic motion information	When the value of page classification (B_{55}) is "0": refer to Table 3-39 "1": refer to Table 3-40

(Notification No. 306, Annexed Table 2)

When the seismic motion information is not fed, the page classification must be "0" and all of the seismic motion information must be "1."

The current time must be expressed by a binary number system with its elapsed seconds starting from the reference year, month, day, hour, minute, and second separately defined, and low 31 bits are assigned by MSB first.

[Description]
When transmitting the seismic motion warning information, checking the time of receivers against the output time information enables us to confirm the reliability of the seismic motion warning information received in the receivers compatible with the automated starting equipped with a time adjustment function through TOT (Time Offset Table), communication lines, etc.

Note that, in the seismic motion information, the bit assignment for the information to be transmitted varies depending on the codes of page classification. It is possible for receivers to know which information is transmitted by the confirmation of page classifications. When the page classification is "0," the information for the target area of the seismic motion warning is transmitted as shown in Table 3-39. When the page classification is "1," the information for the epicenter of the seismic motion warning is transmitted as shown in Table 3-40. However, both of the page classifications "0" and "1" seismic motion information are not necessarily transmitted.

ARIB STD-B31

(1) Seismic motion information for page classification "0"
If the page classification is "0," this classification must mean the information indicative of the seismic motion warning target area. Table 3-39 shows the bit assignment to areas. The bit assigned to the areas including the seismic motion warning target areas must be "0," while the bit assigned to the areas not including the seismic motion warning target areas must be "1." Note that if the seismic motion information is not fed, the bit must be "1" in all areas.

Table 3-39: Seismic Motion Information for Page Classification "0"

Bit	Area	Bit	Area	Bit	Area
B_{56}	Hokkaido Center	B_{75}	Niigata Prefecture	B_{94}	Hiroshima Prefecture
B_{57}	Hokkaido South	B_{76}	Toyama Prefecture	B_{95}	Tokushima Prefecture
B_{58}	Hokkaido North	B_{77}	Ishikawa Prefecture	B_{96}	Kagawa Prefecture
B_{59}	Hokkaido East	B_{78}	Fukui Prefecture	B_{97}	Ehime Prefecture
B_{60}	Aomori Prefecture	B_{79}	Yamanashi Prefecture	B_{98}	Kochi Prefecture
B_{61}	Iwate Prefecture	B_{80}	Nagano Prefecture	B_{99}	Yamaguchi Prefecture
B_{62}	Miyagi Prefecture	B_{81}	Gifu Prefecture	B_{100}	Fukuoka Prefecture
B_{63}	Akita Prefecture	B_{82}	Shizuoka Prefecture	B_{101}	Saga Prefecture
B_{64}	Yamagata Prefecture	B_{83}	Aichi Prefecture	B_{102}	Nagasaki Prefecture
B_{65}	Fukushima Prefecture	B_{84}	Mie Prefecture	B_{103}	Kumamoto Prefecture
B_{66}	Ibaraki Prefecture	B_{85}	Shiga Prefecture	B_{104}	Oita Prefecture
B_{67}	Tochigi Prefecture	B_{86}	Kyoto Prefecture	B_{105}	Miyazaki Prefecture
B_{68}	Gunma Prefecture	B_{87}	Osaka Prefecture	B_{106}	Kagoshima
B_{69}	Saitama Prefecture	B_{88}	Hyogo Prefecture	B_{107}	Amami Islands
B_{70}	Chiba Prefecture	B_{89}	Nara Prefecture	B_{108}	Okinawa main islands
B_{71}	Tokyo	B_{90}	Wakayama Prefecture	B_{109}	Daito Island
B_{72}	Izu Islands	B_{91}	Tottori Prefecture	B_{110}	Miyako Island
B_{73}	Ogasawara	B_{92}	Shimane Prefecture	B_{111}	Yaeyama
B_{74}	Kanagawa Prefecture	B_{93}	Okayama Prefecture		

Note 1) Hokkaido Center refers to Akabira-shi, Ashibetsu-shi, Ishikari-shi, Iwamizawa-shi, Utashinai-shi, Eniwa-shi, Ebetsu-shi, Otaru-shi, Kitahiroshima-shi, Sapporo-shi, Sunagawa-shi, Takikawa-shi, Chitose-shi, Bibai-shi, Fukagawa-shi, Mikasa-shi and Yubari-shi, and areas within the jurisdiction of Ishikari, Shiribeshi, and Sorachi General Subprefectural Bureaus.
Note 2) Hokkaido South refers to Date-shi, Tomakomai-shi, Noboribetsu-shi, Hakodate-shi, Hokuto-shi and Muroran-shi, and areas within the jurisdiction of Iburi, Oshima, Hidaka, and Hiyama General Subprefectural Bureaus.
Note 3) Hokkaido North refers to Asahikawa-shi, Shibetsu-shi, Nayoro-shi, Furano-shi, Rumoi-shi and Wakkanai-shi, and areas within the jurisdiction of Kamikawa, Souya, and Rumoi General Subprefectural Bureaus.
Note 4) Hokkaido East refers to Abashiri-shi, Obihiro-shi, Kitami-shi, Kushiro-shi, Nemuro-shi and Monbetsu-shi, and areas within the jurisdiction of Okhotsk, Kushiro, Tokachi, and Nemuro General Subprefectural Bureaus.
Note 5) Tokyo refers to the Tokyo Metropolitan Area (excluding areas within the jurisdiction of the Oshima, Ogasawara, Hachijo Island, and Miyake Island Branch Offices).
Note 6) Izu Islands refers to areas within the jurisdiction of the Oshima, Hachijo Island, and Miyake Island Branch Offices (excluding Sumisuto Island, Torishima Island, and Bayonaise Rocks).
Note 7) Ogasawara refers to areas within the jurisdiction of the Ogasawara Islands Branch Office.

Note 8) Kagoshima refers to Kagoshima Prefecture (excluding Amami-shi and Oshima District).
Note 9) Amami Islands refers to Amami-shi and Oshima District.
Note 10) Okinawa main islands refers to Itoman-shi, Urazoe-shi, Uruma-shi, Okinawa-shi, Ginowan-shi, Tomigusuku-shi, Nago-shi, Naha-shi, Nanjo-shi, Kunigami District, Shimajiri District (excluding Kitadaito-mura and Minamidaito-mura), and Nakagami District.
Note 11) Daito Island refers to Shimajiri District (restricted to Kitadaito-mura and Minamidaito-mura).
Note 12) Miyako Island refers to Miyakojima-shi and Miyako District.
Note 13) Yaeyama refers to Ishigaki-shi and Yaeyama District.

(Notification No. 306, Annexed Table 2, Annexed Statement 1)

[Description]

When multiple seismic motion warnings are generated simultaneously (the total number is two at maximum), there may be the cases where the page classification "0" seismic motion information (area information) is fed with the first one and the second one being fed independently. In this case, the update flag is not updated when the output of seismic motion warning information (area information) is changed from the first one to the second one or from the second one to the first one.

ARIB STD-B31

(2) Seismic motion information for page classification "1"
Table 3-40 shows the seismic motion information for page classification "1."

Table 3-40: Seismic Motion Information for Page Classification "1"

Bit assignment		Explanation
B_{56}	Total amount of seismic motion information	This is used to identify the total number of the seismic motion information being transmitted. When the total number are 1 and 2, "0" and "1" must be used respectively.
B_{57}	Seismic motion information identification	This is used to identify the seismic motion information being transmitted.
$B_{58}-B_{66}$	Seismic motion warning identification(Note)	This is used to identify the seismic motion warning.
B_{67}	Information type	This is used for the identification of types of seismic motion warnings. "0" must be indicated when the seismic motion information shows that a seismic motion warning was issued, while "1" must be indicated when the information shows that the seismic motion warning was cancelled. Note that $B_{68}-B_{110}$ must all be "1" when the information shows that the seismic motion warning was cancelled.
B_{68}	Northern latitude and southern latitude flag	"0" and "1" indicate northern latitude and southern latitude, respectively.
$B_{69}-B_{78}$	Latitude information(Note)	This is the domain used to indicate the latitude of an epicenter, and the value shall be determined by 10 times the latitude, which is expressed using a binary system.
B_{79}	West longitude and east longitude flag	"0" and "1" indicate east latitude and west latitude, respectively.
$B_{80}-B_{90}$	Longitude information(Note)	This is the domain used to indicate the longitude of an epicenter, and the value shall be determined by 10 times the longitude, which is expressed using a binary system.
$B_{91}-B_{100}$	Depth information(Note)	This is used to indicate the depth of an epicenter. The value shall be the depth (km), which is expressed using a binary system.
$B_{101}-B_{110}$	Occurrence time(Note)	This is used to indicate the occurrence time of seismic motion.
B_{111}	Reserved	This must be "1."

Note: Numerical values must be expressed by a binary system and assigned by MSB first.
(Notification No. 306, Annexed Table 2, Annexed Statement 2)

The seismic motion information identification for B_{57} must be "0" if the seismic motion information being transmitted is the first one, while that must be "1" if the information is the second one.

The occurrence time is determined on the basis of the reference year, month, day, hour, minute, and second identical to the current time indicated in $B_{24}-B_{54}$, and the elapsed seconds from the reference time is expressed by a binary system in which low 10 bits are assigned by MSB first.

[Description]
For "seismic motion warning identification," nine bits are assigned to identify the seismic motion warning information when multiple seismic motion warnings are generated. When discriminating multiple seismic motion warning information based on the time (on the second time scale), the use of nine bits seismic motion warning identification allows the identification of the seismic motion warning information for the past eight minutes and 32 seconds.

ARIB STD-B31

A comparison between the current time of B_{24}–B_{54} and the occurrence time of B_{101}–B_{110} makes it possible to know the elapsed number of seconds from the occurrence of the seismic motion.

3.16.6.5.2 Detailed seismic motion warning information for signal identification "100"/"101"/"110"

This is used for future extension, and must be "1" in all cases.

3.16.6.5.3 Detailed seismic motion warning information for signal identification "111"(Note)

Table 3-41 shows the bit assignment for the detailed seismic motion warning information for the signal identification "111" (the case where the signal identification indicates "detailed seismic motion warning information is not available").

Table 3-41: Detailed Seismic Motion Warning Information for Signal Identification "111"

Bit assignment	Explanation	
B_{24}–B_{55}	Reserved	Must be "1" in all cases
B_{56}–B_{66}	Identification of broadcasting organizations	Code used to identify broadcasting organizations
B_{67}–B_{111}	Reserved	Must be "1" in all cases

(Notification No. 306, Annexed Table 3)

Note: When the start/ending flag is "11," the signal identification "111" is fed.

[Description]
Broadcasting company identification 11 bits are uniquely assigned to broadcasting organizations across the country. The broadcasting organizations that send the seismic motion warning information can be identified by this AC signal only.

3.16.6.6 CRC

CRC bits must be generated from B_{21}–B_{111} of the seismic motion warning information by using the generating polynomial shown in Fig. 3-35, and the initial value of each register of the circuit must be "0."

Generating polynomial: $g(x) = x^{10} + x^9 + x^5 + x^4 + x + 1$

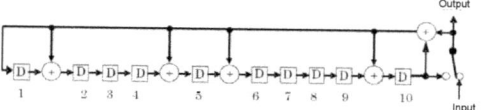

D : Represents an 1-bit delay element
⊕ : Represents an EXCLUSIVE-OR arithmetic element

Fig.: 3-35: CRC Generating Circuit

ARIB STD-B31

(Notification No. 306, Note 8)

[Description]
The information on detailed seismic motion warning information is important information and is required to have a high degree of reliability. Therefore, after decoding with the error-correction codes indicated in Section 3.16.6.7, the detection of errors by CRC shall be made possible.

3.16.6.7 Parity Bit

Parity bits shall be generated from B_{17}–B_{121} of the seismic motion warning information by the shortened (187,105) code of the (273,191) difference-set cyclic code. The generating polynomial of the (273,191) difference-set cyclic code shall be as follows.

$$\text{Generating polynomial: } g(x) = x^{82} + x^{77} + x^{76} + x^{71} + x^{67} + x^{66} + x^{56} + x^{52} + x^{48} + x^{40} + x^{36} + x^{34} + x^{24} + x^{22} + x^{18} + x^{10} + x^{4} + 1$$

(Notification No. 306, Note 9)

[Description]
The information on the seismic motion warning information is important information and is required to have a high degree of reliability. Therefore, the information is protected by the error-correction code using different-set cyclic code, as is the case with TMCC. Configuration identification and synchronizing signals shall be excluded from the error-correction, and the shortened (187,105) codes of the (273,191) difference-set cyclic codes shall be used.

3.16.7 Modulation scheme

The modulation of AC carriers shall be implemented through DBPSK. (See Section 3.13.4)

ARIB STD-B31

Chapter 4: Frequency Utilization Requirements

4.1 Frequency bandwidth and others

A frequency bandwidth of 5.7 MHz must be used for digital terrestrial television broadcasting. The carrier frequency must be the center frequency of the frequency bandwidth.

(Ordinance Article 19, Radio Equipment Regulations Annexed Table 2 No.1, No10-2(1))

[Description]

The frequency bandwidth must be 5.7 MHz when the OFDM carrier bandwidth is 5.572..MHz with 4-kHz spacings between carrier frequencies in Mode 1. This bandwidth must apply regardless of which mode is chosen, and has been selected to ensure that the bandwidth of 5.610 MHz has some margin to determine that each carrier of the uppermost and lowermost in the 5.572..MHz bandwidth includes 99% of energy.

The center frequency is the frequency of the carrier at the center, among an odd number of OFDM carriers.

4.2 Permissible transmission-frequency deviation

The permissible transmission-frequency deviation must be 1 Hz.

Note 1: Excluding those provided in Note 2, a deviation of 500 Hz is allowed if the Minister for Internal Affairs and Communications approves it on the grounds that it will not substantially hinder the efficient use of radio waves.

Note 2: Broadcasting is conducted only by means of relaying the broadcasting programs of other broadcasting stations.
(a) Power applied to antenna transmission lines more than 0.5W: 3kHz
(b) Power applied to antenna transmission lines more than 0.05W and 0.5W or less: 10kHz
(c) Power applied to antenna transmission lines 0.05W or less: 20kHz (Notification No.68)

Note 3: Other than as provided in the above, in two or more broadcasting stations configured as a single frequency network which means a group of stations in the case of transmitting using radio waves with the same frequency and the same broadcasting programs as those of other stations in the same broadcasting service area ("Broadcasting Service Area" means such Broadcasting Service Area as prescribed in Article 2-2, paragraph (2), item (ii) of the Broadcast Act [Act No.132 of 1950]), the relative permissible transmission-frequency deviation between those two or more broadcasting stations should be within 10Hz.

(Radio Equipment Regulations Annexed Table 1, 7-10, Note 21, Note 49.
Notification No.68)

4.3 IFFT sampling frequency and permissible deviation

The IFFT sampling frequency for use with OFDM for digital terrestrial television broadcasting must be as follows:

fs = 512/63 MHz (8.126984 MHz)

Note also that the permissible deviation must be ±0.3 ppm.

ARIB STD-B31

(Ordinance Article 20-3)

[Description]
This deviation has been determined to ensure that the frequency deviation (caused by IFFT sample frequency error) of the carrier at each end of the bandwidths is 1 Hz or less.

4.4 Transmission-spectrum mask

The transmission-spectrum limit mask is specified as shown below in Fig. 4-1. The related break points for the spectrum mask are listed in Table 4-1.

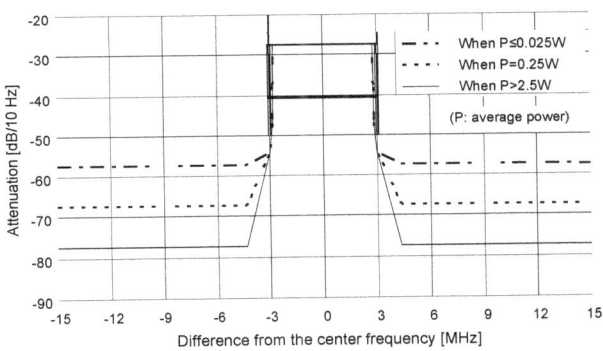

Fig. 4-1: Transmission-spectrum limit mask for digital terrestrial television broadcasting

Table 4-1: Breakpoints for transmission-spectrum mask

Difference from the center frequency (MHz)	Attenuation relative to average power P (dB/10 kHz)	Type of stipulation
±2.79	-27.4	Upper limit
±2.86	-47.4	Upper limit
±3.00	-54.4	Upper limit
±4.36	-77.4[*1*2]	Upper limit

*1 If the frequency corresponding to an adjacent channel number (the channel number between 13 and 62 that is one number different from the channel number of the television broadcasting corresponding to the allocated frequency in the Plan for the Available Frequencies Allocated to Broadcasting stipulated in item (ii) of paragraph (2) of Article 7 of the Radio Law) is not used for standard television broadcasting (excluding digital broadcasting and restricted to the effective radiation power that is less than ten times the own effective radiation power) within the own broadcasting area, the following specifications should be applied:
·(73.4+10logP) dB/10 kHz in the case of radio equipment whose transmission power is

ARIB STD-B31

more than 0.25 W and equal to or less than 2.5 W;
-67.4 dB/10 kHz in the case of radio equipment whose transmission power (excluding the case of *2) is 0.25 W or less.
*2 If the frequency corresponding to an adjacent channel number is not used for standard television broadcasting (excluding digital broadcasting) within one's own broadcasting area, the following specifications should be applied:
-(73.4+10logP) dB/10kHz in the case of radio equipment whose transmission power is more than 0.025W and less than 0.25W;
-57.4 dB/10kHz in the case of radio equipment whose transmission power is 0.025W or less.

Note: For the adjacent channels of radio equipment that amplifies multiple waves together, an attenuation of -27.4 dB/10 kHz relative to average power P can be set as the upper limit regardless of the above table.

(Radio Equipment Regulations Annexed Figure 4-8-8)

The above specifications are accompanied with transitional measures (supplementary provisions to the Radio Equipment Regulations ··Ministerial Ordinance No. 119 issued by the Ministry of Internal Affairs and Communications in 2005).

[Description]
If an adjacent channel is used for standard television broadcasting (excluding digital broadcasting and restricted to the effective radiation power that is less than ten times the own effective radiation power) within the own broadcasting area, the solid line of Fig. 4-1 (attenuation relative to average power P is -77.4 dB/10 kHz at the frequencies of +/-4.36 MHz from the center frequency) should be applied regardless of the value of P.

4.5 Maximum permitted power level of spurious emission or unwanted emission

The power supplied to antenna transmission line	Maximum permitted power level of spurious emission in out-of-band domain	Maximum permitted power level of unwanted emission in spurious domain
Above 25 W	20 mW or less, and 60 dB* lower than the average power of the fundamental frequency	12 mW or less, and 60 dB lower than the average power of the fundamental frequency
Above 1 W, and 25 W or less	25 µW or less	25 µW or less
1 W or less	100 µW or less	

* For the maximum permitted power level of spurious emission in the out-of-band region for transmission equipment whose transmission power exceeds 8 kW, the values specified in Section 4.4 shall be used.

(Radio Equipment Regulations Annexed Table 3, Item 5(6))

The above specifications are accompanied with transitional measures (supplementary provisions to the Radio Equipment Regulations··Ministerial Ordinance No. 119 issued by the Ministry of Internal Affairs and Communications in 2005).

ARIB STD-B31

Annex A: Transmission Parameters and Data Rates for 7MHz and 8MHz Bandwidth Systems

The ISDB-T system can be extended to the systems with 7MHz or 8MHz bandwidth by increasing the signal bandwidth or the carrier spacings of the 6MHz bandwidth system by 7/6 or 8/6 times, respectively. When extended this way, the FFT sampling frequency is also increased by 7/6 or 8/6 times, while this leads to a decrease in the effective symbol length by 6/7 or 6/8 times, respectively. Note that the broadcasting TS transmission clock is four times the FFT sampling clock, and the same shall be applied to 7MHz and 8MHz bandwidth systems.

Table A·1 through Table A·4 show OFDM segment parameters, transmission signal parameters, data rates per a segment, and total data rates for all 13 segments of the 7MHz bandwidth system. Note that in a similar way, Table A·5 through Table A·8 show parameters and data rates of the 8MHz bandwidth system.

ARIB STD-B31

Table A-1: OFDM-Segment Parameters (7MHz Bandwidth System)

Mode		Mode 1		Mode 2		Mode 3	
Segment bandwidth (Bws)		7000/14 = 500 kHz					
Spacings between carrier frequencies (Cs)		Bws/108 = 4.629... kHz		Bws/216 = 2.314... kHz		Bws/432 = 1.157... kHz	
Number of carriers	Total count	108	108	216	216	432	432
	Data	96	96	192	192	384	384
	SP[*1]	9	0	18	0	36	0
	CP[*1]	0	1	0	1	0	1
	TMCC[*2]	1	5	2	10	4	20
	AC1[*3]	2	2	4	4	8	8
	AC2[*3]	0	4	0	9	0	19
Carrier modulation scheme		QPSK 16QAM 64QAM	DQPSK	QPSK 16QAM 64QAM	DQPSK	QPSK 16QAM 64QAM	DQPSK
Symbols per frame		204					
Effective symbol length		216 μs		432 μs		864 μs	
Guard interval		54 μs (1/4), 27 μs (1/8), 13.5 μs (1/16), 6.75 μs (1/32)		108 μs (1/4), 54 μs (1/8), 27 μs (1/16), 13.5 μs (1/32)		216 μs (1/4), 108 μs (1/8), 54 μs (1/16), 27 μs (1/32)	
Symbol length		270 μs (1/4), 243 μs (1/8), 229.5 μs (1/16), 222.75 μs (1/32)		540 μs (1/4), 486 μs (1/8), 459 μs (1/16), 445.5 μs (1/32)		1080 μs (1/4), 972 μs (1/8), 918 μs (1/16), 891 μs (1/32)	
Frame length		55.08 ms (1/4), 49.572 ms (1/8), 46.818 ms (1/16), 45.441 ms (1/32)		110.16 ms (1/4), 99.144 ms (1/8), 93.636 ms (1/16), 90.882 ms (1/32)		220.32 ms (1/4), 198.288 ms (1/8), 187.272 ms (1/16), 181.764 ms (1/32)	
FFT sampling frequency		2048/216 = 9.481481... MHz					
Inner code		Convolutional code (1/2, 2/3, 3/4, 5/6, 7/8)					
Outer code		RS (204,188)					

*1: SP (Scattered Pilot) and CP (Continual Pilot) are used by the receiver for synchronization and demodulation purposes.
*2: TMCC (Transmission and Multiplexing Configuration Control) is control information.
*3: AC (Auxiliary Channel) is used to transmit additional information for broadcasting. AC1 is available in an equal number in all segments, while AC2 is available only in differential modulated segments.

Table A-2: Transmission Signal Parameters (7MHz Bandwidth System)

Mode		Mode 1	Mode 2	Mode 3
Number of OFDM segment(N_s)		13		
Bandwidth (Bw)		$B_{ws} \times N_s + C_s$ = 6.504...MHz	$B_{ws} \times N_s + C_s$ = 6.502...MHz	$B_{ws} \times N_s + C_s$ = 6.501...MHz
Number of segment of differential modulation		n_d		
Number of segment of coherent modulation		n_s ($n_s+n_d=N_s$)		
Spacings between carrier frequencies (C_s)		$B_{ws}/108$ = 4.629...kHz	$B_{ws}/216$ = 2.314...kHz	$B_{ws}/432$ = 1.157...kHz
Number of carriers	Total count	$108 \times N_s + 1 = 1405$	$216 \times N_s + 1 = 2809$	$432 \times N_s + 1 = 5617$
	Data	$96 \times N_s = 1248$	$192 \times N_s = 2496$	$384 \times N_s = 4992$
	SP	$9 \times n_s$	$18 \times n_s$	$36 \times n_s$
	CP[*1]	$n_d + 1$	$n_d + 1$	$n_d + 1$
	TMCC	$n_s + 5 \times n_d$	$2 \times n_s + 10 \times n_d$	$4 \times n_s + 20 \times n_d$
	AC1	$2 \times N_s = 26$	$4 \times N_s = 52$	$8 \times N_s = 104$
	AC2	$4 \times n_d$	$9 \times n_d$	$19 \times n_d$
Carrier modulation scheme		QPSK, 16QAM, 64QAM, DQPSK		
Symbols per frame		204		
Effective symbol length		216 μs	432 μs	864 μs
Guard interval		54 μs (1/4), 27 μs (1/8), 13.5 μs (1/16), 6.75 μs (1/32)	108 μs (1/4), 54 μs (1/8), 27 μs (1/16), 13.5 μs (1/32)	216 μs (1/4), 108 μs (1/8), 54 μs (1/16), 27 μs (1/32)
Symbol length		270 μs (1/4), 243 μs (1/8), 229.5 μs (1/16), 222.75 μs (1/32)	540 μs (1/4), 486 μs (1/8), 459 μs (1/16), 445.5 μs (1/32)	1080 μs (1/4), 972 μs (1/8), 918 μs (1/16), 891 μs (1/32)
Frame length		55.08 ms (1/4), 49.572 ms (1/8), 46.818 ms (1/16), 45.441 ms (1/32)	110.16 ms (1/4), 99.144 ms (1/8), 93.636 ms (1/16), 90.882 ms (1/32)	220.32 ms (1/4), 198.288 ms (1/8), 187.272 ms (1/16), 181.764 ms (1/32)
Interleave	Frequency	セグメント間およびセグメント内周波数インターリーブ		
	Time	I=0 (0 symbols), I=4 (380 symbols), I=8 (760 symbols), I=16 (1520 symbols)	I=0 (0 symbols), I=2 (190 symbols), I=4 (380 symbols), I=8 (760 symbols)	I=0 (0 symbols), I=1 (95 symbols), I=2 (190 symbols), I=4 (380 symbols)
Inner code[*2]		Convolutional code (1/2, 2/3, 3/4, 5/6, 7/8)		
Byte interleave		Convolutional byte interleave every 12 bytes		
Outer code		RS (204,188)		

*1: The number of CPs represents the sum of those CPs in segments, plus one CP added to the right of the entire bandwidth.

*2: The inner code is taken as a convolutional code in which the mother-code with a constraint length of 7 (number of states: 64) and a coding rate of 1/2 is punctured.

ARIB STD-B31

Table A-3: Data Rate per a Single Segment (7MHz Bandwidth System)

Carrier modulation	Convolutional code	Number of TSPs transmitted [1] (Mode 1/2/3)	Data Rates (kbit/s) [2]			
			Guard interval ratio 1/4	Guard interval ratio 1/8	Guard interval ratio 1/16	Guard interval ratio 1/32
DQPSK QPSK	1/2	12 / 24 / 48	327.66	364.07	385.49	397.17
	2/3	16 / 32 / 64	436.89	485.43	513.99	529.56
	3/4	18 / 36 / 72	491.50	546.11	578.23	595.76
	5/6	20 / 40 / 80	546.11	606.79	642.48	661.95
	7/8	21 / 42 / 84	573.42	637.13	674.61	695.05
16QAM	1/2	24 / 48 / 96	655.33	728.15	770.98	794.34
	2/3	32 / 64 / 128	873.78	970.87	1027.98	1059.13
	3/4	36 / 72 / 144	983.00	1092.22	1156.47	1191.52
	5/6	40 / 80 / 160	1092.22	1213.58	1284.97	1323.91
	7/8	42 / 84 / 168	1146.84	1274.26	1349.22	1390.11
64QAM	1/2	36 / 72 / 144	983.00	1092.22	1156.47	1191.52
	2/3	48 / 96 / 192	1310.67	1456.30	1541.97	1588.69
	3/4	54 / 108 / 216	1474.50	1638.34	1734.71	1787.28
	5/6	60 / 120 / 240	1638.34	1820.38	1927.46	1985.87
	7/8	63 / 126 / 252	1720.26	1911.40	2023.83	2085.16

[1]: Represents the number of TSPs transmitted per frame
[2]: Represents the data rate (bits) per segment for transmission parameters
Data rate (bits): Number of TSPs transmitted × 188 (bytes/TSP) × 8 (bits/byte) × (1/frame length)

ARIB STD-B31

Table A-4: Total Data Rate[*1] (7MHz Bandwidth System)

Carrier modulation	Convolutional code	Number of TSPs transmitted (Mode 1/2/3)	Data Rates (Mbit/s)			
			Guard interval ratio 1/4	Guard interval ratio 1/8	Guard interval ratio 1/16	Guard interval ratio 1/32
DQPSK QPSK	1/2	156/ 312 / 624	4.259	4.732	5.011	5.163
	2/3	208 / 416 / 832	5.679	6.310	6.681	6.884
	3/4	234 / 468 / 936	6.389	7.099	7.517	7.744
	5/6	260 / 520 / 1040	7.099	7.888	8.352	8.605
	7/8	273 / 546 / 1092	7.454	8.282	8.769	9.035
16QAM	1/2	312 / 624 / 1248	8.519	9.465	10.022	10.326
	2/3	416/ 832 / 1664	11.359	12.621	13.363	13.768
	3/4	468 / 936 / 1872	12.779	14.198	15.034	15.489
	5/6	520/ 1040 / 2080	14.198	15.776	16.704	17.210
	7/8	546/ 1092 / 2184	14.908	16.565	17.539	18.071
64QAM	1/2	468 / 936 / 1872	12.779	14.198	15.034	15.489
	2/3	624 / 1248 / 2496	17.038	18.931	20.045	20.653
	3/4	702 / 1404 / 2808	19.168	21.298	22.551	23.234
	5/6	780 / 1560 / 3120	21.298	23.664	25.057	25.816
	7/8	819 / 1638 / 3276	22.363	24.848	26.309	27.107

*1: This table shows an example of the total data rate in which the same parameters are specified for all 13 segments.
Note that the total data rate during hierarchical transmission varies depending on the hierarchical parameter configuration. In the case shown above, the data volume transmitted by all 13 segments is equal to the sum of all data volumes transmitted by these segments that can be determined based on Table A-3.

ARIB STD-B31

Table A-5: ODFM Segment Parameters (8MHz Bandwidth System)

Mode		Mode 1		Mode 2		Mode 3	
Segment bandwidth (Bws)		\multicolumn{6}{c}{8000/14 = 571.428... kHz}					
Spacings between carrier frequencies (Cs)		Bws/108 = 5.291... kHz		Bws/216 = 2.645... kHz		Bws/432 = 1.322... kHz	
Number of carriers	Total count	108	108	216	216	432	432
	Data	96	96	192	192	384	384
	SP[1]	9	0	18	0	36	0
	CP[1]	0	1	0	1	0	1
	TMCC[2]	1	5	2	10	4	20
	AC1[3]	2	2	4	4	8	8
	AC2[3]	0	4	0	9	0	19
Carrier modulation scheme		QPSK 16QAM 64QAM	DQPSK	QPSK 16QAM 64QAM	DQPSK	QPSK 16QAM 64QAM	DQPSK
Symbols per frame		204					
Effective symbol length		189 μs		378 μs		756 μs	
Guard interval		47.25 μs (1/4), 23.625 μs (1/8), 11.8125 μs (1/16), 5.90625 μs (1/32)		94.5 μs (1/4), 47.25 μs (1/8), 23.625 μs (1/16), 11.8125 μs (1/32)		189 μs (1/4), 94.5 μs (1/8), 47.25 μs (1/16), 23.625 μs (1/32)	
Symbol length		236.25 μs (1/4), 212.625 μs (1/8), 200.8125 μs (1/16), 194.90625 μs (1/32)		472.5 μs (1/4), 425.25 μs (1/8), 401.625 μs (1/16), 389.8125 μs (1/32)		945 μs (1/4), 850.5 μs (1/8), 803.25 μs (1/16), 779.625 μs (1/32)	
Frame length		48.195 ms (1/4), 43.3755 ms (1/8), 40.96575ms(1/16), 39.760875ms(1/32)		96.39 ms (1/4), 86.751 ms (1/8), 81.9315 ms (1/16), 79.52175 ms (1/32)		192.78 ms (1/4), 173.502 ms (1/8), 163.863 ms (1/16), 159.0435 ms (1/32)	
FFT sampling frequency		2048/189 = 10.835978... MHz					
Inner code		Convolutional code (1/2, 2/3, 3/4, 5/6, 7/8)					
Outer code		RS (204,188)					

[1]: SP (Scattered Pilot) and CP (Continual Pilot) are used by the receiver for synchronization and demodulation purposes.
[2]: TMCC (Transmission and Multiplexing Configuration Control) is control information.
[3]: AC (Auxiliary Channel) is used to transmit additional information for broadcasting. AC1 is available in an equal number in all segments, while AC2 is available only in differential modulated segments.

ARIB STD-B31

Table A-6: Transmission Signal Parameters (8MHz Bandwidth System)

Mode		Mode 1	Mode 2	Mode 3
Number of OFDM segments (N_s)		13		
Bandwidth (Bw)		$Bws \times N_s + Cs$ = 7.433...MHz	$Bws \times N_s + Cs$ = 7.431...MHz	$Bws \times N_s + Cs$ = 7.429...MHz
Number of segments of differential modulations		n_d		
Number of segments of coherent modulations		n_s ($n_s+n_d=N_s$)		
Spacings between carrier frequencies (Cs)		$Bws/108$ = 5.291... kHz	$Bws/216$ = 2.645... kHz	$Bws/432$ = 1.322... kHz
Number of carriers	Total count	$108 \times N_s + 1 = 1405$	$216 \times N_s + 1 = 2809$	$432 \times N_s + 1 = 5617$
	Data	$96 \times N_s = 1248$	$192 \times N_s = 2496$	$384 \times N_s = 4992$
	SP	$9 \times n_s$	$18 \times n_s$	$36 \times n_s$
	CP*1	$n_d + 1$	$n_d + 1$	$n_d + 1$
	TMCC	$n_s + 5 \times n_d$	$2 \times n_s + 10 \times n_d$	$4 \times n_s + 20 \times n_d$
	AC1	$2 \times N_s = 26$	$4 \times N_s = 52$	$8 \times N_s = 104$
	AC2	$4 \times n_d$	$9 \times n_d$	$19 \times n_d$
Carrier modulation scheme		QPSK, 16QAM, 64QAM, DQPSK		
Symbols per frame		204		
Effective symbol length		189 μs	378 μs	756 μs
Guard interval		47.25 μs (1/4), 23.625 μs (1/8), 11.8125 μs (1/16), 5.90625 μs (1/32)	94.5 μs (1/4), 47.25 μs (1/8), 23.625 μs (1/16), 11.8125 μs (1/32)	189 μs (1/4), 94.5 μs (1/8), 47.25 μs (1/16), 23.625 μs (1/32)
Symbol length		236.25 μs (1/4), 212.625 μs (1/8), 200.8125 μs (1/16), 194.90625 μs (1/32)	472.5 μs (1/4), 425.25 μs (1/8), 401.625 μs (1/16), 389.8125 μs (1/32)	945 μs (1/4), 850.5 μs (1/8), 803.25 μs (1/16), 779.625 μs (1/32)
Frame length		48.195 ms (1/4), 43.3755 ms (1/8), 40.96575ms(1/16), 39.760875ms(1/32)	96.39 ms (1/4), 86.751 ms (1/8), 81.9315 ms (1/16), 79.52175 ms (1/32)	192.78 ms (1/4), 173.502 ms (1/8), 163.863 ms (1/16), 159.0435 ms (1/32)
Interleave	Frequency	Inter-segment and intra-segment frequency interleave		
	Time	I=0 (0 symbols), I=4 (380 symbols), I=8 (760 symbols), I=16 (1520 symbols)	I=0 (0 symbols), I=2 (190 symbols), I=4 (380 symbols), I=8 (760 symbols)	I=0 (0 symbols), I=1 (95 symbols), I=2 (190 symbols), I=4 (380 symbols)
Inner code *2		Convolutional code (1/2, 2/3, 3/4, 5/6, 7/8)		
Byte interleave		Convolutional byte interleave every 12 bytes		
Outer code		RS (204,188)		

*1: The number of CPs represents the sum of those CPs in segments, plus one CP added to the right of the entire bandwidth.

*2: The inner code is taken as a convolutional code in which the mother-code with a constraint length of 7 (number of states: 64) and a coding rate of 1/2 is punctured.

ARIB STD-B31

Table A-7: Data Rate per a Single Segment (8MHz Bandwidth System)

Carrier modulation	Convolutional code	Number of TSPs transmitted *1 (Mode 1/2/3)	Data Rates (kbit/s) *2			
			Guard interval ratio 1/4	Guard interval ratio 1/8	Guard interval ratio 1/16	Guard interval ratio 1/32
DQPSK QPSK	1/2	12/ 24 / 48	374.47	416.08	440.56	453.91
	2/3	16/ 32 / 64	499.30	554.78	587.41	605.21
	3/4	18/ 36 / 72	561.71	624.13	660.84	680.87
	5/6	20/ 40 / 80	624.13	693.47	734.27	756.52
	7/8	21/ 42 / 84	655.33	728.15	770.98	794.34
16QAM	1/2	24/ 48 / 96	748.95	832.17	881.12	907.82
	2/3	32/ 64 / 128	998.60	1109.56	1174.83	1210.43
	3/4	36/ 72 / 144	1123.43	1248.26	1321.68	1361.74
	5/6	40/ 80 / 160	1248.26	1386.95	1468.54	1513.04
	7/8	42/ 84 / 168	1310.67	1456.30	1541.97	1588.69
64QAM	1/2	36/ 72 / 144	1123.43	1248.26	1321.68	1361.74
	2/3	48/ 96 / 192	1497.91	1664.34	1762.25	1815.65
	3/4	54/ 108 / 216	1685.15	1872.39	1982.53	2042.61
	5/6	60/ 120 / 240	1872.39	2080.43	2202.81	2269.56
	7/8	63/ 126 / 252	1966.01	2184.45	2312.95	2383.04

*1: Represents the number of TSPs transmitted per frame
*2: Represents the data rate (bits) per segment for transmission parameters
Data rate (bits): Number of TSPs transmitted × 188 (bytes/TSP) × 8 (bits/byte) × (1/frame length)

ARIB STD-B31

Table A-8: Total Data Rate[*1] (8MHz Bandwidth System)

Carrier modulation	Convolutional code	Number of TSPs transmitted (Mode 1/2/3)	Data Rate(Mbit/s)			
			Guard interval ratio 1/4	Guard interval ratio 1/8	Guard interval ratio 1/16	Guard interval ratio 1/32
DQPSK	1/2	156/ 312 / 624	4.868	5.409	5.727	5.900
	2/3	208 / 416 / 832	6.490	7.212	7.636	7.867
	3/4	234 / 468 / 936	7.302	8.113	8.590	8.851
QPSK	5/6	260 / 520 / 1040	8.113	9.015	9.545	9.834
	7/8	273 / 546 / 1092	8.519	9.465	10.022	10.326
16QAM	1/2	312 / 624 / 1248	9.736	10.818	11.454	11.801
	2/3	416/ 832 / 1664	12.981	14.424	15.272	15.735
	3/4	468 / 936 / 1872	14.604	16.227	17.181	17.702
	5/6	520/ 1040 / 2080	16.227	18.030	19.091	19.669
	7/8	546/ 1092 / 2184	17.038	18.931	20.045	20.653
64QAM	1/2	468 / 936 / 1872	14.604	16.227	17.181	17.702
	2/3	624 / 1248 / 2496	19.472	21.636	22.909	23.603
	3/4	702 / 1404 / 2808	21.907	24.341	25.772	26.553
	5/6	780 / 1560 / 3120	24.341	27.045	28.636	29.504
	7/8	819 / 1638 / 3276	25.558	28.397	30.068	30.979

*1: This table shows an example of the total data rate in which the same parameters are specified for all 13 segments.
Note that the total data rate during hierarchical transmission varies depending on the hierarchical parameter configuration. In the case shown above, the data volume transmitted by all 13 segments is equal to the sum of all data volumes transmitted by these segments that can be determined based on Table A-7.

ARIB STD-B31

www.ingramcontent.com/pod-product-compliance
Lightning Source LLC
Chambersburg PA
CBHW052151300426
44115CB00011B/1626